D1163632

THE THIRD "R"

THE THIRD "R"

MATHEMATICS TEACHING FOR GRADES K-8

GERALD R. RISING
STATE UNIVERSITY OF NEW YORK AT BUFFALO

JOSEPH B. HARKIN
STATE UNIVERSITY OF NEW YORK COLLEGE AT BROCKPORT

WADSWORTH PUBLISHING COMPANY, INC.
BELMONT, CALIFORNIA

EDUCATION EDITOR: ROGER PETERSON

PRODUCTION EDITOR: CONNIE MARTIN

DESIGNER: HEDY McADAMS

ILLUSTRATOR: MARTHA WESTON

Printed in the United States of America

1 2 3 4 5 6 7 8 9 10—82 81 80 79 78

Library of Congress Cataloging in Publication Data

Rising, Gerald R.
The Third "R".

Includes index.
1. Mathematics—Study and teaching—(Elementary). I. Harkin, Joseph B., 1926– joint author. II. Title.
QA135.5-R57 372.7 77-19012
ISBN 0-534-00567-5

CONTENTS

A NOTE TO THE INSTRUCTOR

The elementary school teachers you will be teaching will usually have interests in specific grades. Individuals plan to teach fifth grade or second grade, seventh grade or kindergarten. Only a very few wish to prepare themselves for teaching mathematics for kindergarten through eighth grade, the range covered by this text. This book provides a general format for teaching mathematics in elementary school, with examples from all grades. To satisfy their interests in specific grade levels, individual teachers should refer to school mathematics texts and teacher's editions for the grades in which their interests lie. We have used this procedure in our own classes with considerable success. Students have had little difficulty borrowing texts from schools in which they observe, plan to student teach, or in some cases already teach. Where students have had difficulty locating such books, textbook salesmen have been helpful with loans. We urge you to insure that your teachers obtain these texts early in your course.

A teacher's guide for this text is available from Wadsworth Publishing Company, 10 Davis Drive, Belmont, California 94002. This guide contains teaching suggestions and answers to exercises.

This is the first edition of a text radically different from its competitors in goals, scope, and attitude toward its readers, your students. We invite your reactions to its use and your suggestions for revisions.

ACKNOWLEDGMENTS

The authors would like to thank the following for their help: Robert Ashlock, University of Maryland; Francis R. Brown, Illinois State University at Normal; James V. Brum, Herbert H. Lehman College; Gary E. Downs, Iowa State University; Allen C. Friebel, California State University, San Jose; Roland F. Grey, University of British Columbia; Larry L. Hatfield, University of Georgia; W. Robert Houston, University of Houston; Joe Moray, San Francisco State University; and Lauren Woodby, Michigan State University.

PREFACE FOR CLASSROOM TEACHERS

This is a book about teaching mathematics in elementary school. Most of you will be teaching many subjects of which mathematics is just one: reading and language arts, social studies, science, and in many cases even music and physical education. We naturally feel that mathematics is of primary importance, coequal with reading, for mathematics lies at the heart of all quantitative and logical thinking. But at the same time we recognize that mathematics can be only part of your interest and responsibility.

Most textbooks on elementary school teaching methods provide a few examples of elementary school mathematics, with only superficial treatment of how to teach it. We depart significantly from that format. Instead we attempt to communicate to you a broader view of school mathematics at this level and to provide you with a rich variety of teaching ideas directly related to this subject. Through exercises, you are encouraged to relate these ideas and techniques directly to the grade level at which you plan to teach. In particular, we expect you to obtain and make extensive use of a teacher's edition of a mathematics text for your teaching level, preferably one you will be using in your teaching. By this means we seek to personalize the program for you, to tailor this course to your needs.

In this book you will be treated as serious students. We know that most of you bring to your reading of this text a foundation of pedagogy from other courses. Here you will relate some of those ideas specifically to mathematics instruction. You will also be challenged by the mathematical content of this text. No prerequisites beyond elementary school mathematics are required of you, but you will find yourself forced to think deeply about even primary grade mathematics exercises. In so challenging you we have several goals: (1) to give you confidence in your ability to attack significant problems, (2) to increase your respect for the content of elementary school mathematics, and (3) to increase your respect for the youngsters you will be teaching, many of whom can solve these same challenging problems. We are confident that you will measure up to these challenges, and hope that you will then provide your students some of the same intellectual mind-stretching that can come only from mathematics.

This book is divided into four parts. In the first we introduce you to our broader view of mathematics and provide some general psychological principles that help form the basis for later chapters. In part two we will be concerned with teaching not only geometry and arithmetic, the two major content strands of elementary school mathematics, but also structure and logic, the glue that holds mathematical thinking together. In part three we will analyze the instructional program from the perspective of various teaching methods. Then in the last part you will confront these ideas, taking into consideration the broad range of students in the classroom. In appendices we recommend a few books for your school library and for your own professional library, as well as sources of teaching materials.

The real test of this or any other methods text is how it affects your teaching. Based on our use of earlier drafts of these materials with prospective and in-service elementary school teachers, and their comments to us, we feel that serious study of this book will improve your teaching of mathematics. But you are the important link. You have a significant and demanding task ahead of you and you can make major contributions to many children. On you will depend the future; we count on you with confidence.

We append here one final note on gender. In preparing this text we and our editors have sought to communicate ideas with both clarity and style. You will be the ultimate judge of how well we have succeeded. On the matter of gender, however, we have found ourselves caught between a strong commitment to equality of the sexes, and our desire to avoid the lockjaw usage *he or she* or an unsexed substitute like *one.* Whenever possible we have structured sentences in a way that avoids sex bias. Occasionally we have resorted to *he or she.* And occasionally we have used the masculine pronoun *he,* meaning that pronoun only as a formal substitution for *he or she.* We invite any reader who is dissatisfied with our "system" to substitute *she, he or she, she or he,* or *he* wherever he comes across a pronoun. God knows that there is no satisfactory solution. We only pray that She approves of ours.

THE THIRD "R"

PART 1

CONCRETE

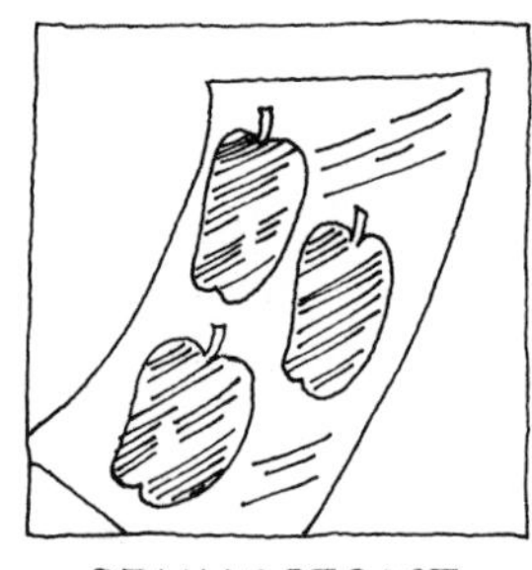
SEMIABSTRACT

ABSTRACT

BACKGROUND

In this first part the stage will be set for the more direct attack on mathematics teaching problems in the sections that follow. In the first chapter you will be introduced to some of the kinds of thinking that are found in contemporary mathematics programs. These ideas will be conveyed largely through illustrative examples. The second chapter draws together many of the important ideas of psychology that relate to teaching and learning. These ideas provide a basis in theory—sometimes in competing or even conflicting theories—for thinking about mathematics instruction. It will become clear as you read this chapter that although psychology provides some interesting ideas and a useful framework for organizing them, you will need to interpret these ideas in light of your own experience and common sense. Also, you will need to apply them to the particular mathematical goals you seek and the specific students you are teaching.

CHAPTER ONE

MATHEMATICS AND THE ELEMENTARY SCHOOL TEACHER

MATHEMATICS, TEACHERS, AND STUDENTS

Beginning teachers are often deeply concerned about their ability to help children learn mathematics. While confident that they can teach reading, social studies, and the other subjects in the elementary school curriculum, they fear the special demands placed on them in teaching the third "r," 'rithmetic. This concern is usually based on a feeling of inadequacy. Asked about their reasons, prospective teachers typically respond, "I was never a good mathematics student myself," or, "I avoided mathematics after I found that it didn't interest me, and now I believe that my background is weak," or, "I just never liked it: too much memorization."

In response to these widely held concerns we offer some evidence based on our own work with both prospective and in-service teachers:

1. The basic content of elementary school mathematics is completely within your intellectual range if you completed high school, to say nothing of college. You know how to add, subtract, multiply, and divide. Those skills, rusty though they may be, form a satisfactory basis for learning to teach mathematics.

2. Contrary to common belief, experienced teachers rate mathematics as highly as reading, *first* in personal preference and in satisfaction of accomplishment.

This is not to suggest that teaching mathematics is a snap and that there is no need to prepare. Quite the opposite is true. Mathematics is often poorly taught in elementary schools, sometimes by the very teachers who believe they are doing their best work in this area. This is due to misperceptions by teachers and children of what constitutes mathematics. The widely held belief that mathematics is a skill, strictly limited to computation, is as limiting and erroneous a notion as would be the assumption that the study of literature is confined to technical aspects like spelling and pronunciation.

It is in fact the authors' basic tenet that mathematics is the most basic liberal art, a subject whose social and cultural values are especially important in elementary school because it is so accessible to children. These youngsters are unprepared to meet many of the abstract ideas of literature and science because they still lack the skills and background. In elementary school they must first develop those skills, reading in particular. But mathematics is different. Almost from their first day in school children can be confronted with intellectual challenges in mathematics that they can *meet* and *solve.* Herein lies the ultimate value of the elementary school mathematics program. When students are given the opportunity to master challenging ideas and problems by thoughtful teachers, they develop intellectual power and motivation that are deeply humane and relate to all other learning.

A FIRST EXAMPLE

To demonstrate what we are talking about, we offer the following example developed and taught by Frederique Papy. Primary-grade students are introduced, perhaps in story form, to a playground full of children. On the chalkboard the playground is represented by a loop and the children by dots, as in figure 1. (This is already an important abstraction, but one that children understand without hesitation.) Now the children on the playground are "told" to point to their sister or sisters if there are any there. Madame Papy

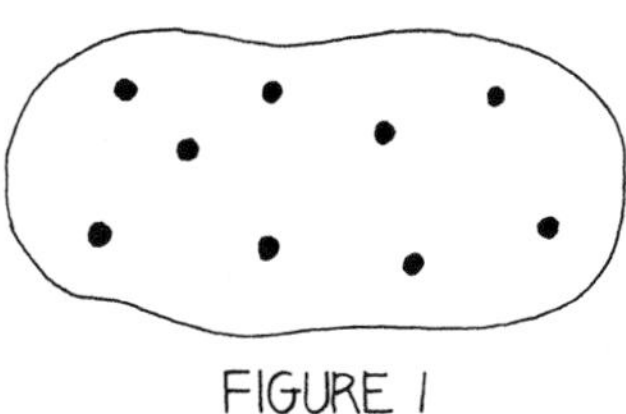

FIGURE 1

uses arrows to represent the pointing children, as in figure 2. Next the students are told that exactly one arrow is missing. They are asked to tell where it is and why. Can you find it? The youngsters do so quickly, and a

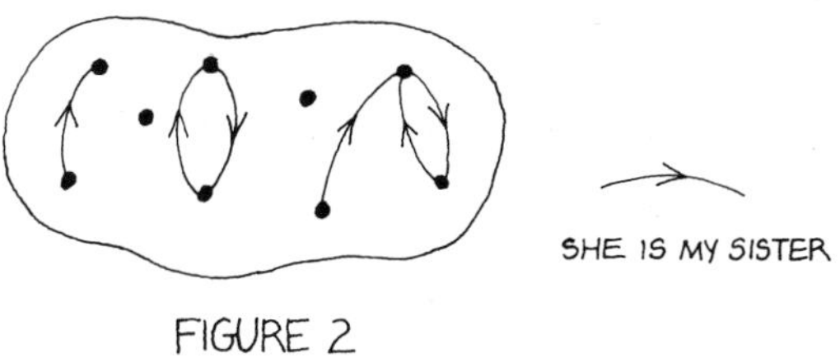

FIGURE 2

child completes the diagram, as in figure 3. Their explanations show a good understanding of what mathematicians more formally call *transitivity.* Next

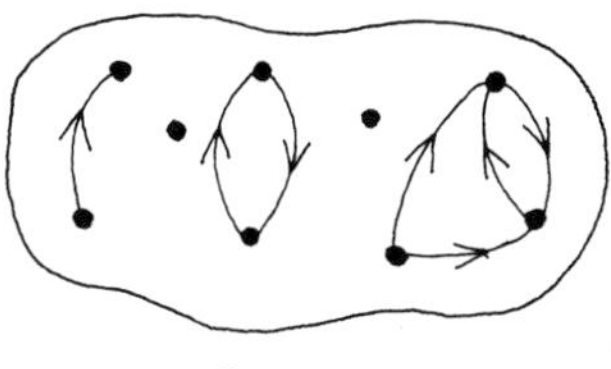

FIGURE 3

the children are asked: Which dots must represent girls? Which could be either boys or girls? And finally, which *must* represent boys? (You, too, should answer.) A correct response to this last question demonstrates good intuitive understanding of indirect reasoning, the kind of reasoning that is difficult for many tenth-grade geometry students to master in a more formal setting. The explanation usually goes something like this: "She's a girl because the arrow is pointing at her. If the other dot that the arrow comes from was a girl, an arrow would point back." And so the two boys are identified.

Please note several things about that lesson. First, it relates to the world of the children, so it is therefore meaningful and interesting to them. Second, important and deep mathematical concepts, including relations, transitivity, and indirect reasoning, are brought into clear focus by the simple pedagogical device of the diagram. Third, no background of undeveloped skill is required. The intuitive perceptions of the children are quite adequate for the task when it is presented in this form. This last point is especially important because it relates to the broader view of mathematics on which this text is constructed.

Perhaps it is hard for you to recognize this kind of problem as mathematics. There is no computation. There are no numbers. There are no mathematical terms. (Our textual comments about such terms as transitivity would not, of course, be part of the lesson with children.) How then is it mathematics? Our best answer at this point is that it would be recognized by professional mathematicians as both a powerful example of a mathematical structure and a method of mathematical proof.[1]

Viewed in this broad sense, mathematics does indeed relate to humanistic values. Here is logical reasoning, basic to argument or discourse in any field; abstraction, a process important to problem solving in all subjects; and intellectual challenge, a rich source for intellectual growth and academic motivation.

But lest we go too far, we must point out that mathematics is not all arrow diagrams. We chose this first example precisely because it is so different from the traditional, narrow view of mathematics. While computa-

---

[1]In fact arrow diagrams or Papygrams, after Frederique and her husband George, also an internationally famous mathematician and teacher, are used extensively in advanced mathematics texts. See, for example, Saunders MacLane and Garrett Birkhoff, *Algebra* (New York: Macmillan, 1967), a book for university mathematics majors and graduate students.

tional algorithms such as long division and the sums and times tables are still very important to elementary school mathematics, these no longer constitute *all* of school mathematics. Only when skills grow out of the broader study of concepts and structure can the study of skills actually be effective in mathematics programs.

A SECOND EXAMPLE

We turn now to an example that does involve computation.

EXAMPLE

A simplified football scoring system allows 3 points for a field goal and 7 points for a touchdown. It is evident that a team cannot score 2 or 4 points in this game. What is the *largest* total number of points that would be impossible for a team to score because of the scoring restrictions?

You should attempt to solve this problem yourself. You might attack it by first listing scores, and then crossing out scores you cannot achieve, like 2, and looping scores you can, like 3.

1 ~~2~~ (3) 4 5 6 7 8 9 10
11 12 13 14 15 16 17 . . .

What is the maximum inadmissable score? Can you prove that your result is correct? Read on only after you have answered at least the first of these questions.

Consider this problem and the thinking involved. Computation? Certainly. You probably used the addition combinations $3 + 3$, $3 + 3 + 3$, $3 + 7$, $3 + 3 + 3 + 3$, $3 + 3 + 7$, $7 + 7$, $3 + 3 + 3 + 3 + 3$, $3 + 3 + 3 + 7$, $3 + 7 + 7$, to loop the additional numbers.

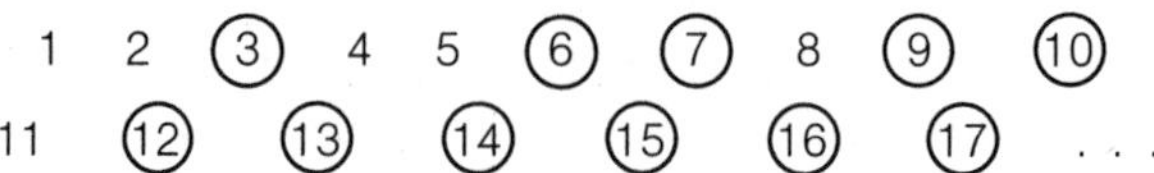

You may then have stopped, satisfied that 11 is the answer to the problem. That seems reasonable because scores above 11 seem to be attained regularly. But you may also have gone further to satisfy yourself that the three scores in a row, 12, 13, and 14, together with the 3-point field goal, complete the problem by providing a proof. Diagrammatically, it might appear like this:

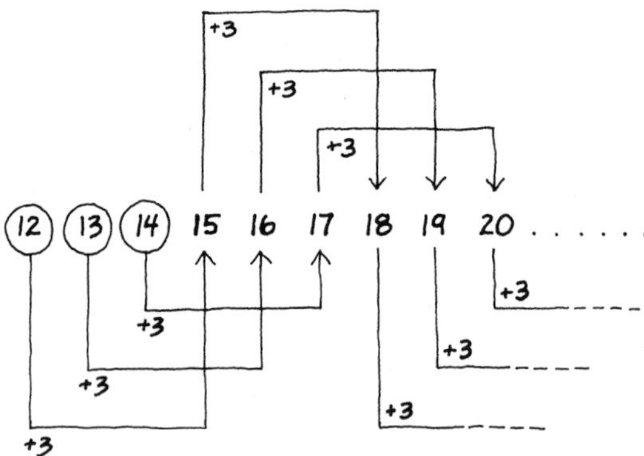

This procedure would establish a logical basis for your intuitive solution.

This problem provides an opportunity to practice computation, and (for better students) to use logic to prove the result. Furthermore, it provides these activities in the context of an interesting and reasonable setting, and suggests additional problems and questions:

> What if the scores for a field goal and a touchdown are 5 and 8, respectively? 4 and 7?
>
> What happens if 1 is an allowable score?
>
> What if the scores are 3 and 6? What is difficult about these scores?
>
> What kinds of scores give *no* maximum unobtainable total?

Can you discover a rule that tells you the answer directly for any pair of scores (except those for which there is no answer)?

This last question takes students to a higher level of organization. Now they must consider their answers to previous questions, solved by direct trial, to find a pattern.

3, 7 → 11 (points → highest score *not* allowed)

5, 8 → 27

4, 7 → 17

If they don't succeed, they can try new pairs of scores, discovering

2, 3 → 1	4, 5 → 11
2, 5 → 3	5, 6 → 19
3, 4 → 5	8, 11 → 69
3, 5 → 7	7, 10 → 53

These patterns lead finally to an unexpected and little-known general result: the highest unobtainable score is the difference between the product of the two scores and their sum. Applied to the first problem: $(3 \times 7) - (3 + 7) = 11$. This last is of course a long way from the initial problem, but it should suggest to the reader how a more thoughtful approach to computation-generating exercises can lead to exciting mathematics.

AN EXAMPLE SUITABLE FOR ANY GRADE

The previous example and its results were appropriate to intermediate grades. Here is a quite different one, designed for primary grades and above. It is adapted from material developed by David Page for The Arithmetic Project.[2]

Consider the array:

30	31	32 . . .							
20	21	22	23	24	25	26	27	28	29
10	11	12	13	14	15	16	17	18	19
	1	2	3	4	5	6	7	8	9

and some moves on the array, designated by arrows:

$$6\uparrow = 16$$

$$22\rightarrow = 23.$$

(Thus ↑ means go to the number above, and → means go to the number to the right, and diagonal arrows (↗, ↘) have parallel meanings. Children don't need this explanation.)

Now answer some questions:

$$17 \quad \leftarrow = \_\_\_\_$$

$$52 \quad \downarrow = \_\_\_\_$$

$$75 \quad \nearrow = \_\_\_\_$$

---

[2]For additional materials from this center, which offers exciting in-service and preservice courses, information may be obtained from The Arithmetic Project. See Appendix C.

____ ↘ = 59

12 ____ = 21 (What arrow?)

43 → → = ____

61 ↑↑↓↑↑↓ = ____

36 →↑←↓ = ____

39 ____ = 57 Use two arrows.
Use three arrows.
Use only diagonal arrows, etc.

Notice how students get a feel for the structure of our numeration system in an interesting way. And notice, too, how many different ways this idea can take you:

1. Some questions involve choice. In the problem 29 → = ____, the answer could be 30, 20, or just "off the chart" (so 29 → ← = 29 still), or "breakdown" or "tilt."[3]

2. Other arrays could be used.

16	17	18	19	20
11	12	13	14	15
6	7	8	9	10
1	2	3	4	5

18 ↗ = 24

[3]Notice that in this last case *only*, the commutative law fails, that is → ← ≠ ← →, since 29 → ← = "breakdown," but 29 ← → = 29.

7	8	9	10
4	5	6	
2	3		
1			

18 ↗ = 25

20	7	8	9	10
19	6	1	2	11
18	5	4	3	12
17	16	15	14	13

18 ↗ = 6

3. You could build your own arrays. For example, you might start with the grid below and fill it in using the following rules:

↑ means −2 and → means +5

↓ means +2 and ← means −5

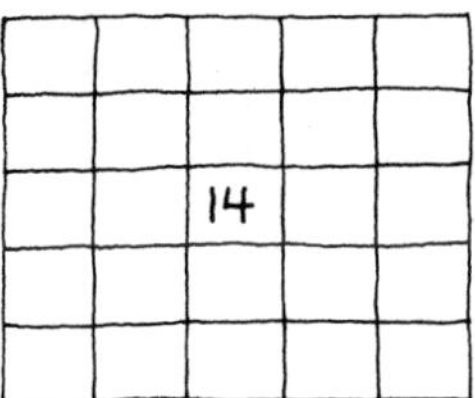

What then would each of the following mean on this grid?

↗ means ______ ↙ means ______

↘ means ______ ↖ means ______

These examples of what Page calls "maneuvers on lattices" provide the student with many things: computation practice, insight into structure, appreciation for the consistency of mathematics, self-confidence, and perhaps most of all *fun.* In the pages ahead we want to give you some feeling for your role in organizing activities that address these kinds of concerns.

A PROBLEM OF THE "REAL WORLD"

Much has been said about the value of problem solving in the "real world." Children are often more motivated to solve such problems since they can identify with them. However, this is not always the case; even problems with applications can be dull.

Consider the following information:[4]

Too often the problems associated with this kind of information are too simple, such as: How much do 1 pencil and 1 eraser cost? But there are other questions that force children to investigate as well as calculate:

What is the most you can spend?

What amounts would be impossible to charge up to 23¢?

A clerk is hired who cannot do arithmetic. Make a table for him that shows charges.

---

[4]This problem was devised by Robert Wirtz.

ERASERS

PENCILS	0	1	2	3
0				
1				
2		11¢		
3				

Assuming a purchase is made, what is the largest number of coins in change you can have if you started with 25¢?

TEACHERS OF ELEMENTARY SCHOOL MATHEMATICS

In this text, we do not ask that you have a strong mathematical background. Some of you have that; others do not. Rather we ask for your serious attention to nontrivial problems of both mathematics and pedagogy. We ask for an open, willing approach to new ideas and new problems, for we believe that to teach mathematics well you must do some mathematics yourself. And we also ask you to have fun with mathematics, to meet its challenges in the same way you confront crossword puzzles, card games, or athletic contests. You will be repaid in measure equal to your response; and your students will gain proportionally.

Your role as a classroom teacher is of primary importance, not only in developing intellectual skills, but also in fostering attitudes. A major block to learning mathematics is a general fear of the subject, technically termed *mathephobia.* We identify several sources of mathephobia:

1. Belief that the subject is inherently difficult

2. Boring memorization and rote procedures (like long division)

3. Lack of creative activities

Regarding point 1, success in mathematics should be difficult for very few students to attain. For most, because of its logical consistency and its intimate relationship with the real world of experience, mathematics can be *easy*. The key is sensitive teaching, which we will address throughout this text. Points 2 and 3 are really opposite sides of the same coin. They relate to a restricted view of mathematics that is widespread among both adults and students. In too many classrooms mathematics is indeed viewed as rote computation and memorization. Elementary school mathematics is often reduced to mere memorization of four-digit "telephone numbers" like 3407 and 3412, addition and multiplication facts that have no connection with the child's world. It is the responsibility of the teacher to see that this limited view of mathematics is not communicated to students.

In the following chapters, we will address the problems of teaching mathematics to children in this broader context. Mathematics will be considered as far more than computation. Teaching mathematics includes fostering creativity and positive attitudes toward the subject that today is both queen and handmaiden to the sciences.

EXERCISES

1. Here is a rather difficult exercise that is equally challenging to elementary school students (who understand the terms) and to adults. It is offered here to stress the idea that serious intellectual challenges are not restricted to high school, college, or graduate school. You will need to review the different kinds of triangles.

An acute triangle is a triangle all of whose angles are acute, that is, less than a right angle (90°).

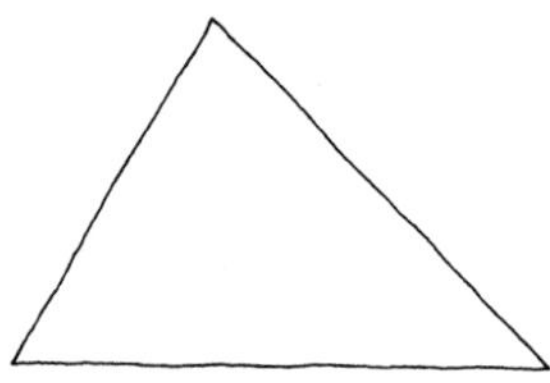

A right triangle contains one right angle and two acute angles.

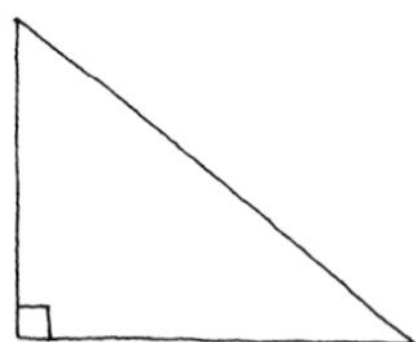

An obtuse triangle contains one obtuse angle and two acute angles. (An obtuse angle is greater than 90°.)

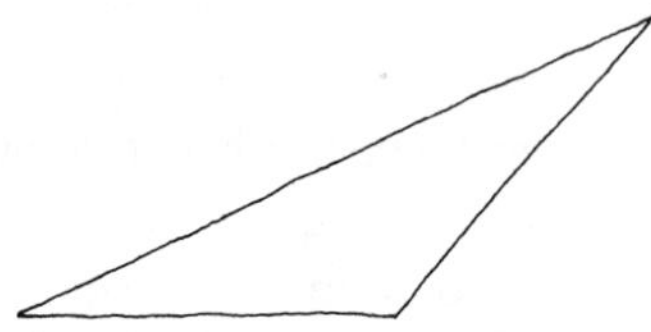

Here is an acute triangle whose interior is separated by three segments into four acute triangles.

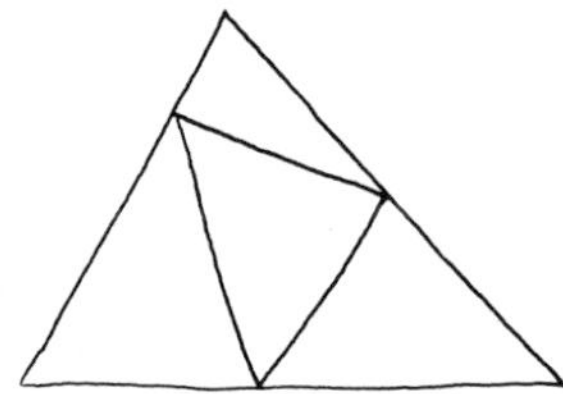

Challenge: Draw an obtuse triangle. In its interior draw enough segments so that the interior is separated into *only* acute triangles. Remember, this is a difficult exercise. It *is* possible, but if you are unsuccessful after five or ten minutes, stop!

2. Now comment on exercise 1. Is it an advanced mathematical concept that makes the problem so difficult? (In our experience about the same proportion of sixth-grade *students* as high school *teachers* solve this problem.)

3. David L. Silverman, in a delightful book on games called *Your Move* (New York: McGraw-Hill, 1971), describes "Woolworth (The Five-and-Ten-Cent-Game)." It is played by two people. One places his nickel and dime on the leftmost space of the appropriate track; the other, on the opposite end. A move consists of advancing or retreating either one of your two coins one or more spaces in its track, but not joining or passing your opponent's coin. Players alternate. When one player can no longer move and is squeezed into his original position, the other player wins his 15¢.

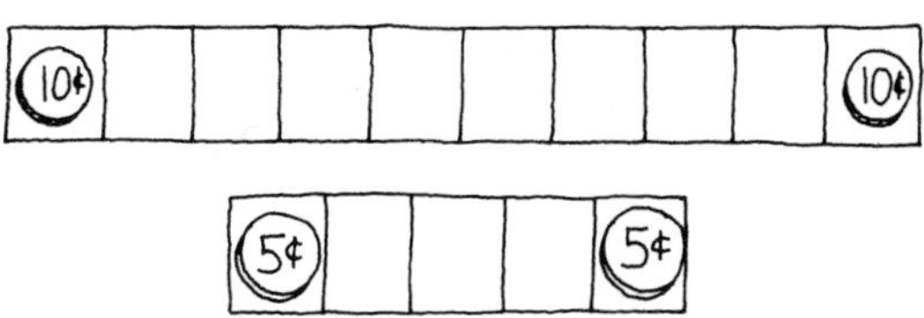

Challenge: You move first. What strategy assures you of a win? (*Hint:* Unless you are absolutely brilliant or have seen the game before, you must collect data to solve the problem. Find an opponent and play the game several times for practice. Don't gamble until you're sure of yourself.)

4. Considering our broader view of mathematics, the activity of exercise 3 is quite acceptable. Disregarding any prior prejudice for or against this view, try to justify it.

5. Now return to more prosaic matters. Check your ability to calculate:

(a) $\begin{array}{r} 938 \\ \times\ 307 \\ \hline \end{array}$

(b) $583\overline{)1667963}$

(c) $\begin{array}{r} 20\frac{1}{6} \\ -16\frac{3}{4} \\ \hline \end{array}$

(d) $9.38 \times 30{,}700$

(e) $5.83\overline{)166.7963}$

(f) 30% of 57

(g) $\frac{3}{8} \times 5\frac{1}{3}$

(h) $\frac{3}{8} \div 5\frac{1}{3}$

Note: If you can calculate these answers, you should have no difficulty with any of the computation that lies ahead in this course or in your elementary school teaching. If you cannot solve specific exercises, make note of them. Later when we refer to elementary school textbooks, make it your business to look up those techniques of which you are not sure. Check your answers on page 20.

6. Check your ability to apply your knowledge about computation using a few nonstandard examples. Rather than attempt to recall algorithms (procedures), use common sense.

(a) Order from small to large:

$\frac{3}{4}, \frac{2}{3}, \frac{4}{7}, \frac{3}{5}.$

(b) Find $\sqrt{10}$ to the nearest tenth. The symbol $\sqrt{\ }$ (square root) means the positive number which multiplied by itself gives the value enclosed. For example, $\sqrt{16} = 4$, because $4 \times 4 = 16$.

(c) What integer follows next after one thousand ninety-nine?

(d) Find the number midway between 37.3 and 150.

(e) What number divided by $3/7$ gives $3/7$?

7. Try to find a way to check your work on exercise 6. Assume for a few moments that the correct answers to that exercise are of extreme importance to you. (On them hinges your freedom, a job after graduation, peace in our time, or this semester's tuition.) Can you assure yourself that you have correct solutions? Beware especially of exercises that appear easy.

8. It is our claim that almost all of you, if you were suddenly marooned on a desert island, could reclaim lost arithmetic skills, and even develop further mathematics on your own when you really needed it. If we are right, what forces would be at work? Were you able to make those same forces work for you in exercise 7? Why or why not? How does this affect your thinking about teaching and learning?

9. Try to discover how many scores are unattainable in the football scoring problem posed on page 9. First explore the case for scores of 3 and 7. Then experiment with other scores in an attempt to find and test a general formula.

Answers to exercise 5: (a) 287966, (b) 2861, (c) $3\frac{5}{12}$, (d) 287966, (e) 28.61, (f) 17.1, (g) 2, (h) $9/128$.

CHAPTER TWO

PSYCHOLOGY AND MATHEMATICS TEACHING

In chapter 1 we urged you to reassess your own mathematics background and to broaden your view of the subject. We will return often to the view of mathematics that was raised in that chapter. Now, however, we turn to characteristics of the learners with whom you will work. Of even more importance to teaching than an understanding of mathematics is an understanding of your students, and of yourself as you interact with them.

Consider two children: a kindergarten student, self-centered, lacking basic conceptual and social skills, his thinking fixed on concrete objects, essentially bounded by immediate perception; an eighth-grader, socially and conceptually alert, concerned with the question, Why?, already beginning to understand formal logical reasoning, and ready to deal with the more abstract demands of secondary schools. A few minutes spent in observing these two children will reveal striking cognitive differences, as well as social and physical differences. It becomes evident that the elementary school classroom is a place of change. We wish to emphasize in this chapter that not all of that change is in school learning, but that in fact all school learning must be carefully related to changes in the basic characteristics of children.

We examine in this chapter then some aspects of psychology as they relate to school learning and teaching of mathematics. Our goal is to provide some basics, not to survey the field of psychology. You should interpret these theories for yourself and try to fit them into your personal psychology of instruction.

STAGES OF COGNITIVE DEVELOPMENT

The Swiss psychologist Jean Piaget has described stages of cognitive (thought) development in children. Piaget and his followers suggest that physical growth, especially that of the maturing nervous system (including the brain), as well as broadened experience and social interaction, bring about a progression from one developmental stage to another. (Thus, one can expect children with physical disorders or with limitations in experience or social interaction to be slower, while normal children exposed to a rich environment will progress more rapidly.)

The four basic stages with their associated typical age levels are shown in the following table.

average boundaries (age in years)	*grade*	*stages*
Birth		
		Sensory Motor. The child is gaining control of complex motor activities such as crawling and of the rudiments of language.
2		
		Preoperational. The child focuses on himself, considers only one attribute at a time, has little sense of either sequence or cause and effect, and can describe only concrete perceptions.
6–7	1 or 2	
		Concrete Operations. The child is developing systematic thought based on concrete objects and restricted to simple, distinct tasks. He develops the notion of conservation of attributes such as length, volume, weight, and time. (Conservation here refers to stability, as in the example of a line segment remaining unchanged in length when the paper on which it is drawn is rotated.) However, he views each attribute separately and does not see separate systems forming an integrated whole; he cannot handle subtleties.
11–12	6 or 7	
		Formal or *Logical Operations.* The adolescent has a fuller grasp of orderly systems, which he is learning to integrate. He can deal with possibilities as well as with reality.

The chart makes it apparent that the elementary school student moves through preoperational, concrete operational, and formal operational stages, spending the greatest time in the concrete operational stage. The elementary school curriculum, and the mathematics program in particular, is thus largely tied to a child's development of systematic thought based on concrete and sensory objects. At the same time it should provide a basis for the formal operations to come.

Piaget's stages are based on generalized patterns, and individual children may depart from the age and grade divisions. But little success has been achieved in attempts to "teach" children into more advanced stages before they are old enough for those stages. An interesting example of this kind of attempt is offered by the Swedish scientist J. Smedslund, who taught children in the preoperational stage a unit on conservation of volume. He molded a piece of clay into different shapes, demonstrating by water displacement that the volume remained unchanged (was conserved), as in the diagram below. The children seemed to understand.

But then Smedslund gave the clay demonstration again, secretly pinching off a piece so that the volume was changed at the same time the shape was distorted. The children were quite willing to accept this contradiction. Whereas earlier they had generalized that the shape did not alter the volume, they now generalized that (today) the shape did change the volume. Their understanding of conservation of volume was only superficial. (Older children, more secure in their understanding of conservation, questioned the experiment's outcome.) Still, educators in the United States have been so

In the conservation of volume experiment, a clay ball is carefully lowered into a beaker full of water (1), which flows into a measuring cup (2). The ball is then distorted and the experiment repeated (3,4). The equal measures in the cups (2,4) demonstrate that the distorted clay displaces the same volume.

concerned with accelerating the stages that such attempts have come to be known as American Piaget.

The teacher, then, should be alert to the limitations of children and their readiness for various classroom activities. That does not mean, however, that the mathematics program should be tightly restricted to the child's current stage. Recall in this regard the roles of both experience and social interaction in facilitating progress from one step to the next. Rather the teacher should recognize the need to tie abstractions to concrete experiences throughout the elementary grades.

CONCRETE, SEMIABSTRACT, AND ABSTRACT

Consider this idea more carefully. For many years educators have referred to three levels of exposition: concrete, semiabstract, and abstract. Physical objects, such as the apples on the teacher's desk in the figure, fall into the concrete category. Semiabstract ideas (a picture of three apples) are one step removed from the concrete. The abstract is essentially disassociated from physical objects: the concept of the number three, the general notion common to three apples, three cows, or three pencils. It should be evident from the definitions of these concepts that they form a psychologically ordered hierarchy.

CONCRETE

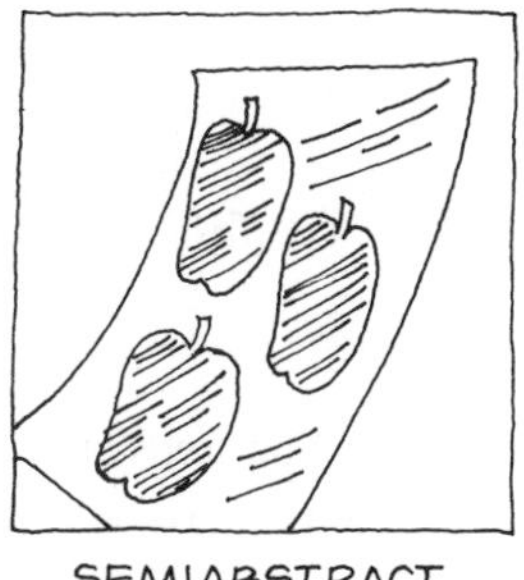
SEMIABSTRACT

ABSTRACT

Reading parallels mathematics in this regard. The schoolyard tree is a concrete object, a rebus symbol is semiabstract, and the word *tree* is abstract. Note how the word *tree* generalizes physical objects and drawings,

REBUS SYMBOL

although no specific physical appearance is associated with it. The abstract word *tree* may call up a variety of mental images, but it is tied to no single one—exactly the case with most mathematical abstractions.[1]

Rather than worrying about distinctions between these conceptual levels, you should concern yourself with the hierarchy of thinking. For example, while a counting frame or abacus is certainly a concrete device, it more often plays a role at the semiabstract level, since it is a more general representation of counting or numeration. To demonstrate what we mean, note in the figure that the counters form a concrete display related by strict counting to the addition facts

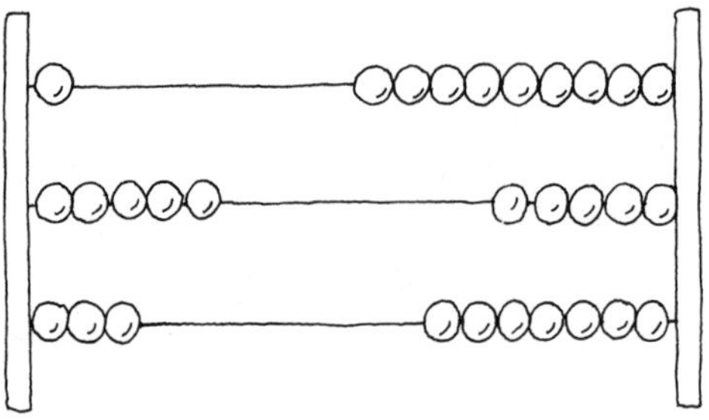

COUNTING FRAME

$$1 + 9 = 10,$$

$$5 + 5 = 10, \text{ and}$$

$$3 + 7 = 10.$$

But when the top bar represents hundreds, the middle bar tens, and the bottom bar units, the counting frame may be thought of as a semiabstract representation of the number 153 on the left or its tens complement 957 on the right.

[1]Interestingly there are exceptions to this in mathematics: one is the semiabstract *tree diagram* used in probability, which takes its name from its appearance.

Similarly, it may be difficult to assign student activities to specific conceptual levels. A kindergarten child's counting may be almost at the motor level, speaking a sequence of memorized words when passing a finger over objects. Such a child, when asked to count the circles in the following figure, often continues more than once around.

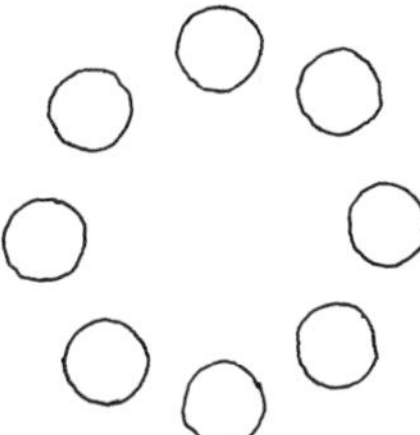

Learning mathematics, as well as reading, involves the development of abstract ideas, and building increasingly higher abstraction levels into complex systems. The development of algebra as generalized arithmetic and of composition as an extension of simple reading and writing are gross examples of this process. But we need not examine such complex processes to see this. The fraction, a higher level abstraction, is built on that of the whole number.[2] Thus the concept of $^{3}/_{7}$ grows out of a prior understanding of the concepts 3 and 7, as well as other ideas.

A KEY PRINCIPLE OF TEACHING: DELAY ABSTRACTION

The message that evolves from Piaget's description of cognitive growth (or from any theory of readiness for learning) is to delay abstractions whenever possible. Be sure that the groundwork has been laid and that the child is

[2]As part of a general policy to avoid notational sophistication we use the word *fraction* to represent both the symbol and the idea. Formalists would have said *rational number* here, reserving the word *fraction* or even *fractional numeral* to represent the symbol.

reasonably in command of basic concrete notions before moving to semiconcrete representations. Similarly, be sure the child has a broad base in semiconcrete representations before moving to abstractions. This extends to higher level abstractions as well.

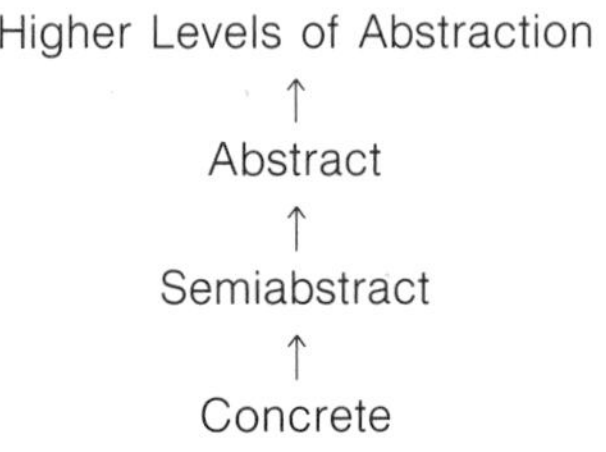

DEVELOPING UNDERSTANDING

This may seem to you like a rather obvious caution. It should be, but it is one on which many teachers and even some curricula and textbooks fail. For example, consider how many students fail to learn to multiply either because they don't understand the basis of multiplication or because they cannot add well. In the first case, they have not had adequate prior experience at concrete and semiabstract levels; and, in the second, they have not mastered prerequisite abstractions.

Some psychologists even extend the idea of concept-building to emotional effects. They claim that children who walk too soon without enough experience crawling may be left with serious psychological deficiencies. That theory may or may not be a valid extension, but it should be evident that the development of skills, concepts, and structures in mathematics leans heavily on cognitive prerequisites. We will return to this idea throughout the book.

At the elementary school level, Piaget's message concerning curriculum is more general, as suggested by the figure. But at preschool and kindergarten levels, the program should be virtually all concrete. As students become ready, the proportion of semiabstract and, later, abstract activity can be increased.

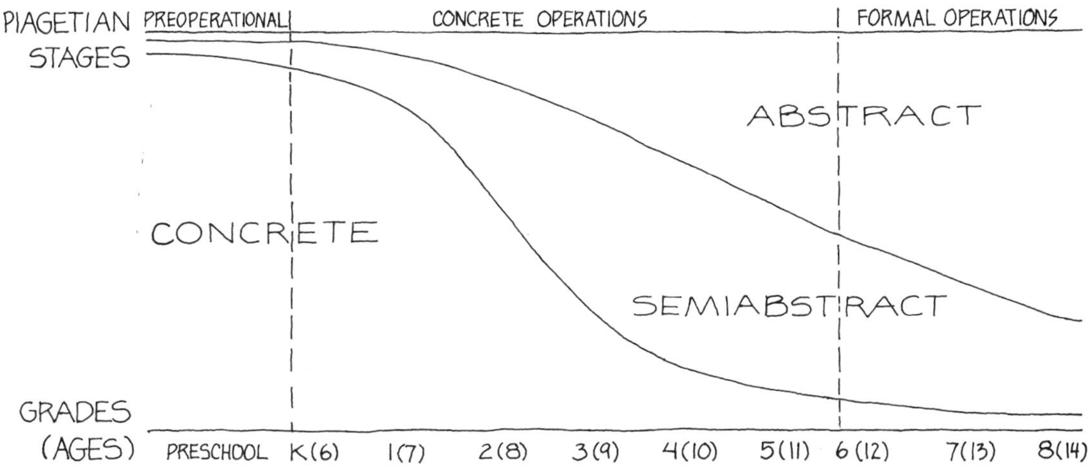

MATHEMATICAL SYMBOLISM AS A PSYCHOLOGICAL PROBLEM

One aspect of mathematics (and reading) instruction that relates to the problem of readiness is the need for symbolism to convey ideas. By their very nature, symbols are either semiabstract or abstract. Since the number zero could be described as a picture of an empty hole (0), a rather specious argument could be made that it is a semiabstract symbol. But few other digits provide a similar argument base.[3]

Think for a moment of the mathematical symbols introduced in most first-grade classes: the digits, $+$, $-$, $=$, often $\neq$, $>$, and $<$. The last two cause special problems because of common perceptual reversals at this age. Some programs even include set notation, with its {, }, $\cup$, and $\cap$; others

[3]One author occasionally finds himself counting the tines on the numeral 3 in column addition. This artifact of early education is an example of a nondebilitating habit that reduces computation speed. It is a reasonable question whether we should be concerned at all with such problems.

introduce parentheses and the solidus (/) or vinculum (—) of fractions. Not only that, but symbols are used in complex ways:

23 is different from 32

2/3 is different from 3/2

$5 - 2$ is different from $2 - 5$

Eugene Nichols, former director of the Project for the Mathematical Development of Children at Florida State University, has a delightful videotape of his work on that project with a first-grader who displayed remarkable logic in confronting symbols. After Nichols had the youngster fill in several exercises of the form

$$6 + 2 = \underline{\qquad},$$

which the boy did with ease, he wrote on his pad

$$5 + 3 = 3 + 5$$

and showed it to the boy. The written response was

$$\cancel{5 + 3} = 3 + 5 = \underline{\quad 8 \quad}.$$

Nichols persisted,

$$5 + 3 = 3 + 5.$$

This time the boy responded

$$\overset{+}{5 + 3 \neq 3 + 5} = \underline{\ \ 16\ \ }.$$

Nichols tried once more

$$5 + 3 = 3 + 5$$

This time the lad squeezed in

$$5 + 3 = \underline{8} \mid 3 + 5 = \underline{\ \ 8\ \ }.$$

At no point did the student budge from his insistence on "=" as an operation symbol[4] rather than a relation symbol.

One of Nichols's former colleagues on the project, Stanley Erlwanger, who also worked with Hassler Whitney at the Princeton Institute for Advanced Study, tells of an even more remarkable incident. He wrote

$$\underline{\qquad} = 5 - 2,$$

and when a bright first-grader didn't respond, Erlwanger told the student, "It is all right to work from right to left." (Students at this age often insist on working left to right, partly as a result of their reading experience.) The boy's eyes brightened and he wrote

$$\underline{\ -3\ } = 5 - 2.$$

[4]Or at least a symbol that demanded that the answer appear to the right.

He did indeed work from right to left, symbol by symbol:

$$2 - 5 = \underline{\ -3\ }.$$

Teachers should be sensitive to these and other problems that arise in the use of symbols. They must realize too that mathematics, supposedly the most fixed and constant of subjects, generates its own problems related to symbols. Some of its symbols are *ambiguous.* The "−" symbol, for example, has three distinct meanings in mathematics:

Subtraction, as in $8 - 3 = 5$

Negative or below zero, as in $-5°$ C (a temperature)

Additive inverse or opposite, as in $-(-3) = 3$

Some symbols are *synonymous;* that is, they have the same meaning.[5] Thus multiplication is displayed as

$$3 \times 5,$$

$$3 \cdot 5,$$

$$3(5),$$

or even, in algebraic notation,

$$ab.$$

---

[5]English usage differs from that of the United States. There, $3.5 = 15$ and $3 \cdot 5 = 3\frac{1}{2}$, exactly the reverse of our symbol usage. Note the inconsistencies in our usage: ab means the product of a and b, but 35 means $3 \cdot 10 + 5$, and $3\frac{1}{2}$ means $3 + \frac{1}{2}$.

Sometimes subtleties of notation cause significant differences in meaning. For example,

$$3 \times 5 + 2 \neq 3 \times (5 + 2),$$

the parentheses not only indicating multiplication, but carrying the additional role of ordering operations. Teachers' responses to these problems will be addressed briefly in the following sections, and in chapters 4 and 6–9.

MAINTAINING AN OVERVIEW

The need for symbols to express ideas at a time when students are not fully prepared for abstractions poses serious problems for the classroom teacher. But such problems are to be expected in creative teaching. Other difficult problems arise from the fragmentation of curriculum into discrete units and daily activities, an inescapable aspect of sequential curriculum development common to all programs. Decisions regarding process (development of intellectual skills) and product (content instruction) also pose serious problems. How does one maintain a proper balance between these two important aspects of teaching?

There is no prescription for responding to these and similar problems, just as there is no prescription for classroom discipline, something all teachers would like to maintain. Subsequent chapters in this text, school mathematics texts, and teachers' manuals to some extent provide a cumulative response. But the teacher with specific problems is still left with piecemeal answers that do not necessarily add up to a unified whole. This is where many teachers fail. They carry out the day-to-day activities of their program with care. They plan and execute each lesson well; students work hard. But something is missing and the instructional program falls short. What is missing may seem pedantic and even trivial, but it is extremely important. It is the teacher stepping back, away from the specifics of the program, to review how the pieces fit together, how the daily and weekly activities relate to the total picture of mathematics learning.

To explore this point further, consider the teaching of *bridging* in addition at the second-grade level. Bridging is an intermediate step in the process of *carrying.*[6] The idea is that you bridge over into the next decade. Thus the addition problems

$$\begin{array}{r}15\\+\ 7\\\hline\end{array}\quad\begin{array}{r}25\\+\ 7\\\hline\end{array}\quad\begin{array}{r}35\\+\ 7\\\hline\end{array}\quad\begin{array}{r}45\\+\ 7\\\hline\end{array}\quad\begin{array}{r}55\\+\ 7\\\hline\end{array}\quad\cdots$$

are examples of bridging related to the fact $5 + 7 = 12$. Many students who can easily answer a problem like

$$\begin{array}{r}29\\+\ 3\\\hline\end{array}$$

by counting "29, 30, 31, 32," will make errors when answering the same exercise by bridging. They may answer 22 or 12 or 31 or even 212 or 312. To the teacher whose attention is fixed on the specific problem, this kind of episode seems to call for review of the procedure, followed by drill. But this is treatment of surface symptoms rather than their root causes. It is aspirin administration for a still treatable intellectual illness.

Now step back and think about this difficulty. Surely when we recall the student's earlier ability to answer correctly, we can think of other things to do. In this instance, a rote procedure is canceling a less abstract procedure. But we want the rote procedure to extend the less abstract procedure. *Solution:* Make the connection between the two.

One of many ways to make this connection is to use beans and bean sticks (beans glued on popsicle sticks). These concrete representations for numbers could be interpreted using both counting and bridging procedures, possibly as shown in the diagrams on the following page. The teacher should make certain that the student sees many such exercises together, counting in each case to stress the relationship between the two procedures. When this

---

[6]*Carrying* is an old-fashioned term that today goes by a variety of names, most often *regrouping.* We see nothing wrong with the older, often more familiar, word.

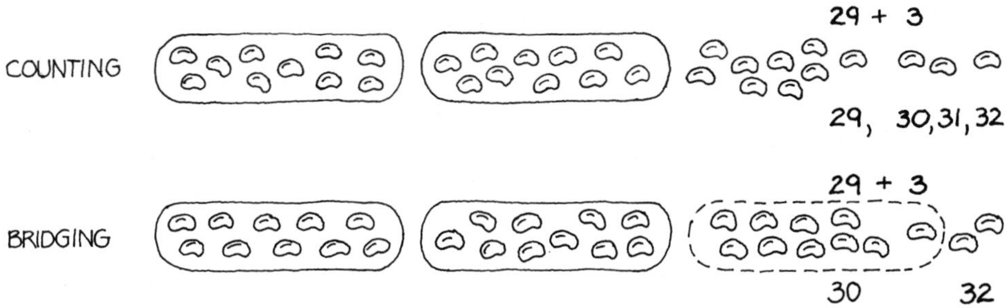

has been accomplished, counting should *support* bridging, which will have an additional conceptual base.

This example illustrates the most important message of this text: We need thoughtful teachers. Teaching requires penetrating diagnosis at all levels, not just at the remedial level. This kind of sensitive pedagogy is especially important to promote a child's movement up the conceptual or abstraction ladder.

A CONTRADICTION

The Harvard psychologist Jerome Bruner has stated, "Any subject can be taught effectively in some intellectually honest form to any child at any stage of development."[7] Does this contradict Piaget? It certainly seems to. How, for example, could you teach the calculus to even the brightest elementary school student? The key to Bruner's statement is the phrase "in some intellectually honest form." Rudiments of calculus do appear in elementary schools in the study of measurement—distance, time, and especially rate—and in initial exposure to infinite processes, for example, $\frac{1}{3} = .333....$

What is most important is the *way* the content is chosen and taught. And that is Bruner's point. His statement and its interpretation in Piagetian terms has led to the concepts depicted by the *spiral curriculum.* The figure on the next page demonstrates how the curriculum returns to topics at later

[7]Jerome Bruner, *The Process of Education* (New York: Vintage Books, 1963), p. 33.

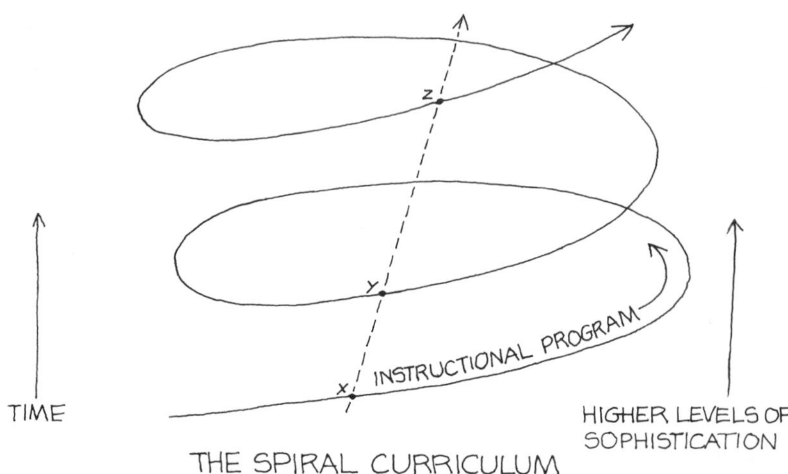

grade levels, but at higher levels of sophistication. Thus a particular concept that appears at x reappears at y and z, on the dotted line.

Elementary textbooks reflect this approach. The organization for each grade level is essentially the same; each topic is reviewed and extended. This provides students with repeated practice, giving them an opportunity to overlearn foundation concepts and skills, which then become essentially automatic and rapid. Students should not have to work out each addition or multiplication fact or process as they attempt higher-grade activities that demand these prerequisite skills.

Teachers should be alert to the danger, as well as the value, of this idea. Such repetition can lead to boredom and attendant classroom discipline problems. In too many classrooms the mathematics program after grade one is overly repetitious. No wonder some students turn away from mathematics. On the other hand, teachers sometimes develop certain topics superficially or even omit them entirely, assuming they will be covered later.

The answer to this dilemma is creative pedagogy. The teacher must find new and interesting ways to approach the same ideas. The potential for a successful program is demonstrated by a remarkable elementary school textbook series, written by Robert Wirtz, Morton Botel, W. W. Sawyer, and Max Beberman. In this series, called *Math Workshop for Children,* the basic ideas are repeated; but at successive grade levels they become progressively more challenging. Other text series have been strongly influenced by this one.

Classroom teachers cannot escape the implications for their own teaching. They should be aware of what was studied in earlier grades, as well as what is to follow. On this basis, they should carefully develop instructional sequences that strengthen student understanding without dampening interest.

TRANSFER

Arden Frandsen defines transfer of training as "the application to new learning tasks or problems of principles, concepts, or skills learned previously in different situations."[8] This concept has had an interesting history in education, particularly in mathematics education. The idea evolved from faculty psychology, the early concept of education as mental training or discipline. The brain was thought to be much like a muscle, whose growth was stimulated by problems of ever-increasing difficulty. Latin was supported as a school subject, not for its historical and linguistic value, but because it trained the mind. The trained mind could eventually apply itself to other more practical things. Similarly mathematics, and in particular geometry, was justified because it could be made challenging.

This extreme view of transfer was rejected by psychologists half a century ago, although it is evident that some mathematics teachers still use this criterion to evaluate their teaching. But generally the reaction was so strong that transfer was all but completely rejected, along with mental discipline and Latin. Geometry, too, lost much of its stature for a time. E. L. Thorndike in particular believed that transfer occurred only where identical elements were present and that the student had to be able to identify the new work as being related to the earlier concepts. This implies that if the logic learned in high school geometry is to be applied to real life situations, then the teacher must demonstrate those applications.

More recently, psychologists and others have stressed that transfer takes place on a much more substantial scale. If it did not, no one could solve original problems, and all science would grind to a halt. The important point is contained in a remark by Ernest Hilgard: "Some transfer of training must occur or there would be no use in developing a foundation for later learn-

---

[8]Arden N. Frandsen, *Educational Psychology* (New York: McGraw-Hill Book Company, 1961), p. 586.

ing."[9] In other words, if we give up the concept of transfer, we might as well give up any idea of a sequential development of curriculum, a concept central to mathematics instruction.

AN ILLUSTRATION OF TRANSFER: INTRODUCTORY ACTIVITIES WITH A GEOBOARD

There is probably no manipulative device that surpasses the geoboard as an instrument to cultivate exploration in mathematics. A spirit of inquiry is essential to the creation of independent thinkers among mathematics students. In this section we consider only a few introductory geoboard activities that illustrate some ideas about transfer. For those who wish to explore this idea further, there is a rich literature related to geoboards.[10]

A geoboard is a square array of nails driven halfway into a block of wood. Rubber bands are stretched around nails to form various polygons. A typical array uses 25 nails. Each student should have his own geoboard and a supply of about a dozen colored rubber bands of various sizes to carry out activities like those described here.

The following activities are appropriate for students at any grade level who have never used a geoboard before. The dialogue is based on observation of many classroom situations.

Teacher: Stretch one of your small rubber bands around four nails close together to form a square.

Responses:

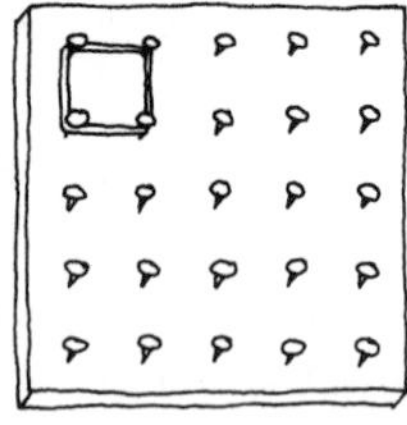

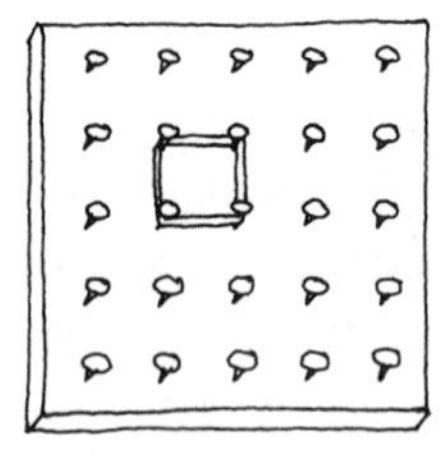

ETC.

[9]Ernest R. Hilgard and Gordon H. Bower, *Theories of Learning* (New York: Appleton-Century-Crofts, 1966), p. 7.

[10]See, for example, John Niman and Robert Postman, *Mathematics on the Geoboard* (New Rochelle, N.Y.: Cuisenaire, 1974).

Teacher: [*After checking student responses and correcting errors*] We'll call that an area of one square unit or just one. Now show me two square units.

Responses:

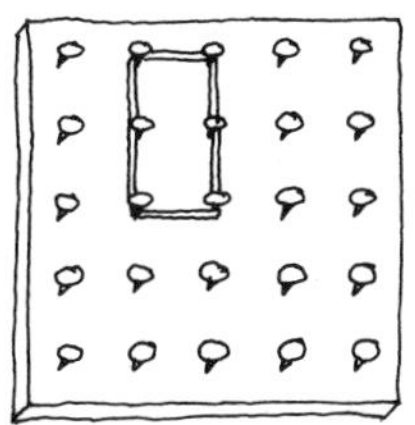

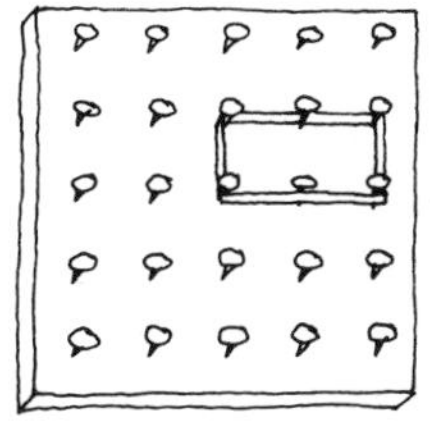

ETC.

[*In our experience this response is guaranteed at any grade level.*]

This exercise might be extended by asking for different ways of showing areas of three and four or more; with practice, the student's facility and confidence increases, and a more difficult challenge can be given.

Teacher: Now make a triangle with area one. [*Errors are usual on first attempts at this, but correct responses fall generally into two categories.*]

Responses:

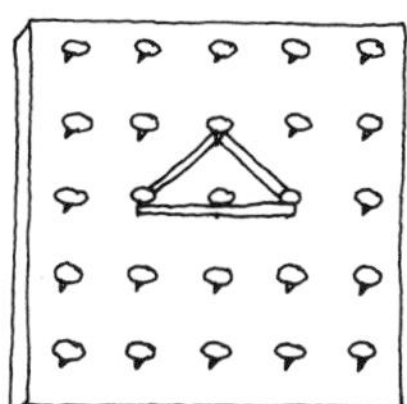

BUILDERS

These names are assigned, based on student explanations for the two answers. Embedders explain their area as half of the two-rectangle area:

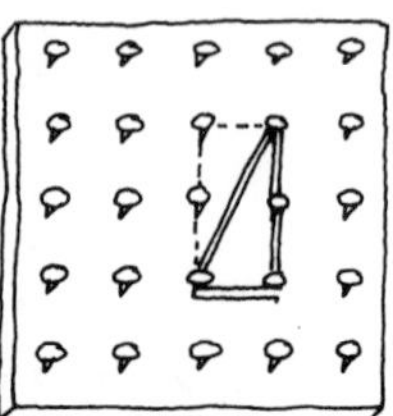

Builders explain their area as the sum of two halves, thus:

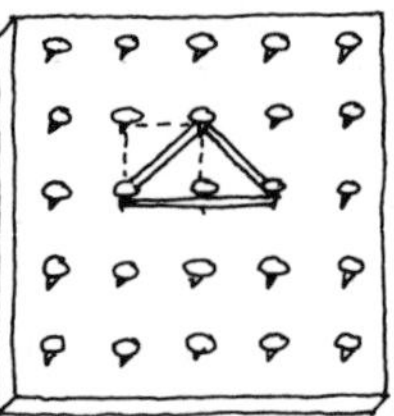

The following inquiry tends to reinforce the notion that there are two distinct responses to questions.

Teacher: On your geoboard make a triangle with the largest possible area.

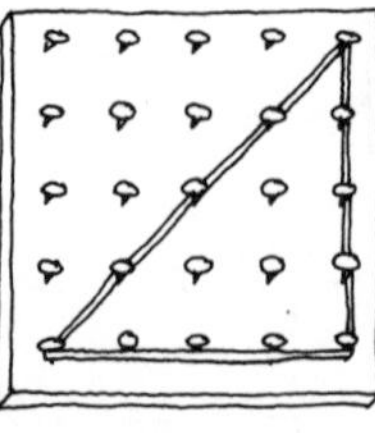

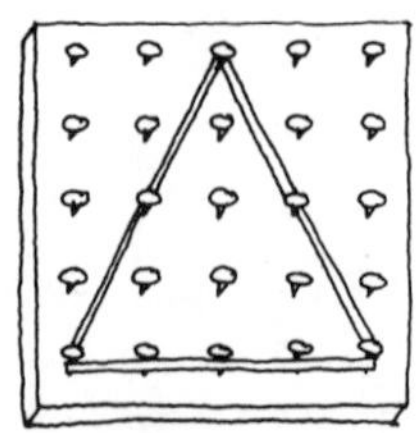

EMBEDDERS BUILDERS

Teacher: What is the area of your triangle?

Student: [*Embedder*] Eight, half of sixteen.

Student: [*Builder*] Eight, four plus four.

Again there are a variety of directions for possible exploration. One possibility is to ask how many differently shaped triangles have this maximum area.

And one final inquiry:

Teacher: I know you can make a square of area one. Now make a square of area four. [*Pause*] Make a square of area two. [*Longer pause*] If you have made a square of area two, try to make one of area three and one of area five.

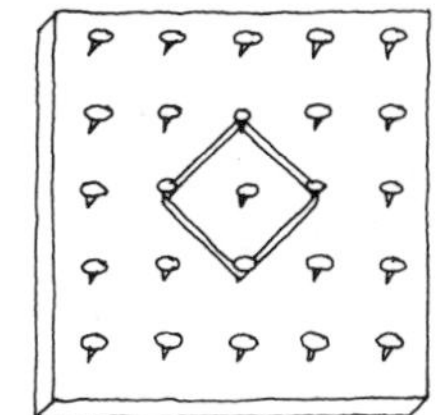

A SQUARE OF AREA TWO

Observing the responses of embedders and builders to the request for a square of area two, you learn immediately that the builders discover this square much more quickly.

There are a number of observations that can be made about this lesson. Perhaps the most important one is that students show a remarkable facility for answering these questions without specific instruction. Assuming that most children have not been exposed to these sorts of problems, their remarkable ability to make a rectangle of area two represents a basic form of transfer. We also saw that the two constructs, embedding and building, had different transferability to new problems. It should be noted that other inquiries could be framed that would give embedders an advantage.

The value of such devices as the geoboard is that students have a concrete tool to help them visualize ideas.[11] Similarly, all concrete devices provide such assistance and continue to be useful throughout school. You will meet many more, especially in chapter 6. You will be asked to explore the geoboard further in the exercises at the end of this chapter.

TWO PSYCHOLOGICAL SCHOOLS

While the idea of readiness, attributed to Piaget, is generally accepted by psychologists, transfer raises issues that separate the psychologists into two distinct camps. The two major psychological schools that relate to teaching are the stimulus-response (S-R) group, often called behaviorists, and the gestalt group. Teachers will do well to synthesize the best from each.

BEHAVIORISM

The earlier stimulus-response connectionism and conditioning theories were drawn together by an important and still-active Harvard psychologist, B. F. Skinner. Put very simply, stimulus-response theory states that organisms, including people, tend to continue along rewarded paths and retreat from punished paths. In one sense, Skinner actually uses the reverse order (response-stimulus) by rewarding approximations of desired behavior.

This basic reorganization has had a striking effect on animal training, which Skinner has demonstrated. Within a short time, he can teach a dog to turn around on command. To do this, he gives the command and rewards the dog's first random movements in the desired direction. At each stage of the training, the dog's motion in the desired direction must be a little stronger in order to receive the reward—a food pellet or encouragement.

---

[11]The word *crutch*, often used here, is unfortunate in that it carries a negative connotation. Under any conditions when a crutch provides an alternative to rote learning, we encourage use of the crutch. Education should lead to the ability to walk alone (conceptual freedom) rather than lying prone (memorization).

(Failures may or may not be punished to extinguish them. In one sense, lack of response may be viewed as punishment, so that in effect all responses are rewarded or punished. Skinner himself plays down the role of punishment.) In a remarkably short time the dog obeys the command to turn around.

Learning, according to this theory, is built up in the same way. The learning process may be thought of as a staircase of small steps. Larger concepts must be broken down into small discrete concepts; major objectives must be approached through a series of short, intermediate steps. An obvious result of this connectionist view of learning is programmed instruction, in which blocks of learning, even entire courses, are presented as a sequence of thousands of steps. Each step is a simple question, relying heavily on previously mastered content. After answering this question, the student immediately checks to see if his answer is correct (is thereby rewarded or punished), and then moves on to the next question.

Skinner suggests that this technique be applied in the classroom as well, that teachers be trained to break their teaching down into smaller, easier-to-master, discrete steps. In other words, he urges teachers to manage their classrooms along the lines of operant conditioning, much like his training of the dog.

A related outcome of the conditioning theory of learning is the current stress on behavioral objectives: You set up instructional goals based on student behavior, and then work back through the program to develop a step-by-step approach to this behavior. This process indicates a hierarchy of prerequisites to achieve the desired behavior, and outlines a programmed path for students to follow. This path becomes the basis for organized classroom activity. Robert Gagné is a contemporary learning theorist who has stressed these kinds of specific task analyses of mathematics learning. He calls them learning hierarchies.

Much laboratory and classroom evidence supports various aspects of Skinnerian learning theory. But it is often criticized in the areas of problem solving and transfer. Skinner and his followers have responded to these criticisms. Solving larger problems, they say, is merely a matter of manipulating variables at a level to which the student has been programmed; no originality is required. An examination of a programmed text demonstrates what is meant by this. If you look only at the first few exercises, they appear trivial, as they should according to the theory. But skip ahead. Without mastering the small intermediate steps, you will find that items a few pages later appear much more difficult. In other words, larger problems are merely the sum of smaller problem increments.

Transfer, for Skinner and his followers, comes when students respond to similar stimuli in different areas. This is quite similar to the identical-elements idea of Thorndike, mentioned earlier.

David Ausubel is another contemporary psychologist whose work is usually associated with the Skinnerian group. While encouraging analyses of learning hierarchies similar to Gagné's, he takes a more extreme position by stressing content knowledge, rather than learning to think, as the central role of the school. But Ausubel adds to the concept of the learning hierarchy the principle of *advance organizer.* Given alternate task sequences to achieve a goal, Ausubel recommends the route that embodies the best overriding principle. James Bidwell has described the application of Gagné's and Ausubel's ideas to teaching division of fractions.[12] Examples of the three procedures for which learning hierarchies have been constructed are given below. Bidwell's preference among advance organizers is the inverse-operation process; he claims that it serves as a stronger organizing principle than the organizers in either the common-denominator or complex-fraction process.

$$\frac{2}{3} \div \frac{4}{5} = \frac{10}{15} \div \frac{12}{15} = \frac{10}{12}$$

COMMON DENOMINATOR

$$\frac{2}{3} \div \frac{4}{5} = \frac{\frac{2}{3}}{\frac{4}{5}} \cdot \frac{15}{15} = \frac{10}{12}$$

COMPLEX FRACTION

$$\frac{2}{3} \div \frac{4}{5} = n$$

means

$$\frac{2}{3} = n \cdot \frac{4}{5}$$

$$\frac{2}{3} \cdot \frac{5}{4} = n \cdot \frac{4}{5} \cdot \frac{5}{4} = n$$

INVERSE OPERATION

[12]"Some Consequences of Learning Theory Applied to Division of Fractions," *School Science and Mathematics* 71 (1971): 426–34.

Benjamin Bloom recommends a complete reorganization of the classroom to accomplish learning tasks.[13] His teachers are encouraged to vary the amount of time spent learning by individual students rather than to accommodate to different levels of achievement, the reverse of common practice. Bloom calls for uniformly high levels of achievement (a constant), with different amounts of time needed by individuals to reach this goal. Mathematics learning, which depends so much on previous attainment, should take into account Bloom's views. The coordination of self-pacing, attendant in this approach, offers considerable challenge to teachers.

Among educational psychologists today, behaviorism is the overriding approach to learning. It has many attractions: simplicity, almost mechanical applicability, short-term demonstrability, and ease of incorporation into teaching materials. Most contemporary elementary school mathematics programs are designed along these lines with topics broken down into careful developmental sequences. We will see now, however, that there are alternatives.

GESTALT

To an increasing number of educators the theories of the behaviorists are dehumanizing. Is teaching the same as animal training? Is learning merely an accumulation of large numbers of discrete details? Gestalt psychologists accuse the Skinnerians of focusing on memorization rather than understanding, on training rather than intellecutal growth, on the superficial end product rather than the organization of thought. The goal of gestalt psychologists is improvement of the thinking process rather than the mechanical, conditioned production of specific output.

The gestalt or field psychologists believe that there are larger learning increments and, in particular, that insight plays an important role in problem solving. A comparison of the two viewpoints is shown in the figure on the following page. Note how the quantum leap in the gestalt diagram replaces the steady upward march in the behaviorist diagram.

---

[13]Benjamin Bloom, "Learning for Mastery," in *Handbook on Formative and Summative Evaluation of Student Learning,* ed. Benjamin Bloom et al., (New York: McGraw-Hill Book Company, 1971), pp. 43–57.

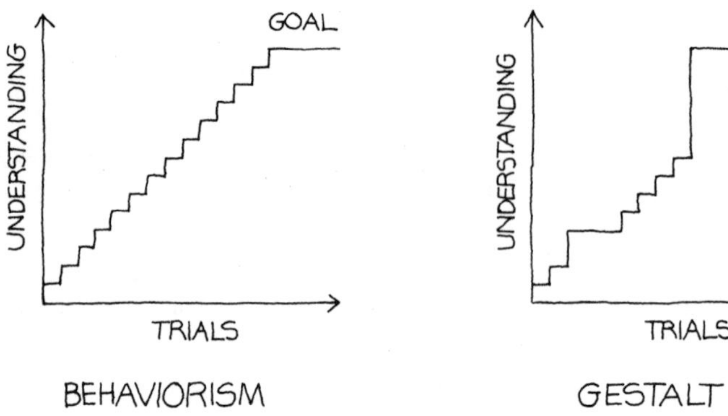

Jacques Hadamard lists a series of four steps in problem solving: (1) preparation, (2) incubation, (3) illumination, and (4) verification.[14] These parallel an earlier sequence suggested by John Dewey. The mathematical literature is full of anecdotal evidence in support of such a sequence: mathematicians to whom concepts crystallized in bed, on walks in the country, for one (Poincaré) even while boarding a carriage.

Obviously, field theorists tend to focus on larger, or more significant, problems. It is hard to place in the behaviorist's mold the challenge exercise of chapter 1, separating the obtuse triangle into acute triangles, which exemplifies a gestalt problem.

One result of gestalt theory is what is often described as teaching for discovery, a topic treated at length in later chapters. In this kind of teaching, the stage is set for students to make significant generalizations and theory extensions. One aspect of this teaching is the "Eureka" syndrome, whereby the discoverer is strongly motivated by success. This encourages him to make further, and often still deeper, explorations.

Peter Caws suggests that a "kind of single-minded concentration that keeps out irrelevant thoughts, and a facility for spotting wrong moves" is

[14]Jacques Hadamard, *Psychology of Invention in the Mathematical Field,* Princeton: Princeton University Press, 1949.

needed in problem solving.[15] Perhaps exaggerating, he says: "As for everybody's not being a genius, the answer may be that everybody . . . is, until inhibiting factors supervene—which almost always happens." From this viewpoint, teachers should help students to raise their level of concentration so that they can make progress in learning, and avoid losing the inborn facilities that helped them learn to walk and talk without formal instruction. Raymond Wilder, in a discussion of the role of intuition in the process of learning and developing mathematics, suggests that we are wrong to teach mathematics as a vast amount of knowledge.[16] Rather we should turn our energies to teaching students to participate in mathematical activity in order to develop the appropriate setting for creative insight. Bruner encourages keeping the learning environment as fluid and individualized as possible, in order to encourage students to generate ideas.

Gestaltists, then, feel that learning takes place in larger increments. While accepting that much learning is the accumulation of experience, they stress the reorganization of past experience and the building of new configurations on old ones.

Some gestalt psychologists have noted better than 100 percent transfer of learning tasks. In other words, as George Katona and others have found, students sometimes do better with a new conceptually related task than with the original one! Does the brain provide some efficiency here that is not part of the input? Computer users know that this kind of serendipity is quite possible—computers often produce unexpected bonuses of information. But is this merely a throwback to faculty psychology: the mind as a muscle? To some it seems to be, but evidence points in other directions. Despite the power of the brain, its inherent inefficiency operates against direct attempts to train it as an athlete trains for a race. It is not enough just to present harder and harder problems. Rather, we must devise educational sequences that provide an appropriate mass of information, as well as explicit directions related to its use. The brain then requires practice of a different type: for example, search patterns, methods of organizing data in problem solving, must be made as efficient as possible.

---

[15]Peter Caws, "The Structure of Discovery," *Science,* 12 December 1969, p. 1377.

[16]Raymond Wilder, "The Role of Intuition," *Science,* 5 May 1967, p. 609.

BRAIN BIMODALITY

Robert Ornstein in his important book *The Psychology of Consciousness* organizes strong experimental evidence for a theory of brain development.[17] Ornstein points out that different parts of the brain play specific roles in body control and cognition. Here is a summary of some of the responsibilities associated with specific hemispheres of the brain for typical people.[18]

Left hemisphere

Control of the right side of the body

Processing of information from the right side of the viewing field (recorded on the left side of each eye interior)

Language

Mathematics

Analytic, convergent, logical thinking; sequence and order[19]

Time

Right hemisphere

Control of the left side of the body

Processing of information from the left visual field (recorded on the right side of each eye interior)

---

[17]Robert Ornstein, *The Psychology of Consciousness* (San Francisco: W. H. Freeman, 1973), esp. chap. 3.

[18]Ornstein suggests that these assignments are based on right-handedness. Left-handers, about 5 percent of the population, are less consistent. He also indicates that brain-injured children may develop differently, another part of the brain assuming extra responsibility for the injured region.

[19]Notice that behaviorism is associated with the left hemisphere and gestalt with the right.

Spatial orientation

Integration and analysis

Holistic and relational, divergent thinking

Creative, intuitive activities

Art

The two hemispheres are connected to each other by the *corpus callosum.* It should be obvious that many complex tasks require communication between the two hemispheres. But when one side of the brain is carrying major responsibility, the other appears to be blocked off by electrical body currents called *alpha waves.*

A specific experiment suggests some of the problems in this area that might concern teachers. Subjects were asked to balance a stick on the index finger of one hand. Average times were recorded for left-hand balance and right-hand balance. Then the same subjects were asked to talk while balancing the stick. Result: Right-hand balancing times *decreased,* while left-hand times *increased.* Ornstein's interpretation is that language, a left hemisphere function, interfered with right-hand balance; but in left-hand (right-hemisphere) balance, language occupied the left hemisphere, effectively cutting down interference.

Research in this area is relatively recent, and will probably be greatly expanded in the near future. But several things, important to teachers and curriculum developers, are already evident.

1. Although Ornstein assigns mathematics to the left hemisphere, important aspects of mathematics, notably spatial (geometrical) relationships, appear to be developed in the right hemisphere.

2. In the traditional elementary school mathematics classroom, virtually all activity is associated with development of left-hemisphere aspects of mathematics. (This is true of other subjects to the point that we might describe schooling as a right-handed, or left-brain-hemisphere, activity.)

3. Many students may be characterized by better development of one hemisphere over the other. In particular, left-handed children may function differently in certain activities.

AN ARGUMENT FOR TEACHING MORE VISUAL ALGORITHMS

We have indicated that the left hemisphere of the brain is specialized for language and mathematical computation, while the right hemisphere deals with the gestalt apprehension of visual, spatial, and artistic structures. Scientists are less clear in their understanding of the mechanisms of communication between those distinct and highly specialized information-processing regions of the brain.

One of the current conjectures about the formal differences between the two modalities is contained in the principle of competitive antagonism between the two. Competitive antagonism asserts that one of two modes of representation in competition for the same resources (the neural system) of an organism, if unregulated, will diminish the utility of the other mode. There is antagonism between mechanisms for gestalt apprehension of visual-spatial relationships (the "big picture"), and those related to analytical strategies necessary for perception and production of language.

There is considerable evidence that concept and structure development in mathematics is dependent on *both* modalities. From the principle of competitive antagonism, we can infer that in the teaching of mathematics regulation of linguistic and visual-spatial experiences is necessary. This, of course, is based on the assumption that a balanced development of language and pictorial mechanisms is desirable.

The essential differences between linguistic and pictorial expressions provide substantial reasons for cultivating both mechanisms. Pictorial representations are usually less abstract than linguistic ones, but they do not have as precise a system for assigning interpretations. Linguistic expressions are superior to pictorial ones in specifying the relative importance of information, in ordering it for processing, and in clearly describing new material. On the other hand, pictorial expressions show structure with far greater lucidity than equivalent linguistic expressions. Note in the figure, for instance, the superiority of the pictorial representation over the algebraic representation of the distributive law. While each mode of presentation has its special

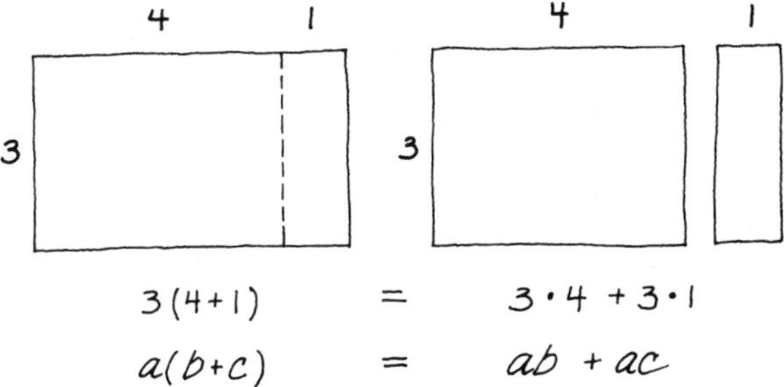

assets, our teaching capabilities are enhanced by relying on a combination of both.

Pedagogy in mathematics then should support both language and visual-spatial skills. While it is yet unclear how much experience is adequate to achieve facility in both domains, we know that linguistic experiences prevail in the current teaching of the algorithms of arithmetic. Thus, for greater balance, we urge that more visual algorithms be included in the mathematics curriculum.

We need not rely merely on neuropsychology for evidence of alternative modes in conceptual and perceptual patterns of organization. Psychoanalytic theory suggests that an individual's style of attentiveness also has an important impact on his conscious experience. Two styles of attentiveness have been characterized, according to the way individuals perceive stimuli. An intense, sharp focus is typical of those who are not tolerant of vagueness in their attention. People of this type concentrate on detail, are unable to let their attention scan, and are reluctant to let their attention be captured. These characteristics make a sharp focuser less susceptible to hunches or creative insights. People prone to this style can rigidly commit themselves to manipulation of information and be quite successful at it. Being confronted by visual patterns that promote the search for visual algorithms forces the intense focuser into a relaxation of this attitude of deliberateness.

Visual experiences, on the other hand, are compatible with a relaxed, more pervasive, style of attention. In a diffuse attentive style, with an absence of sharp focus, sensory images and inspiration dominate. This mode of attention is organized around intake from the environment, rather than its manipulation. Eventually, progressive development of achievement-oriented activity ordinarily causes this diffuse attentive style to be obscured by an active attentive style. A well-designed experience with visual patterns engages the interaction of both attentive modes. Both should then develop physiologically and psychologically to form an organismic whole.

Interaction of the two attentive styles is required for creative synthesis (discovery) in mathematics. There are three distinct stages in the discovery process. First, there is a stage of directed confrontation of the problem. This stage, accompanied by much manipulation and sharply focused attention, leads to a feeling of impasse. At this point, one usually gives up struggling with the problem for a time and diverts attention to other things. During this second stage, while attention is focused away from the problem, the solution manifests itself. The answer suddenly appears. In the third stage, one works over the answer in sharp attentive focus to assess its validity and to integrate it into the cognitive structure. Visual patterns offer a fertile framework in which to successfully realize the three stages of the discovery process.

SOME GENERAL PRECEPTS

The value of psychology to the teacher lies more in the choice of fundamental constructs than in incontrovertible evidence supporting specific modes of teaching. Teachers should spend some time considering philosophical frameworks for their thoughts about teaching. Psychologists have provided a variety of such outlines, as well as volumes of evidence in support of them. Most teachers will not adopt one psychological theory to the exclusion of others. Virtually no psychologist today favors such intellectual isolation. The controversies of several decades ago have largely disappeared from psychology. A teacher may freely choose attractive aspects of various theories, testing each in the real world of the classroom.

Two basic concerns face every classroom teacher: (1) having students learn a specified body of knowledge (product), and (2) having them develop intellectual competence and independence (process). Behaviorists have much to offer teachers about the first type of (guided) learning, but less about the second. The gestalt psychologists' contribution is exactly the reverse. Teachers should draw on both schools, seeking to promote discovery learning whenever possible, while carefully structuring sequences to promote acquisition of knowledge.

The main point here is that philosophical issues should be a central concern of every classroom teacher. Too often we miss the forest for the trees. We trap ourselves in the day-to-day details of instructional programs, obscuring our total view. As a teacher, you should continually challenge yourself with questions about what you believe and why. The remainder of this book draws heavily on the psychological ideas generated in this chapter. You should continually examine your own teaching philosophy in light of these constructs.

We close this chapter with some less controversial precepts that are derived from generally accepted psychological theory and are directly applicable in the classroom. We draw heavily on summaries prepared by Ernest Hilgard and Gordon Bower, and by Goodwin Watson.[20] In the latter case especially, the author suggests that there is common ground between psychologists and teachers and that psychologists can make a positive contribution to the art of teaching.

> Students learn by doing. They should be active, not passive. Too much teacher direction leads to conformity, defiance, or nonparticipation.
>
> Practice is still important. *Overlearning,* practice beyond concept attainment, guarantees retention. But sheer repetition alone is poor practice.
>
> Rewards for desirable responses are preferable to punishment for undesirable responses. Immediate reward is stronger than delayed reward. Often fresh, novel experiences themselves are adequate rewards.
>
> Criticism, failure, and discouragement destroy aspirations, self-confidence, and sense of worth.
>
> Conflicts and frustrations arise inevitably in learning. They should be identified and resolved or accommodated.

---

[20]Ernest Hilgard and Gordon Bower, *Theories of Learning* (New York: Appleton-Century-Crofts, 1966), pp. 562–64; and Goodwin Watson, *What Psychology Can We Trust?* (New York: Bureau of Publication, Teachers College, Columbia University, 1961).

> The difficulty of a problem is determined as much by the way it is presented to students as by its inherent conceptual makeup. Well stated is half-solved.
>
> Thinking is a response to accepted intellectual challenge.
>
> Learning with understanding is more permanent and transferable than learning by rote or formula.
>
> It is important for students to know the goals set for them, as well as their underlying rationale.
>
> Divergent, or open-ended, thinking should be stressed, as well as convergent, or specific-answer, thinking. Developing significant questions is as important an intellectual activity as answering those questions.
>
> Tests can have an inordinate influence on subject matter and teaching methods. Teachers who have process goals should see to it that their tests reflect those goals.
>
> Anxiety levels should be monitored in the classroom. Anxious students may react negatively to comments on progress, while low-anxiety students may benefit from similar comments.
>
> Motives and values strongly affect learning. Relevancy of learning strongly influences student achievement.
>
> Group interactions are important in the classroom. Most students are more concerned about peer response than teacher response.

These, then, are some contributions of the psychologists: general theories with a few specific prescriptions. You must weigh these ideas against your practical experience in the classroom in order to develop your own pragmatic philosophy of mathematics instruction.

EXERCISES

1. Classify each of the following learning activities according to whether it is most influenced by behaviorist or gestalt psychological principles. Do not feel bound by obvious answers. Discuss reasons for your answers.
   - (a) Problem solving
   - (b) Learning the multiplication facts
   - (c) Learning a definition
   - (d) Applying mathematics to the real world
   - (e) Developing logic and structure
   - (f) Learning an algorithm such as long division

2. Choose a topic in an elementary school mathematics textbook and prepare a presentation of the material from a point of view that has elements of both behaviorist and gestalt philosophies.

3. It has been said that pressure to cover a great deal of mathematical content in a course obstructs learning. Discuss this statement.

4. Comment on the statement: "Once the prerequisites are mastered, learning the next task is a snap." If this is true, why is school achievement not much greater?

5. Review your own experiences to respond to the following:
   - (a) Recall an incident where you experienced a "flash of insight."
   - (b) Identify times in your schooling when individual teachers stressed gestalt learning activities.

6. Describe some of the most highly creative students you know. How would you teach students like these?

7. Reconsider Frederique Papy's primary-grade classroom demonstration in chapter 1 from the perspective of this chapter:
   - (a) Do you consider the questions, especially the final one (which dots must represent boys?), as behaviorist or gestalt?
   - (b) How does this example relate to Bruner's comment (quoted on page 35)?
   - (c) How does this example relate to the Piagetian stages? Is it justified or does it contradict Piaget's ideas?

8. Apply the questions of exercise 7 (a–c) to the challenge exercise of chapter 1 (page 18).

9. Two inquiries were left incomplete in the section on the geoboard. Try to construct squares of area three and five on a geoboard (or on a five-by-five lattice). Squares of what area can be constructed?

10. Make up and try to solve three exploration questions related to the geoboard. (Think of activities related to triangles, rectangles, and squares.)

11. Which side of your brain do you think is more highly developed? Justify your answer.

12. Indicate three teaching techniques that would facilitate left-brain-hemisphere development and five, right.

13. Choose a topic in elementary school mathematics. Focus on the grade level that is of specific interest to you as well as one grade below and one above. Evaluate the development of that topic through the three grade levels as it relates to the spiral approach.

14. The statement is made in this chapter that builders will be able to make a square of area two on a geoboard much more quickly than embedders.

(a) Why do you think this is true?

(b) Make up a problem that would be easier for an embedder.

15. Beyond learning differences between embedders and builders, there are those who learn more from a visual viewpoint than from a verbal one, and vice-versa. Give examples of a concept viewed both verbally and visually.

16. How do the embedders vs. builders and the visual vs. verbal distinctions tie in with Ornstein's split-hemisphere theory?

PART 2

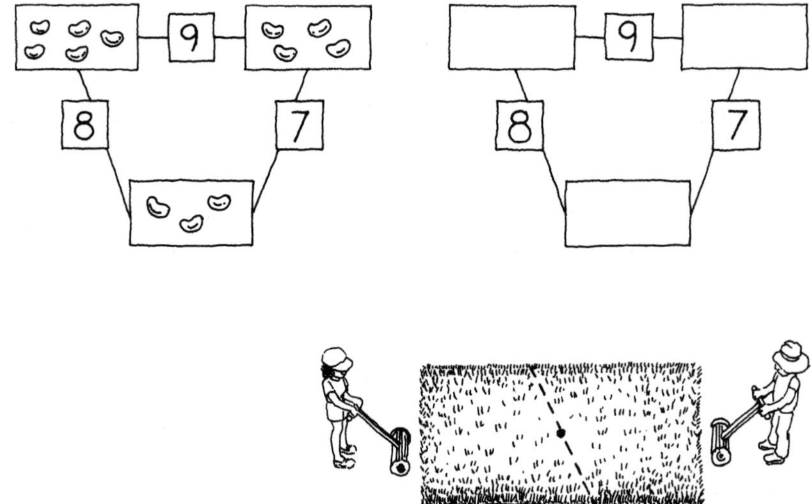

TEACHING THE CONTENT

An often quoted exchange about teaching takes the following form:

I understand you teach mathematics.

I don't teach mathematics; I teach children.

We find this response silly and recommend that in the mathematics classroom teachers teach children mathematics. But although we find these distinctions silly in practice, we will separate content from pedagogy in the sections that follow. This artificial separation will allow you to organize your thinking about these topics before they are synthesized later. In this section, we focus on mathematics content in order to provide a broad overview of what is to be taught.

Chapter 3 is devoted to geometry instruction, 4 to instruction in arithmetic, and 5 to instruction related to structure and logic, the foundations of mathematical understanding. Although we will consider these topics from the viewpoint of content, we will do so by means of examples, which should be examined for their instructional value.

CHAPTER THREE

TEACHING GEOMETRY AND MEASUREMENT

GEOMETRY IN THE SCHOOL PROGRAM

In this and the following two chapters we examine teaching problems related to elementary school mathematics. This broad overview is designed to give you perspective rather than detailed knowledge. The latter should be obtained directly from elementary school texts; the former is necessary to provide a framework for the specific content. This chapter devoted to geometry comes first for three related reasons:

1. Geometry forms a strong foundation for the development of more abstract arithmetic and algebraic aspects of elementary school mathematics.

2. Geometry, because it leans heavily on visual input, provides pedagogical advantages suggested in chapter 2.

3. Geometry provides many problem sources and applications from the real world.

A secondary reason for taking up geometry first relates to an unfortunate phenomenon that is widespread in schools today. Many mathematics teachers identify their role as only that of developing computation skills. They skip text sections, even whole chapters, related to geometry. Because of this, too many youngsters today lack geometric insights. As a result, their mathematics development is careless and unorganized, and the deeper problems suggested in chapter 2 are exacerbated.

Even among teachers who do teach the full mathematics curriculum, many do another type of injustice to geometry. They focus so much attention on the memorization and other borderline mathematics aspects of geometry that students receive a warped and negative view of this topic. Geometry is not merely spelling the word *trapezoid*, defining *perpendicular*, or giving the conversion factor for meters into yards. Even though those activities may force their way into the program, they do not constitute the basic aspects of this important subject. To think of geometry in such terms is bad; to communicate it to students in this limited form is worse.

EXAMPLES OF GEOMETRIC ACTIVITIES

Here are some examples of geometric activities appropriate to elementary school instruction in geometry and measurement.

1. The teacher asks second-grade groups to decide whether the classroom is more or less than twice as long as it is wide. All

standard measuring tools, including meter sticks and rulers, have been carefully removed from the classroom.

2. Students in a third-grade classroom are given an envelope, scissors, and mimeographed sheets, on which the pattern of this figure is duplicated. All youngsters cut their patterns into puzzles of their own individual design. The only restrictions are that they must cut along the lines and cut no more than seven pieces. The students then carefully place the pieces of the puzzle in their envelopes, writing their names on the outside. The teacher collects and redistributes the envelopes, challenging students to reconstruct the original rectangles. When the students finish, they check with the student whose puzzle they solved.

3. A fourth-grade class is discussing angle measure. Having drawn almost one hundred angles on the chalkboard, they now seek ways of classifying the angles and ordering them by size. At carefully chosen times, the teacher standardizes student-developed vocabulary, and introduces the protractor as a standard measuring instrument. (Quarter turn becomes *right angle*, and the words *acute, obtuse, perpendicular,* and *degree* are introduced.) In each case the word or tool fits a developed need. In the context of the discussion, students raise and then resolve the problem of side length being independent of (the mathematician's phrase for "not related to") angle size.

TWO CONGRUENT ANGLES OF DIFFERING SIDE LENGTH

4. In a sixth-grade classroom a student has brought his toy kaleidoscope to school at the teacher's request. Students examine the interior to determine how the instrument works. Their examination will complement their formal study of transformation geometry, in particular, reflections. The teacher has prepared a set of hinged mirrors and protractors so that students can investigate the effects of different size openings on the number of reflections.

HINGED MIRRORS

5. In another sixth-grade class, students are studying polyhedra, that is, solids with polygons for faces. Earlier they collected data to

develop the relationships between number of edges (E), faces (F), and corners (C):

$$F + C = E + 2.$$

The teacher praises the class, telling them that they have discovered a relationship so important that it is given the name of its discoverer: Euler's (pronounced "oiler's") formula for polyhedra.

6. In the same sixth-grade class, the teacher, having placed two cubes of the same size on the desk, picks up one and asks the students to visualize the diagonals of the cube drawn. Teacher and students

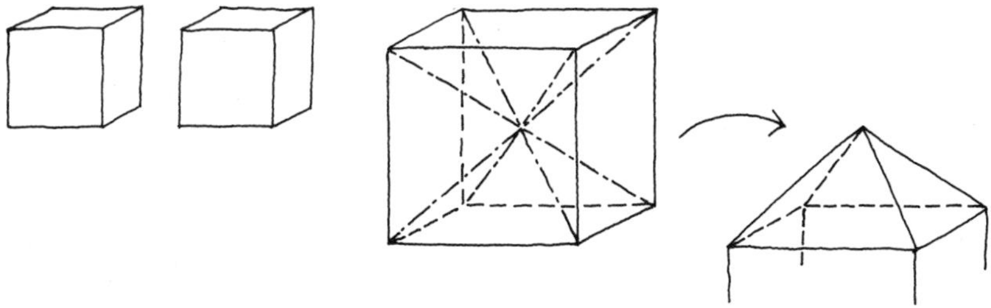

discuss the difference between face diagonals and cube diagonals. The students agree that symmetry would lead these diagonals to meet at the center of the cube. The teacher asks what kind of solid shape is formed by a face and the segments joining that face to the center of the cube. The class agrees that the figure would be a square pyramid. The teacher confirms this by taking apart a model. Addressing the class, the teacher says, "You have done well so far, and I think you are rather good at visualizing figures in three dimensions. But now I have a more difficult problem for you. I am going to place this square pyramid we took from one cube with its square face against the square face of the other cube. (See the figure.) If I did that with all six pyramids to form a single solid, what would that new solid be?" Several students immediately suggest a cube. The teacher says that is a good guess, but urges more careful thinking. He asks the class to think hard about the problem but not to use models to answer until after the next class.

7. A fifth-grade class makes designs with compasses.

8. In a first-grade class, where students are studying rectangles, the teacher has drawn the following figure on the chalkboard:

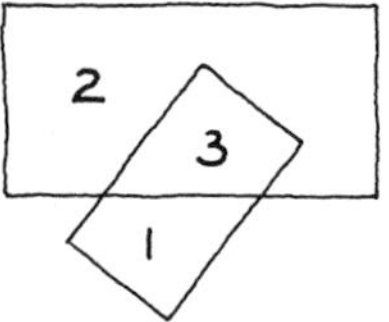

Two students come forward to trace the outlines of the two rectangles. Then the teacher says: "Now suppose each rectangle is a fence. How many separate playgrounds have I enclosed?" The class agrees that there are three. Students come forward to point to them. There is some discussion about the outside being a fourth playground (a discussion encouraged by the teacher), but students agree not to count it, "since it doesn't have a fence around it." The teacher next asks if anyone can suggest how to draw two rectangles and enclose four playgrounds. After some false trials, one student offers the following figure:

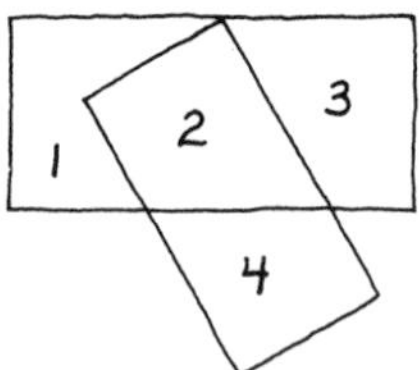

The teacher then asks the class to find all the possibilities for numbers of playgrounds (enclosed regions) formed by two rectangles.

9. In an eighth-grade class, the teacher is developing the area formulas for a parallelogram and a triangle by encouraging students to suggest how to cut the figures and piece them together to form rectangles. By this means the students see not only development of formulas, but also relationships among the figures.

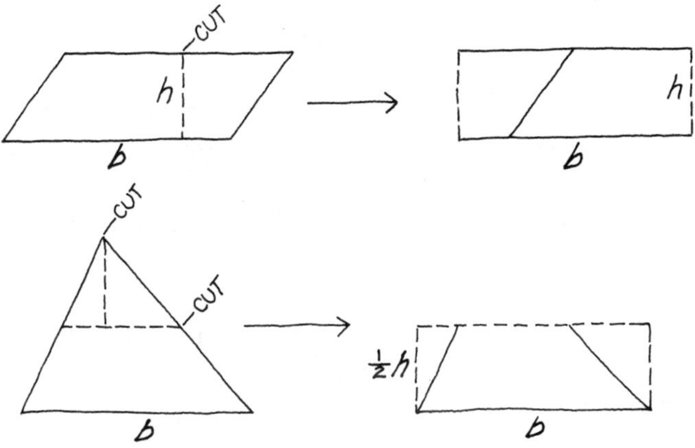

THE DIRECTION OF GEOMETRY INSTRUCTION

The foregoing examples suggest the kinds of goals associated with geometry instruction in the elementary school mathematics program. But these goals are not conducive to formulation of particular classroom exercises. There are a number of specific things we want elementary students to learn; but as soon as we start listing them, the character of the program is apt to change. For example, consider a type of goal statement found in most elementary school programs:

> *Students will be able to identify the following geometric figures: quadrilateral, parallelogram, square, . . .*

The difficulty with such a goal is that it tempts teachers first to tell students what a quadrilateral or a parallelogram is, and then to ask students to repeat back those statements.

Actually, these formal content-specific goals belong in a secondary school mathematics program. Elementary school geometry should be *informal* and *experience-oriented.* Content knowledge should grow naturally out of the students' experiences, as it is needed to help organize their thinking. The failure of curriculum developers and teachers to recognize this has led to such esoteric goals as:

> Students should differentiate between open and closed curves.
>
> Students should be able to draw Venn diagrams to represent relationships between various types of quadrilaterals and triangles.
>
> Students should use proper notation to name or label lines, segments, rays, . . .

Still, a large number of concepts, skills, and structures can be grouped under geometry. In the primary grades, classification of two- and three-dimensional shapes has been traditional. In the upper grades, geometry emerges in four unique directions: (1) more shape-classification schemes and extension of the work of the primary grades, (2) informal geometry based on notions of symmetry, (3) investigations in a coordinate plane, and (4) activities in graph theory.

Measurements of area, volume, and perimeter point up basic relationships between arithmetic and geometry in the measurement of space. In the upper grades, measurements of the probability of an event are usually formulated in the language of geometry.

GEOMETRY AS FUN: A VALUE AND A PROBLEM

Since the geometry program is both activity-oriented and visually oriented, this subject can be fun for students if the more formal aspects are played down by thoughtful teachers. It also can be highly motivating. Gifted students particularly can display their creativity here, and all students can exercise creative skills, thereby developing them. As these are among the most important skills of all learning, their inclusion in the mathematics program should need no justification. With careful planning, students will be encouraged to develop skills, while enjoying the work. But teachers should be alert to the fact that to some students, parents, school administrators, and supervisors *fun* has a negative connotation. They feel that school should be work; students should memorize; students should be taught to respond to multiple-choice objective tests; and students should be taught as they were taught.

The teacher can make several good responses to this attitude:

> Students taught geometry the way we have described respond to goals at higher cognitive levels.
>
> At the same time, students learn the fundamentals of geometry, but in a different context.
>
> Students have an additional advantage of stronger motivation, which is likely to carry over to instruction of more traditional content.

TRANSFORMATION GEOMETRY

A major new direction in geometry instruction today is the incorporation of motion, or transformation, geometry into the curriculum. Motion geometry, as the name implies, is the geometry of movement, as opposed to the static geometry of Euclid. While aspects of this topic are introduced here, the interested reader can explore the topic further in the elementary texts that already incorporate this material.[1]

There are two major aspects of transformation geometry as it is presented in elementary geometry: (1) establishing congruence through tracing, and (2) developing symmetry through self-congruence. The first aspect leads naturally to the second. In the secondary school, transformation geometry is extended to a deeper study of the motions themselves. In the following sections, we outline these elementary school aspects in order to familiarize you with them.

---

[1]See, for example, Clyde Dilley and Walter Rucker, *Heath Elementary Mathematics* (Boston: D.C. Heath, 1976) for grade six.

ESTABLISHING CONGRUENCE THROUGH TRACING

Two figures are said to be congruent if a tracing of one fits exactly over a tracing of the other. To show that the triangles of the following figure are congruent, either one may be traced and the tracing flipped over to fit on

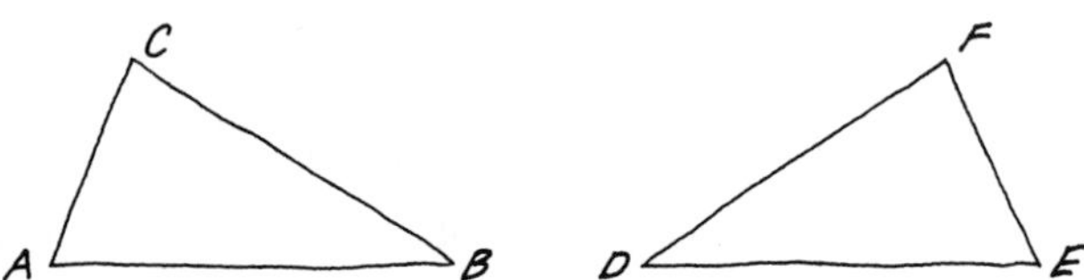

the other. Notation showing how the corners match may be introduced. In this figure,

$$ABC \leftrightarrow EDF,$$

which reads *ABC* corresponds to *EDF*. Order is important.

Of course, when the tracing of one polygon fits over another, so that the polygons are by definition congruent, their corresponding angles and sides also fit, and are congruent as well. Thus when tracing establishes that $\triangle ABC \cong \triangle EDF$ (the symbol $\cong$ means "is congruent to"), the six pairs of corresponding "parts" are also congruent:

$\overline{AB} \cong \overline{ED}$	$\angle A \cong \angle E$
$\overline{BC} \cong \overline{DF}$	$\angle B \cong \angle D$
$\overline{AC} \cong \overline{EF}$	$\angle C \cong \angle F.$

Note that when the order of the correspondence is carefully retained, as

$$ABC \leftrightarrow \text{EDF},$$

$$\triangle ABC \cong \triangle EDF,$$

the above congruent "parts" may be inferred directly from the notation without reference to the figure.

SYMMETRY THROUGH SELF-CONGRUENCE

Every figure is congruent to itself in at least one respect, which is referred to as the identity self-congruence. This congruence applies to a tracing of the figure, which fits the figure exactly as traced. Therefore, in the case of any triangle XYZ,

$$XYZ \leftrightarrow XYZ \quad \text{and} \quad \triangle XYZ \cong \triangle XYZ.$$

But some figures have additional, more interesting kinds of self-congruence. We shall look at two special types.

The first type is *flip self-congruence.* The triangle PQR below has the identity self-congruence:

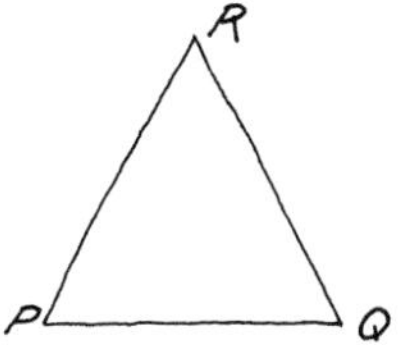

$$PQR \leftrightarrow PQR \quad \text{and} \quad \triangle PQR \cong \triangle PQR,$$

but it also has an additional self-congruence, achieved by flipping over the tracing:

$$PQR \leftrightarrow QPR \qquad \text{with} \qquad \triangle PQR \cong \triangle QPR.$$

Some special properties of this self-congruence are apparent:

$$\angle P \cong \angle Q \qquad \text{and} \qquad \overline{PR} \cong \overline{QR}.$$

Whenever a flip self-congruence occurs, one line of the tracing (although it may not be drawn) is self-congruent. On the figure, the dotted line is self-congruent under the flip self-congruence $PQR \leftrightarrow QPR$. Such a line is called a *line of symmetry.*

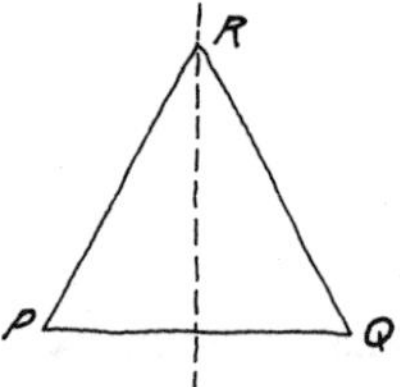

The second special kind of self-congruence is called *half-turn self-congruence.* In this figure the parallelogram (▱) has the identity self-congruence,

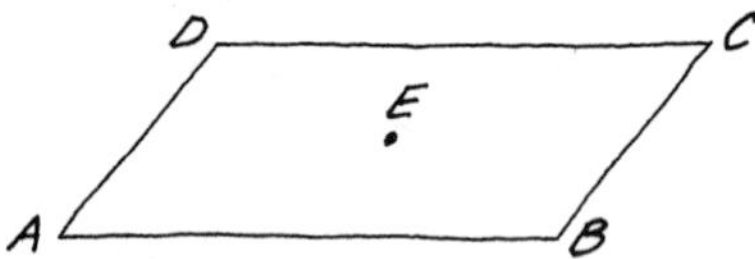

$$ABCD \leftrightarrow ABCD,$$

and also the self-congruence with the correspondence

$$ABCD \leftrightarrow CDAB,$$

which is shown by turning the tracing halfway around the fixed point E. Some properties of this figure, which result from the self-congruence, are

$$\overline{AB} \cong \overline{CD}, \qquad \overline{AD} \cong \overline{BC}, \qquad \angle A \cong \angle C, \qquad \angle B \cong \angle D.$$

The fixed or self-congruent point (E) of a half-turn self-congruence is called a *point of symmetry.*

Additional properties of figures with lines and points of symmetry become evident. For example, on $\square ABCD$, the diagonals $\overline{AC}$ and $\overline{BD}$ would pass through E, the point of symmetry, because opposite corners exchange positions during the half-turn. Thus $\overline{BD} \cong \overline{DB}$ and $\overline{AC} \cong \overline{CA}$. Since the point of symmetry must lie on both of these lines, it must lie at their intersection. And since this is the case, $\overline{DE} \cong \overline{EB}$ and $\overline{AE} \cong \overline{EC}$. You should convince yourself of this by tracing, performing the half-turn and noting how these segments interchange positions. Other congruences of this figure, which arise from its symmetry, are:

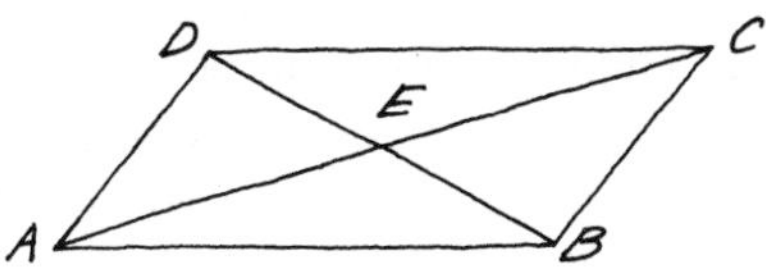

$$\triangle AEB \cong \triangle CED \quad \text{and} \quad \triangle ABC \cong \triangle CDA.$$

In addition, lines that correspond under a half-turn are either parallel:

$$\overline{AB} \leftrightarrow \overline{CD}, \qquad \text{so} \qquad \overline{AB} \parallel \overline{CD}$$

($\parallel$ is the symbol for "is parallel to"), or they are part of the same line, so that

$$\overline{AE} \leftrightarrow \overline{CE}$$

and $\overline{AE}$ and $\overline{CE}$ lie on the same line.[2]

In transformation geometry, figures may be defined by their symmetries. Thus, the two foregoing examples suggest the following definitions:

An *isosceles triangle* is a triangle with a line of symmetry.

A *parallelogram* is a quadrilateral with a point of symmetry.

When these definitions are used, all the properties of the figures result directly from the definition and its associated self-congruences.

THE ROLE OF TRANSFORMATIONS IN THE ELEMENTARY SCHOOL

Our development of transformation geometry has been formal in order to compress its development for this book. This is not, of course, the appropriate development for children. For them development should involve a great deal of drawing and tracing. This hands-on approach gives students a visual and tactile grasp, not only of the concepts of congruence and symmetry, but also of the power of these tools. Students can determine the symmetries of new figures for themselves and derive their properties directly. The advantages of the symmetry definition of a figure over the Euclidian definition (for example, a parallelogram is a quadrilateral with opposite

---

[2]In order to avoid ambiguity here, some transformation geometry definitions of parallel allow a line to be parallel to itself. Then $\overline{AE} \leftrightarrow \overline{CE}$ does not lead to an exception.

sides parallel) are evident in the classroom. While children who have studied motion geometry quickly develop all the properties of the figure, children not familiar with this technique lack the feel for these properties.

ANOTHER DIRECTION FOR MOTION GEOMETRY: SYMMETRIES OF AN EQUILATERAL TRIANGLE

By another avenue, motion geometry can lead to deeper understanding of such algebraic structures as groups. Such ideas are introduced informally at the primary school level, and later formalized in secondary school and college. Here are a series of classroom activities, suitable to middle grades, which relate to symmetries of an equilateral triangle. You should try the investigations yourself.

Students cut out an equilateral triangle about ten centimeters, or four inches, on an edge. On another sheet of paper they trace the same triangle. Students color the edges of the cut-out triangle, on front and back, one red, one green, and one blue; they use the same colors for the frame triangle, as shown in the figure. They then label the corners of the frame triangle *T* (for top), *L* (for left), and *R* (for right). Next, they are told to carry out the investigations listed below.

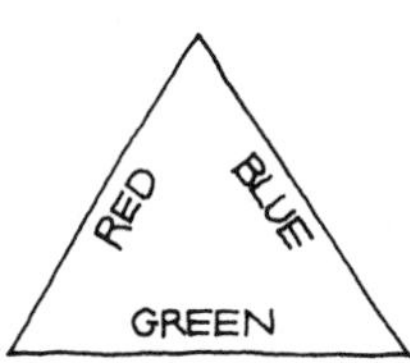

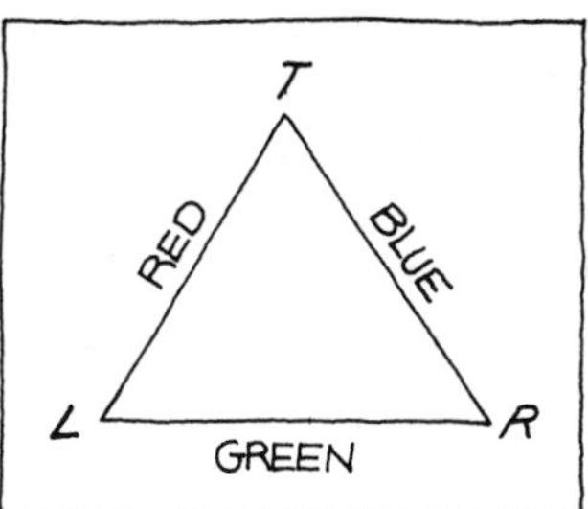

1. Fit the triangle into the frame in all possible positions. (Don't forget you can flip it over.) Record the different color matches in the following table.

your triangle	*frame triangle*		
	red	*green*	*blue*
position 1			
2			
3			
4			
5			
6			

2. Place the triangle on the frame so that the colors match, red to red, green to green, and blue to blue. On your table frame (investigation 1), label this position I, for identity or identical. Stick a pin through the center of the triangle and frame in this position. Turn your triangle counterclockwise $\frac{1}{3}$ turn until the triangle and frame fit again. Find this position on your chart and label it $T_{1/3}$ (or, in higher grades, $T_{120°}$).

3. Start again from the identity position (triangle and frame colors matching), and turn your triangle $\frac{2}{3}$ turn counterclockwise. Label this position on your chart $T_{2/3}$ (or $T_{240°}$).

4. Start again from the identity position. Keeping the corner T in the same position, flip your triangle over. (L and R will reverse.) On the table, label this new position F_T. This notation means flip with T remaining fixed.

5. Use the procedure of investigation 4 to find and label F_L and F_R on your chart. (Be sure to start from the identity position.) You should now have all six positions labeled: I, $T_{1/3}$, $T_{2/3}$, F_T, F_L, and F_R.

6. Make a second table like the following:

SECOND

FIRST

1 \ 2	I	$T_{\frac{1}{3}}$	$T_{\frac{2}{3}}$	F_T	F_L	F_R
I				↓		
$T_{\frac{1}{3}}$				↓		
$T_{\frac{2}{3}}$	- - -	- - -	- - →	F_R		
F_T						
F_L						
F_R						

So that you can see how to complete the table, we will work out the entry that is across from $T_{2/3}$ and below F_T as an example.

(a) Place your triangle in the frame in the identity position.

(b) Make the move on the left: $T_{2/3}$ (Recall that this means to turn your triangle $\frac{2}{3}$ of a turn counterclockwise.)

(c) From this position make the move at the top, F_T. If you have made these two moves correctly your result should be the position you called F_R. Enter this in the table.

Students who have completed this activity will have worked out the structure for a rather complex system. From this structure they can extract properties suggested by the following questions:

1. The example above may be recorded (the symbol $\circ$ is read "followed by"):

$$T_{2/3} \circ F_T = F_R.$$

From your table find

$$F_L \circ F_R = \_\_\_\_,$$

$$F_R \circ F_R = \_\_\_\_, \qquad \text{etc.}$$

2. The inverse of a motion is the motion that "undoes" it or that returns the triangle to the identity. What are the inverses of each of the six motions?

3. What is the result of I (identity) followed by any motion? Any motion followed by I?

4. Does order matter? For example, do these motions give the same result?

$$T_{1/3} \circ F_L$$

$$F_L \circ T_{1/3}$$

While these activities take students deep into mathematics, they retain ties to concrete manipulation so that abstract concepts remain within their reach.

We have included the above example to demonstrate again how serious mathematical ideas can be brought within reach of young children (in this case, about grade 3) by means of concrete activities. But another aspect of this example should not be overlooked. Here a class group can work together to develop the structure of a simple concrete operation. In doing this, they experience how a mathematician works in carrying out the abstraction process. Even when this is not made explicit to the students (as it probably would not be), it is a useful experience for them.

INVESTIGATIONS IN A COORDINATE PLANE

Another new topic studied in the intermediate grades is coordinate geometry. To illustrate how this topic might be developed informally, here is a story-centered approach. Again notice how the story and the games cover the topic, while maintaining a concrete base. We assume in this section that students have been introduced to negative integers. If they have not, some sections should be skipped.

LOCATING POINTS

On the grid are two points called *O* and *P*. Geo-boy is an inhabitant of the world of this grid. Suppose he is now standing at *O*. He has to meet geo-girl in a short time at *P*. His immediate problem is to find the shortest path from *O* to *P*. In this grid world you have to walk along streets (represented by lines), but you can turn at corner points, usually in any of four directions (up, down, left, or right). Shortcuts are not allowed; you can't go across a square, but must go around the outside. Draw several routes geo-boy might take in going from *O* to *P*.

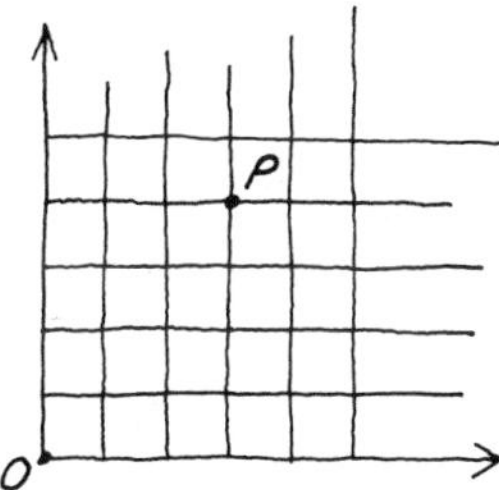

Measuring length in blocks, what is the shortest route you can find? Is there more than one path that has this length? How many? Is there a longest route from *O* to *P*? If you follow the rule that you can't go over the same block twice, then is there a longest path? How long is it? Draw it. Find a shortest path from *O* to *P* with the fewest turns. There are two such routes. Here they are:

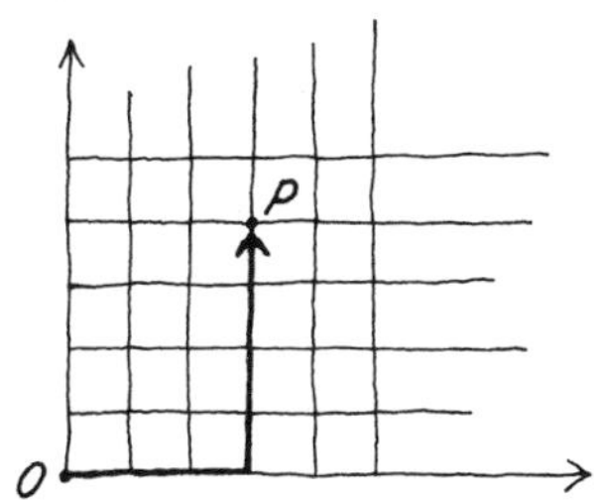

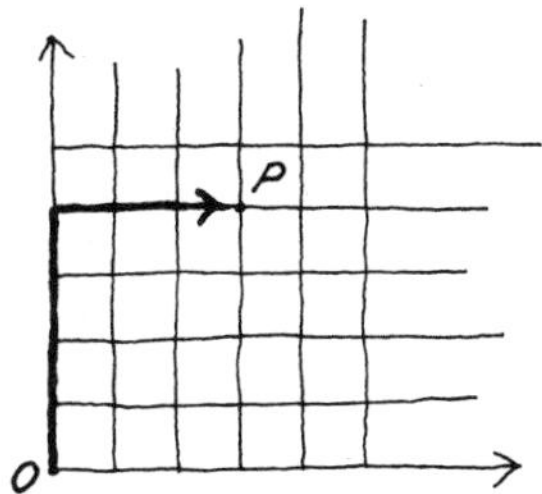

Along comes geo-buddy. He wants to meet geo-boy and geo-girl later at *P* but doesn't know how to get to *P*. If you make the agreement that in grid world you always move to the right (or left) before going up (or down), then your directions to geo-buddy would be the following: Go three right and then four up. If we call *O* by the name (0,0), then how should we name *P*? Remember that the first number in the name of *P* tells how far to go right from *O*, and the second number indicates how far up. Let us agree to write the name for *P* this way: (3,4).

Geo-boy is now at *P* (3,4). He and geo-girl decide to take a walk and avoid geo-buddy who is at *B* (1,3). They take the path shown in the figure. They take this path because they want to stay at least two blocks (on foot) from geo-buddy at all times. Mark in some of the locations of corners that they pass on their walk.

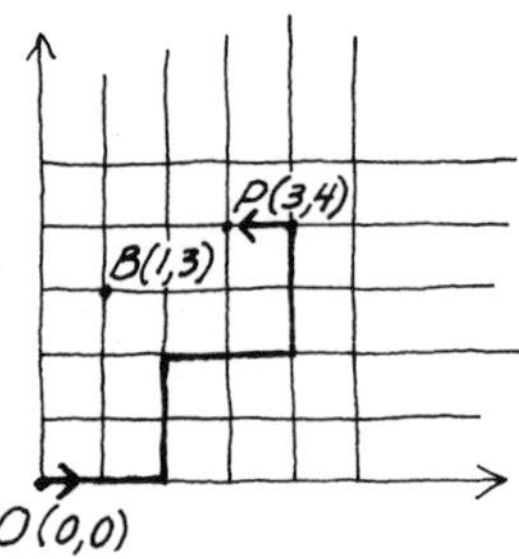

WEST SIDE STORY

Urban sprawl takes place in geo-world. Geo-boy realizes one day that his world has a west side as well as an east side. Geo-buddy and geo-boy agree that since positives were used to locate corners east that negatives

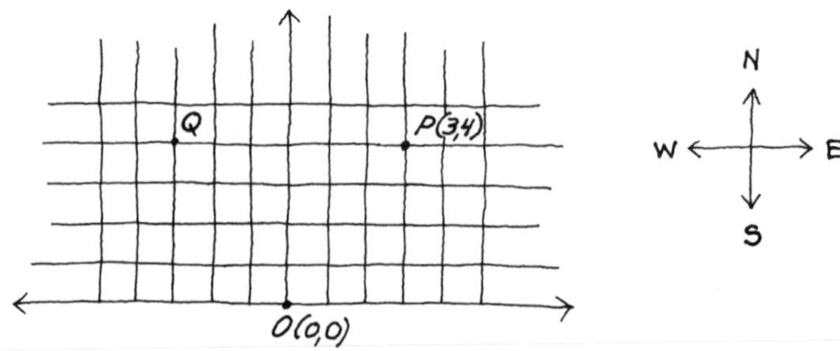

should be used to locate corners west. Since all corners are north, the second number in each address will remain positive. *Q* is as far west and at the same height north as *P* is east and north. What is the address of *Q*?

Geo-girl is stranded at a west-side corner that is exactly six blocks from *P* (3,4). Geo-boy is at *P* trying to decide how many places he will have to explore in order to find her. Locate those corners and give their addresses.

TIC-TAC-TOE—FOUR-IN-A-ROW

Make a grid that looks like the following:

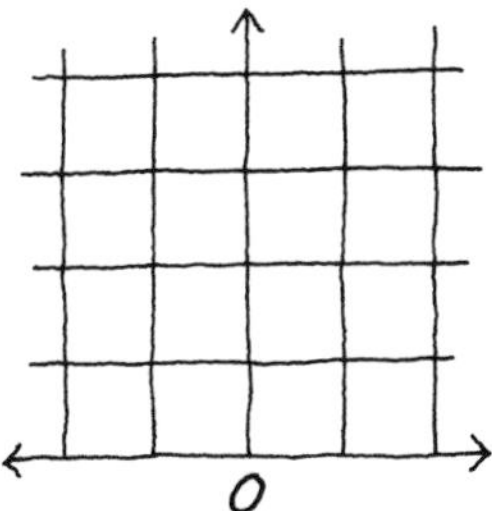

Two players or teams are needed for this game. One player will be the *X* and the other the *O*. The first player to get four corners in a row wins. These are examples of winners:

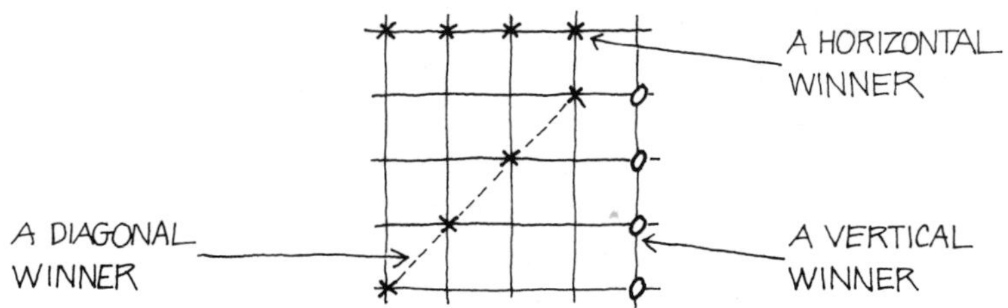

Each player takes a turn. Player *A* tells his opponent, Player *B*, two numbers, which represent a corner. Player *B* must mark the corner for Player *A* with an *X*. If Player *B* locates it incorrectly, Player *A* correctly marks his choice and takes another turn. If Player *B* marks it correctly, then it is his turn to give Player *A* a two-number address to locate. Player *A* will mark Player *B*'s corner with an *O*. If a player gives an address not on the grid or a corner already occupied, he loses a turn. Play a friend to see who is the best tic-tac-toe—four-in-a-row player.

Now make five-by-five grids using the whole geo-world to play tic-tac-toe—four-in-a-row. We make the following agreement about addresses:

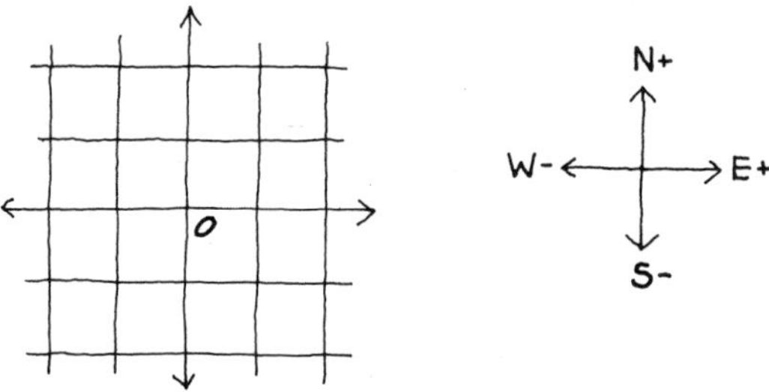

Play your friend again to see who will be champion on the new grid.

MEASUREMENT AND THE METRIC SYSTEM

The measurement process involves two distinct steps, the first of which is usually forgotten:

1. A standard unit is arbitrarily established. Some standard units are meter, inch, degree of temperature (Fahrenheit or Celsius), hour, gram, ounce, liter, and quart.[3]

2. The thing to be measured is compared with the standard unit. The resulting measure is the number of units, for example 4 meters, 37° C (normal body temperature), 90 minutes, or 1½ hours.

---

[3]We simplify this discussion by omitting derived units, such as miles per hour, that interrelate two or more defined units.

Many modern programs stress this first step by citing some of the problems that result from lack of standard units. One way to do this is to discuss some historical problems:

> In the Middle Ages many measurement units were based on the size of the current king. Measures such as the foot and the span changed every time a new king came to power, or every time one crossed a national boundary.
>
> Until about 1900 practically every town in the United States had its own time, which could differ by a few minutes from that of neighboring towns. As cross-country railroads were introduced, lack of a common time made scheduling extremely difficult.
>
> Even the length of a mile, until about 1900, varied by about 10 percent depending on whose definition was used.

A second way of demonstrating the arbitrary nature of units of measure is to measure something using various students as the basis. For example, the dimensions of the classroom may be measured by two groups, the first using as the unit of length a small student's foot and the second a large student's foot. The measurements may then be compared to see how they are different, and (in the upper grades) how they are similar. (Ratios of lengths are retained even though the lengths themselves differ.) Using these means, students will become aware of the need for standardized units.

The measurement system in common use in the United States is still the English system, but the metric system is making increasing inroads. In 1866 the metric system was made legal in this country, in 1893–94 metric units were adopted as "fundamental," and in 1975 an act encouraging (though not mandating) conversion was passed. Meanwhile major U.S. industries including IBM, General Motors, Ford, Caterpillar Tractor, International Harvester, Honeywell, 3M, and John Deere are converting to metrics. Companies with international business were early supporters of conversion, since virtually all of the rest of the world has already shifted to the metric system.

A major responsibility for conversion from English to metric measurement has been assigned to the schools, the logic being that it is easier to teach than to reteach. Children brought up on metrics will be comfortable with this system as adults. The only difficulty with this is the fact that applications outside of school continue to utilize Fahrenheit temperature, pints, quarts, pecks and bushels, feet, yards and miles, ounces, pounds and tons, teaspoons, cups and gallons. Despite this and the slow adoption of metrics, the metric system will probably prevail within about twenty years.

Why metrics? The power of the metric system lies in its relation to our decimal system of numeration. Recall in this regard how easy it is to multiply or divide by 10, 100, 1,000, etc. Within the metric system all conversions involve multiples of ten.[4] In addition, once a basic unit is learned for each type of measure, the conversion prefixes remain the same. We will demonstrate this in the following paragraphs.

The units that will serve as a basis for your instruction are:

Linear measure:	the meter (Canadian: metre)
Mass:	the gram
Volume or capacity:	the liter (Canadian: litre)
Temperature:	the degree Celsius

For linear measure, mass, and volume standard prefixes indicate multiples of these units. The four most commonly used are:

milli-	$\frac{1}{1,000}$	
centi-	$\frac{1}{100}$	
deci-	$\frac{1}{10}$	(Beware: deka means 10.)
kilo-	1,000	

[4]The one dimension not metricated is time, for which the standard definitions remain: 60 sec. = 1 min., 60 min. = 1 hr., 24 hrs. = 1 day, 7 days = 1 wk., 12 mo. = 365¼ days = 1 year, but (finally) 100 years = 1 century.

Thus a centimeter is $\frac{1}{100}$ meter, a kilogram is 1,000 grams, a milliliter is $\frac{1}{1,000}$ liter, a decimeter is $\frac{1}{10}$ meter, and so on. Of course the reciprocals of these are also true: a meter is 100 centimeters, a gram is $\frac{1}{1,000}$ kilogram, a liter is 1,000 milliliters, and there are 10 decimeters in a meter. These simple relationships allow conversions like the following:

325 centimeters = 3.25 meters

2.5 kilometers = 2500 meters

150 grams = .15 kilogram

Note that all of these conversions merely involve shifting the decimal point.

When students have the opportunity to measure with these units and work with them in many problems, they become familiar with their size. Actually, your students may become more comfortable with the units than you are.

You should not encourage conversion between metric and English measure. For students at this young age, we don't want a dual system with changes back and forth; rather we want students to work within the system. The conversion factors are so complicated that they discourage study of the new system. But it will be useful for you to have a gross estimate of the size of some of the common measures:

The meter is slightly longer than the yard.

The kilometer is ⅝ mile (2 km = 1 mi. is usually close enough).

There are about 2½ centimeters to the inch.

The kilogram is about 2.2 pounds.

The liter is slightly more than a quart.

Each degree Celsius is almost twice each Fahrenheit degree.

$$0^\circ \text{ C} = 32^\circ \text{ F (freezing)}$$

$$37^\circ \text{ C} = 98.6^\circ \text{ F (body temperature)}$$

$$100^\circ \text{ C} = 212^\circ \text{ F (boiling)}$$

These relationships will help you to think about the new measures.

Area and volume units are derived multiples of linear units, and are found by squaring and cubing them. For example:

10 centimeters (cm) = 1 decimeter (dm).

Squaring produces

$(10 \text{ cm})^2 = (1 \text{ dm})^2$ or

$100 \text{ cm}^2 = 1 \text{ dm}^2$ (read "square centimeter," etc.).

and by cubing,

$(10 \text{ cm})^3 = (1 \text{ dm})^3$ or

$1{,}000 \text{ cm}^3 = 1 \text{ dm}^3$ (read "cubic centimeters," etc.).

A convenient volume relationship is:

$1 \text{ dm}^3 = 1$ liter.

And a convenient weight relationship is:

$$1 \text{ cm}^3 \text{ of water weighs 1 gram.}$$

This information may seem very complicated and confusing, but once you become accustomed to working with this system, it will be much easier than working in English units. One of the major difficulties is to overcome your own natural resistance to change.

We conclude this section with two very different notes that apply directly to the personal and practical problems of measurement.

Several years ago, when the English converted to metric, they converted their coinage as well. In the old system

$$12 \text{ pence (cents)} = 1 \text{ shilling}$$

but in the new system

5 (new) pence = 1 shilling.[5]

Shortly after the conversion, while one of the authors of this book was in England, he asked a shopkeeper what she thought about the change. "Not too bad," she said, "but I still wonder what they did with those seven extra pennies."

Roy Gallant, in his delightful little book, *Man the Measurer,*[6] tells about the binary nature of some volume units:

---

[5]In the new system, the shilling retains the same relationship to the pound that our nickel does to the dollar: 20 shillings = 1 pound; thus the shilling is not really a metric unit, the cent is.

[6]See Appendix A.

> *Two* ros, *or* mouthfuls, *made an English* handful *(also called a* jigger*). Two handfuls were a* jack *(also called a* jackpot*). Two jacks were a* jill. *Two jills made a* cup. *Two cups made a* pint *(called a* mug *or a* jug*). Two pints made a* quart. *Two quarts made a* pottle. *Two pottles were a* gallon. *Two gallons made a* pail. *Two pails made a* peck. *Two pecks made a* bushel. *Two bushels were a* strike. *Two strikes were a* coomb. *Two coombs made a* cask. *Two casks were a* barrel. *Two barrels made a* hogshead. *Two hogsheads made a* pipe, *and two pipes made a* tun.

At least we don't have that list to memorize.

TEACHING METRICS

Metric measurement is taught in the same way as the English system—by measuring things and using the results in appropriate ways. Here are some questions that can be asked of students:

> How tall are you in centimeters?
>
> How much do you weigh in kilograms?
>
> What are the room dimensions in meters? What are the areas of the walls, the floor, and the ceiling? What is the volume of the room? How much air does this allow for each of us?
>
> Name some things that are about a meter in length.
>
> Who has the longest reach (fingertip to fingertip with arms outstretched)?
>
> How far is it around the playground? (A meter wheel, a wheel one meter in circumference, is a useful device for this kind of measurement. These can be easily made if necessary.)

METER WHEEL

Guess the distance around the school building in inches. Check. Who came closest?

Make a map of the school-yard.

Lie on a large sheet of paper marked off in squares. Have a classmate trace your outline. Estimate the area of the silhouette as closely as possible.

How much does a pencil weigh? An eraser? A piece of chalk? A baseball mitt? A shoe?

How much does a soft drink bottle weigh when full? When empty? How much did the soft drink weigh?

How many liters were in the soft drink bottle?

Bring in containers from home. Record on each how many liters it holds.

These kinds of activities may be extended to the limits of a teacher's creativity and resourcefulness. Textbook teacher's manuals make additional suggestions. These activities, together with standard textbook exercises, will provide your youngsters with the kinds of experiences they need to feel comfortable with metric measurement.

GOALS OF MEASUREMENT INSTRUCTION

In summary, the aims of instruction in measurement include:

Student understanding of the need for standard measurement units, as well as their arbitrary nature.

Student facility with metric and English units, with greater stress on metrics.

Student mastery of conversion techniques within the metric system. (See chapter 9 for a fuller discussion of conversion.)

Student feeling for measurement approximations.

Notice that the newer goals of measurement focus on more general and informal understanding, postponing specifics to higher grades and secondary schools, where responsibility for this is shared with the science teacher.

THE NUMBER LINE

No discussion of geometry for the elementary school would be complete today without noting the ubiquitous number line. This is an extremely important pedagogical device that provides a basic link between geometry and measurement on one hand, and arithmetic (and later, algebra) on the other. Many teachers, especially those in primary grades, have an enlarged number line on permanent display, often above a chalkboard at the front of the classroom. Some teachers begin each school year with a class project to construct a new number line. Each student must practice carefully, and when called on write a number at the appropriate place on the line. For many children, this exercise is also helpful in that it forces them to enlarge those tiny, cramped figures they usually produce.

First and foremost the number line provides a visual display of the ordered counting numbers. Initially, some children will refer to it when they forget the number sequence. This is a reasonable regression to the concrete, which soon becomes unnecessary. Recall in this regard that the number names and symbols (numerals) are arbitrary and carry no mathematical meaning in themselves. Thus, for example, the number two is also *zwei* (German), *dos* (Spanish), and so on. Allowing students to refer to the number line takes some of the false importance away from the task of learning to count. We want children to learn the number sequence, but they should not be threatened by the task.

Far more than a mere crutch, the number line provides a continuing basic tool for teaching. Although the design of the line may be changed to incorporate more sophisticated uses in later grades, it will be essentially the same device. For example, it may later be extended to include negative numbers or fractions.

Consider some other basic uses of this valuable tool:

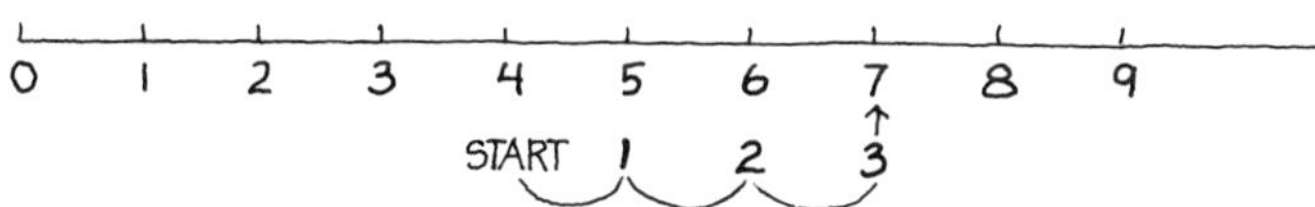

Addition by counting on. The student can add 4 + 3 by starting with 4 and counting three more spaces. This technique of addition is learned by many children on their own or is taught by siblings or parents before children enter school. Many can add without referring to the number line because they have the number sequence so well in mind. But even for such children, this kind of exercise is valuable, since it teaches them to add lengths, associating addition with measurement. From the very beginning, children should become aware that this technique is not restricted to small numbers. It will add to student understanding of addition to use the method to find 21 + 4, 29 + 5, and 12 + 13.

Adding one, two, and three by single visual jumps.

Slide rule addition with two number lines. Two meter sticks are excellent for this purpose. These are marked in centimeters to 100 to permit addition of lengths for all sums of 100 or less. To add 23 + 39, for example, the second meter stick is placed so that its left end corresponds to 23 on the first stick. Above 39 (on the second stick) students read the sum 62 (on the first). Clearly, this is a lesson in adding lengths.

Multiples of two by hops along the line.

Subtraction by counting backwards. To subtract 7 − 3, start with 7, and count back 3 spaces to the answer 4.

Finding one less, two less, and three less by single jumps.

Subtraction by slide rule. Reverse the second number line (meter stick).

Subtraction as finding the missing addend (or more formally as the inverse of addition).

7 − 4 = _____ is the same problem as 4 + _____ = 7
or _____ + 4 = 7.

Thus, subtraction may also be performed by locating 4 and 7 on the number line and counting the spaces between them. This process is identical to the illustration for 4 + 3 above.

Adding several numbers.

Mixed addition and subtraction by counting forward and backward as indicated by the signs.

Multiplication by measures. More than extending the hops for multiples of two, this can give insight into what multiplication is about. You (but not the children) may think of multiplication in the following way:

(a) You know $x \cdot 1 = x$; *any number times 1 is the same number.* Think of this as *using one as the unit of measure.*

(b) Multiplying by another number, say 3, then involves using 3 as the unit of measure. Thus $5 \cdot 3$ means laying off on the number line five three-lengths.

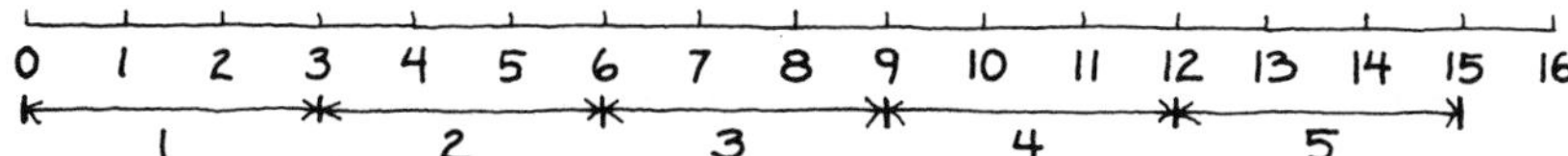

In exactly the same way, 5 · 2½ means using 2½ as the unit length and measuring off five of them.

Division by measures. Once the idea of multiplication is understood as multiple application of measures, you can use the idea for division as well. Dividing 15 by 3 is counting the number of units of three-length that make up 15. By this means, it is easy to see that 15 ÷ 2½ = 6. Try it.

Multiplication and division by scaling. You can also accomplish multiplication and division by a specific multiplier or divisor, say 3, through comparison of two number lines, as in the illustration.

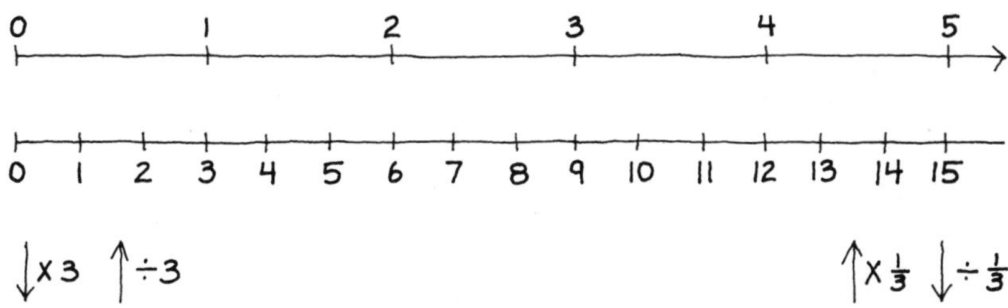

Note that the zeros correspond and that opposite 1 on the top line is the multiplier 3 on the bottom. The space from zero to three is then separated into three equal spaces (on the second line), and the rest of the line is laid out. The sequence is as follows:

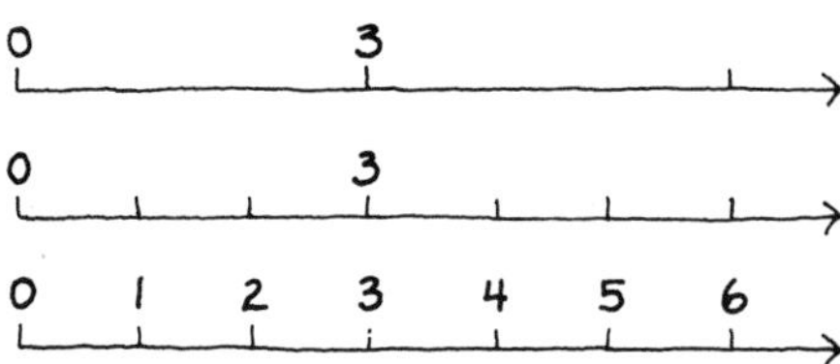

We wish to stress that it is *not* necessary to know the multiples before you start, as these first figures might imply. The vertical arrows indicate the directions for multiplying and dividing by 3. Also note that the reverse arrows indicate multiplication and division by ⅓. Thus the following kinds of exercises may be carried out using the scale.

$2 \times 3 =$ ____	$\frac{2}{3} \div \frac{1}{3} =$ ____
$12 \div 3 =$ ____	$3\frac{1}{3} \times 3 =$ ____
$6 \times \frac{1}{3} =$ ____	$7 \times \frac{1}{3} =$ ____
$5 \div \frac{1}{3} =$ ____	$\frac{1}{3} \times 3 =$ ____
$4\frac{1}{2} \div 3 =$ ____	$3 \div \frac{1}{3} =$ ____

Of course this scale works only for 3. Another scale would be necessary for 4, and additional scales for each new multiplier-divisor.

Regression from algorithms. The number line provides a constant checking device as new procedures are introduced. "Is that the same answer you would get using the number line?" is the key question. Later, as algorithms allow students to solve more complex exercises, comparison with the number line will demonstrate the power of the algorithm, especially how it saves time.

Beginning teachers need not feel that they must devise uses for the number line on their own. Every contemporary text incorporates this tool in its program, with numerous suggestions for its use.

SOME TEACHING SUGGESTIONS

We have stressed the informal and activity-oriented nature of geometry in the elementary school. We have also noted how content specifics, such as definitions, should grow naturally out of the students' need to pin down ideas. Unfortunately, teachers will find that most contemporary textbooks stress the opposite, content-oriented view. This imposes an extra burden on teachers, who must modify such programs to suit their students' best interests.

Geometry provides the best avenue to student creativity in the elementary school, but at the same time, demands creative instruction on the part of the teacher. For this reason, teachers should draw upon a variety of resources in collecting interesting and appropriate geometric challenges for their students. The more you do this, and the more you reorganize and utilize these materials for your own classroom, the easier it will be to create new activities.

EXERCISES

1. Answer the question posed in example 6 on pages 65–66. Check your answer by constructing a model.

2. Give as many additional answers as you can think of for the question in example 8 on page 66.

3. Determine how you could cut a trapezoid (2 sides parallel, as in figure) in order to re-form it into a rectangle. Show how this leads to an area formula for the trapezoid. (See example 9, page 67.)

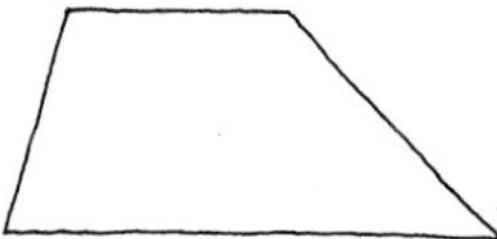

4. Determine all the symmetries of each of the following polygons, and give the properties that those symmetries (and the related self-congruences) generate:

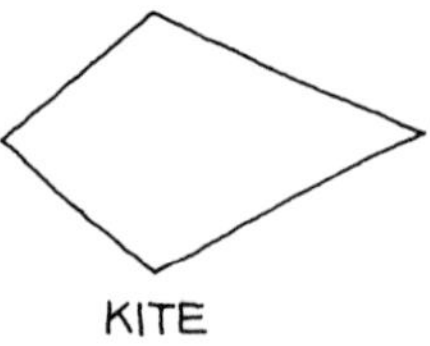

KITE

ISOCELES TRAPEZOID

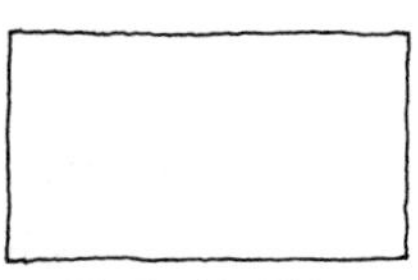

RECTANGLE

RHOMBUS

SQUARE

EQUILATERAL TRIANGLE

5. Review the geometry sections of a text for the grade in which you are most interested. Tell some ways you would modify the content to reflect the views of this chapter. Consider in particular transformation geometry approaches.

6. Review the measurement sections of a text for the grade in which you are most interested. Tell some ways you would modify the content to reflect the views of this chapter.

7. Read an article in a recent issue of the *Arithmetic Teacher* on teaching geometry. Choose one that provides specific teaching ideas. Indicate two ideas that you would use in your own instructional program.

8. How could the following concepts be introduced by means of folding a plain sheet of paper?
   (a) Line
   (b) Angle
   (c) Perpendicular
   (d) Right angle
   (e) Angle bisector
   (f) Midpoint

9. Look up one of the following topics in an encyclopedia. Indicate how you might use ideas related to it in your instructional program.
   (a) Geodesics and geodesic domes
   (b) Symmetry in nature
   (c) Fibonacci numbers and phyllotaxis

10. How could a number line be used to develop the idea that

$$\frac{4}{6} = \frac{2}{3}?$$

11. Review the treatment of the number line in a text for the grade in which you are most interested. Indicate ways in which you could modify the content to include a broader use of the number line.

12. Choose two of the examples of geometric activity discussed in this chapter. Modify each to focus on your particular grade level.

13. After you have made the modifications in exercise 12, pose three problems relating to each example. Try some of your exercises on a child. What are the results?

14. Read the entry for *number* in *Encyclopedia Britannica Junior.* How are geometry and arithmetic related in this article?

15. Devise scales for multiplying and dividing by 5 (and $\frac{1}{5}$). Use the method outlined in pages 93–94. Make up and solve a variety of exercises with your scales.

CHAPTER FOUR

TEACHING ARITHMETIC

ARITHMETIC IS CENTRAL TO ELEMENTARY SCHOOL MATHEMATICS

While geometry has an important role in the elementary school mathematics curriculum, arithmetic is still at center stage. In fact, until only recently mathematics for grades K–8 was designated arithmetic—the third of the three R's: reading, 'riting, and 'rithmetic.

While we try to ensure that arithmetic is only one part of a larger program, we recognize the importance of providing all students with the tools of computation: the ability to add, subtract, multiply, and divide both natural numbers and fractions.[1] Even more, we stress that those skills must be operational; students must be able to apply them to real problems. (We return to this last point in chapter 9.)

With such straightforward goals, one would think that by now we would have an instructional program that would assure every child competence in arithmetic skills. Unfortunately that is not the case. Thousands of students, even after repeating essentially the same K–6 content in grades 7–9, still cannot calculate; some fail at the most rudimentary level.

"NEW MATH" AND ARITHMETIC SKILLS

Many critics blame the so-called new math for the lack of student competence in arithmetic. They argue, for example, that:

> Introduction of new topics has diluted the major emphasis on computation.
>
> Drill has been neglected.
>
> Teachers have overstressed "why" to the disservice of "how to."
>
> Speed and accuracy have been so neglected that students today do not compare with students of yesteryear.

As in so many school controversies there are two sides to each of these points. We believe that there have been certain misguided excesses in teaching the new math. But the new math introduced in textbooks and curricula should be only part of the classroom instructional program. The classroom teacher should take responsibility for maintaining the balance that the critics have suggested is lost.

Unfortunately, some teachers have been led to think that any drill is bad, though proponents of the new math merely called for meaningful and

---

[1]We include here, of course, decimal fractions, commonly called decimals. We also encourage instruction in all rational numbers, both positive and negative, particularly the positive and negative integers.

interesting drill to replace drill-for-drill's-sake. Others have been led to believe that "why" is indeed the end-all, that students can muscle their way through all problems by working from basic relationships. But neither new nor old math texts are to blame, since all have exercises that reinforce concepts and extended exercise sets that provide computational practice.

At the root of this controversy is the fact that arithmetic has always borne the brunt of criticism about educational deficiencies. In some ways, the deficiencies of the new math differ from those of older programs, which focused heavily on rote drill. Some prefer to put up with the deficiencies of the new math, simply because there is less emphasis on drill. However, the real point is that the classroom needs a careful balance between drill and reasoning. While thoughtful, meaningful arithmetic should be developed, children should also have plenty of opportunity to use and to reinforce their skills in meaningful ways.

FOUR CLASSROOM INCIDENTS

We will now consider four classroom incidents, the first attributed to Warwick Sawyer, the middle two to Robert Wirtz, on whom we draw heavily in this chapter, and the last to Stanley Erlwanger.

Warwick Sawyer tells of asking a sixth-grade class to give him an example of where they might need to use the multiplication fact $6 \times 4 = 24$ outside of school. No response. Finally in desperation Sawyer suggested that the students think of their mothers in a market. One youngster finally raised her hand. "My mother went to the market," she offered, "and bought six times four is twenty-four cans of peas."

Robert Wirtz tells of watching a second-grade boy answer a series of exercises in a workbook, each following the general pattern:

$$9 + 6 = 9 + (1 + \_\_\_\_) = (9 + 1) + \_\_\_\_ = 10 + \_\_\_\_ = \_\_\_\_.$$

These exercises were clearly designed to promote conceptual development of sums in the teens. But the youngster beat the system, filling in the blanks right to left!

Wirtz also tells of tutoring a third-grade girl identified by her teacher as weak in multiplication. He checked her on some easy combinations:

"2 × 9?" "18." "3 × 4?" "12." But then "4 × 9?" "37." "I'm not sure of that last one," said Wirtz. "Can you show me a way to check your answer?" The student had none. She didn't know that she could add four 9s or nine 4s, or of any other way to reconstruct the exercise. Wirtz turned and wrote on the chalkboard:

$$4 \times 9 = 37$$

and then marked *x*'s in the following array:

x x x x x

x x x x

He asked the youngster if she would agree that the *x*'s could represent 1 × 9. She agreed. He added a second, third, and fourth set of 9 *x*'s, asking each time if the student agreed that he had made nine more marks and that he represented successively 2 × 9, 3 × 9, and finally 4 × 9. She did. The diagram now appeared:

$$4 \times 9 = 37$$

x x x x x

x x x x|x

x x x x x

x x x|x x

x x x x x

x x|x x x

x x x x x

x

"How many x's are there?" Wirtz asked. The student carefully counted, not taking the anticipated shortcut of counting by fives, and responded, "36." "Ah," said Wirtz handing the girl his chalk, "will you please correct the exercise." The girl confidently turned to the chalkboard and marked an additional x.

Finally, Stanley Erlwanger tells of a sixth-grade youngster who had progressed with considerable success through an individualized instruction program. The student responded to the following questions by filling in the blanks:

.3 + .2 = __.5__

3. + 2. = __5.__

But, when he extended this technique to a third question, the student wrote

3. + .2 = __.5.__

These four examples each carry an important message. (You will be asked to identify specific problems related to them in the exercises at the end of the chapter.) Together they suggest how easy it is for us to fail to communicate with our students, or to send them the wrong information even when we do communicate.

NUMBER CONCEPTS OF ARITHMETIC

We turn now to a brief overview of concepts addressed in modern arithmetic programs. An understanding of these general concerns will give you a measure to evaluate the details of programs for a specific grade or even within a specific unit. Solely for the purpose of organization, we separate the discussion into two parts: number systems and structure of algorithms. In any instructional program, the second of these is closely associated with the first.

NUMBER SYSTEMS

The number systems of arithmetic relate to the following sets of numbers:

Counting numbers or natural numbers: 1, 2, 3, 4, . . .

Nonnegative integers or whole numbers:[2] 0, 1, 2, 3, 4, . . .

Nonnegative rationals or nonnegative fractions, for example, 0, $\frac{1}{2}$, $1\frac{1}{3}$, $\frac{7}{8}$, 5.

Integers: 0, 1, -1, 2, -2, 3, -3, . . .

Rationals, for example: 0, $-\frac{1}{2}$, $\frac{1}{2}$, $1\frac{1}{3}$, $-1\frac{1}{3}$, -7, 5.

A simple semiconcrete device for displaying these sets of numbers is our friend from chapter 3, the number line. Here we carefully plot only the points that are included in a particular system, recognizing that in teaching, the line itself is usually drawn at each stage:

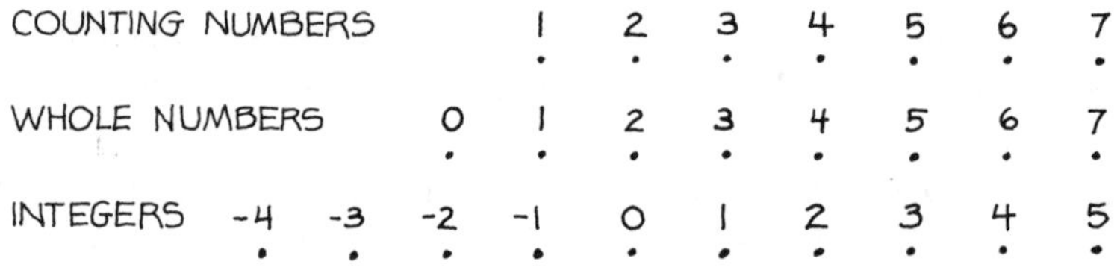

COUNTING NUMBERS				1	2	3	4	5	6	7
WHOLE NUMBERS			0	1	2	3	4	5	6	7
INTEGERS	-4	-3	-2	-1	0	1	2	3	4	5

Now the intermediate points necessary for more accurate measurement are filled in:[3]

---

[2]In some textbook series, in particular Scott, Foresman, these are designated as natural numbers, but not as counting numbers. Here we follow more common usage. See our later comment on "nonnegatives."

[3]Even though the rational lines appear to be complete, theoretically they are not until the real numbers, like $\sqrt{2}$ and π, are included. However, the real number system is not appropriate content for elementary school.

NON-NEGATIVE RATIONALS 0 1 2 3 4 5 6 7

RATIONALS -4 -3 -2 -1 0 1 2 3 4 5

These sets of numbers, along with their particular definitions of equality, their specific operations (addition, subtraction, multiplication, and division, when appropriate), and their order properties ($-5 < 7$, for example) constitute the number systems of arithmetic.

A major goal of arithmetic is to provide students with an understanding of these systems, starting with the counting numbers and building through the others, so that by the end of grade 8 they understand the rational number system. Students in grades K–6 will deal primarily with positive numbers and zero, which we have been careful to call nonnegatives.[4] They will be introduced to the integers, but will not study them extensively. It is useful for teachers to understand the progression and the formal development of these systems, which are included in commonly offered mathematics courses for elementary school teachers. It is less vital that students understand the distinctions between these systems. Although they provide a basis of organization for instruction, they do not provide many useful ideas for students.

A further word about these systems is appropriate. Some mathematics educators have long felt that every aspect of mathematics learning should be firmly based in concepts when first introduced. This is foolish, and classroom teachers should not fall into this trap. Counting is an obvious case in point. Most students enter school with rote counting skills; some can count to 100 and beyond. This skill is at the level of memorized counting, and may not even involve counting objects. It is like the ability to recite the words of a song, a television ad, or a prayer. But, nonetheless, it is a useful skill on which to build later ideas even before it is shored up with further conceptual understanding.

---

[4]We recommend against using the word *nonnegatives* with students; the term *whole numbers* avoids it. Similarly, the context will usually make clear whether the rationals or the nonnegative subset of the rationals is being employed. Thus a fifth-grade text may have a chapter entitled "Rational Numbers," when actually it only considers positive rationals and zero. We support this, as well as use of the word *fraction* as a synonym for *rational numbers,* which avoids technical number-numeral differences.

It has recently been argued that the basis for children's counting is *ordinality* rather than *cardinality*. Ordinality refers to order, and is usually identified by words like first, second, and so on. Cardinality refers to what we usually classify as counting, specifically answering the question, how many? At this writing, this fact has not yet been reflected in primary-grade textbooks, and should especially be of concern to kindergarten teachers. Teachers should emphasize exercises that help students extend their ordered idea of counting to the cardinal concept of counting objects in groups.[5]

Suppose, for example, a first-grade teacher draws a number line on the chalkboard and calls on students to name points.

For the point designated by the arrow, a student might at this stage suggest "7." Why not? At this time it is the seventh number designated! Our choice here is arbitrary, and we should be fair in pointing that out to students (or at least to this student). We number in counting order here from left to right. Other times we may order right to left or down to up, but always in physical order. Similarly our choice of equal intervals is arbitrary. Later in school students will meet logarithmic and other scales where the divisions are not equal; but here, for many very good reasons, we want equal divisions.

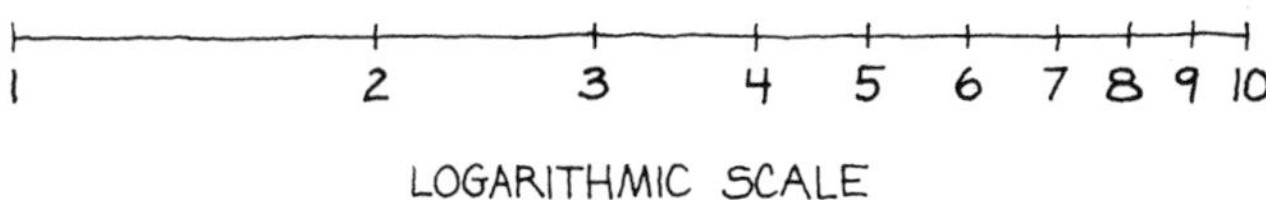

LOGARITHMIC SCALE

[5]In this regard, one author recalls his son's experience showing his puppy in a dog show. He placed third out of three. Elated, he announced, "Dad, I hope next time there will be ten dogs so I can win tenth prize."

STRUCTURE OF ALGORITHMS

An algorithm is a fixed procedure for computing or for solving a mathematical problem. Arithmetic abounds in algorithms. There are addition algorithms, subtraction algorithms, multiplication algorithms, division algorithms, square root algorithms, and an algorithm for converting fractions to decimals, to name only a few. You can compare an algorithm to a routine, like the one you follow in the morning in getting up and going to school. You simply carry out a sequence of activities, often with little or no conscious thought. In the same way, most of us carry out an algorithm like long division with little thought as to why it works. Since we are reasonably efficient and reasonably accurate, we don't bother with the why of the process each time we use it.

We hope you can see the danger, which in some cases overbalances the advantages, of the routine process. What happens if we forget, or if we make a systematic error? What happens if we want to check our work? What if we want to extend the algorithm to broader categories, like division of decimals? Compare this again with the routine for going to school. You are always prepared to move from rote, unthinking activity back to conscious activity. If the coffee boils over, for example, you aren't locked into the rest of your program. If you take an extended vacation, you are free to reorganize your program on return. Why? Because you always have a conceptual grasp of what is occurring, and you can move from rote to reasoned processing. Too many students lack this ability in dealing with arithmetic processes.

But do not carry this too far. Recall the story of the centipede who, when asked by the ant how he so marvelously synchronized all those legs, found that when he thought about it he could no longer walk. We would err in the same way if we demanded that students constantly go back to first principles. (Would you like to be asked to explain long division in terms of counting?) Still, we should help students gain a conceptual grasp of the algorithms they will use.

Algorithms are usually taught step-by-step from simple to complex stages, and from simple to complex examples. Opportunities for student error and lack of understanding lurk around every corner. Here is where alert, individualized, and sensitive monitoring of students is essential. Every teacher should take the opportunity to sit down with individual students to observe their computations and talk with them about their procedures. Even so, it is quite possible to overlook serious misconceptions. We asked a student how he arrived at the 5 in his correct subtraction answer:

$$\begin{array}{r} 62 \\ -\ 37 \\ \hline 25 \end{array}$$

He said, "I couldn't subtract seven from two so I subtracted the two from the seven." It turned out that this procedure, which of course produced many errors, did not result in incorrect answers in the next column to the left, for he added, "When I have to subtract upside down I change the six to five."

One specific suggestion about teaching algorithms: Before you start teaching the first steps, trace the full development of the process for yourself. This will give you better perspective on your specific tasks, and will help you to see that many steps that may not initially seem important will later be of paramount importance. Failure to do this may lead you to slide over these steps, and may result in later problems.

WHICH ALGORITHM SHOULD YOU USE?

The question of which algorithm to use is of great interest to theorists, both curriculum developers and researchers in mathematics education. There are many alternatives to consider. Here are a few different approaches to "borrowing" in subtraction, using the example:

$$\begin{array}{r} 43 \\ -\ 27 \\ \hline \end{array}$$

You cannot subtract 7 from 3, so:

METHOD 1. You borrow 10 from 40, subtract 7 from the resulting 13, and then subtract 20 from 30.

METHOD 2. Add 10 to both terms, giving 40 + 13 and 30 + 7. Now subtract 7 from 13 and 30 from 40. (This method, called equal additions, is especially useful in problems like 3,718 − 1,999. Just add one to each and the problem becomes 3,719 − 2,000.)

METHOD 3. Consider the number line. We travel from 27 to 43. 3 gets us to 30, 10 more to 40, and 3 to 43. Adding 3 + 10 + 3, the answer is 16.

METHOD 4. You *can* subtract 7 from 3. You get 20 + −4 = 16.

There are many others, including a method often used in mechanical computers called adding the complement. Consider the following subtraction:

$$\begin{array}{r} 73{,}256{,}722{,}894 \\ -\ 27{,}802{,}996{,}481 \\ \hline \end{array}$$

Replace the digits in the number being subtracted by their difference from 9, and add. Thus $2 \rightarrow 9 - 2 = 7$; $7 \rightarrow 9 - 7 = 2$; $8 \rightarrow 9 - 8 = 1$, and so on. Add:

$$\begin{array}{r} 73{,}256{,}722{,}894 \\ +\ 72{,}197{,}003{,}518 \\ \hline 145{,}453{,}726{,}412 \end{array}$$

Taking the 1 from the left, and adding it to the units digit gives the answer:

145,453,726,412 = 45,453,726,413

+

You may feel that one would have to hate subtraction to use this method, but note that it does reduce the number of machine operations, eliminating subtraction in the process.

There are two widely used methods of division as well. Most readers are familiar with the algorithm that deals only with leftmost digits in the dividend. For example, in the division:

$$27\overline{)62{,}475}$$

the student would think "62 ÷ 27" or perhaps "62,000 ÷ 27" to obtain the first digit in the quotient. Alternatively, the so-called Greenfield method considers the whole dividend at each stage, subtracting (and counting) multiples of 27 from the division. A computation might appear as:

	27)62,475	
	− 27,000	1,000
	35,475	
	− 27,000	1,000
	8,475	
	− 5,400	200
	3,075	
	− 2,700	100
	375	
	− 270	10
	105	
	− 81	3
REMAINDER	24	2,313 QUOTIENT

The literature of mathematics education is replete with arguments in support of various algorithms. Experiments have been carried out to provide empirical support for one algorithm or another. Most experiments indicate only that no significant difference between different methods can be demonstrated. To complicate matters, many experimenters are either authors of texts that use one of the algorithms or they developed the algorithm themselves—thus even positive results would need independent confirmation.

While we believe that the various algorithms should be of interest to the classroom teacher, we also contend that only in rare cases should teachers substitute their own algorithms for the one developed in the textbook on which the program is based. To do so is to invite trouble. In any program, a particular algorithm should be a specific part of the total picture. Whatever was learned before will help to support the algorithm; the algorithm itself will aid further development. Substitution of different algorithms places several specific responsibilities on teachers:

1. Teachers must establish prerequisites for the algorithm and see to it that all steps are fully developed.

2. They must be alert in subsequent instruction to both curricular and logical implications of the change.

3. They must communicate these changes to teachers in the following grades.

This is a major responsibility, which we do not recommend to teachers. Even when teachers are convinced they must make such changes, we feel they should do so only in full communication with the school administration and curriculum supervisors.

We offer one last example of an algorithm, which may suggest the difficulty of deciding on the merits of one procedure over another. Certainly one of the most difficult algorithms of elementary school is the one for addition of fractions, as in the following:

$$\frac{2}{7} + \frac{3}{8}.$$

Adults who can produce that sum are unusual. (Some would say that they are in fact limited to those who are mathematicians or mathematics teachers.) But consider the following simple algorithm:

1. Add the cross products.[6] Write the sum above the fraction bar in the answer.

2. Multiply the bottoms.[7] Write the product below the fraction bar in the answer.

The calculation could look like this:

$$\frac{2}{7} + \frac{3}{8} = \frac{2 \cdot 8 + 3 \cdot 7}{7 \cdot 8} = \frac{37}{56}.$$

Why all the fuss if it is that easy? The fuss is based on at least three arguments:

1. Without some justification for its use, the algorithm is eminently forgettable.

2. In fact, the problem does not involve merely remembering the procedure; it is one of confusing several procedures. For example, since

$$\frac{2}{3} \times \frac{1}{5} = \frac{2 \times 1}{3 \times 5},$$

why isn't

$$\frac{2}{3} + \frac{1}{5} = \frac{2 + 1}{3 + 5}?$$

---

[6]Cross products are those that you probably recall from your study of proportions. In the proportion $\frac{2}{3} = \frac{4}{x}$ you multiply the top of one side by the bottom of the other and set it equal to the product of the other pair of terms, obtaining $2x = 12$. The procedure is the same here, except that you add the results.

[7]Purists would certainly prefer denominators here.

3. In practical applications the algorithm turns out to be inefficient and even counterproductive. Consider, for example,

$$\frac{3}{8} + \frac{5}{16}.$$

Compare solving the problem using the algorithm to the more reasonable solution of utilizing common denominators to obtain

$$\frac{6}{16} + \frac{5}{16} = \frac{11}{16}.$$

Algorithm questions are complex and controversial. We recommend leaving them to textbook writers and curriculum researchers. The one instance we would suggest departing from this recommendation is in the case of remediation. When a student is completely blocked along an avenue, exploring another may be in order. Any gain may well justify later complications. The analogy here is with radical surgery.

THE ROLE OF THE TEXTBOOK IN TEACHING ARITHMETIC

Although arithmetic content of elementary school is familiar to most teachers, few anticipate the complexities of teaching procedures associated with familiar algorithms. Consider in this regard how you would proceed if you were asked to teach a primary-school child the subtraction process or an intermediate-grade student the long division procedure. Even an experienced teacher would find it difficult to include all the steps necessary to head off student problems. Here is where a textbook provides an important pedagogical crutch, in this case for the teacher. Contemporary texts have been carefully designed and sequenced to develop computational skills. This is their strong point. An experienced teacher will usually follow the general development of a text, ad-libbing additional content and occasionally even departing from the sequence. Until thoroughly familiar with the sequence, a beginner would do well to follow it very closely. Our classroom observation indicates that failure to do this often leads to serious difficulties, which can be exacerbated by the teacher's failure to identify deficiencies in the instructional program.[8]

Following a sequence of presentation does not mean, however, that you should restrict a program to that format. Common sense is in order here. When something doesn't work and students fail to grasp an idea, reteaching, quite possibly using a different technique, is certainly required. Supplementary texts are always useful as resources for different techniques.

ALTERNATIVE CREATIVE APPROACHES

Some very fine teachers are able to present instructional programs that contradict virtually everything in the last section. Consider the following episode. The teacher is talking with a fourth-grade student who has mastered multiplication but has had only minimal contact with division in any form.

Student: My brother in sixth grade does problems like this. (*Writes on the chalkboard*)

$$31\overline{)6{,}234}$$

Will we study how to do that this year?

Teacher: No, but you're so good at multiplying I think I can show you how to do that kind of division. Want to try?

Student: Okay.

---

[8]This does not mean that one must follow the text presentation religiously, but rather that you should not introduce conflicting algorithms or depart from the sequence in such a way that you introduce topics for which prerequisites have not been taught.

Teacher: Here's a problem. (*Writes on the chalkboard*)

$$23\overline{)38{,}654{,}298{,}621{,}530{,}600{,}521{,}734{,}568}$$

I'll start. Whenever you think you see what I'm doing, I'll let you take over. If you have a question, ask.

The teacher carefully proceeds, pointing to the numbers, but saying nothing. The student asks a question or two, but soon takes over, and after a few mistakes carries on with growing confidence.

This story is not apocryphal. *Some* teachers working with *some* students under *some* circumstances can bring off a technique like this. In the example, the student's interest in surprising an older brother was the motivating factor. But this is not an isolated case. This technique is a central feature of the program in many British primary schools. There students meet problems in the classroom that require development of more sophisticated tools. For instance, a third-grade group might be asked what their classroom would weigh if it were completely filled with sand. It should be evident that in addition to developing measurement ideas and the concept of proportion, the calculations would stretch the students' skills beyond what they have already achieved.

Even though it directly opposes the sequential teaching proposed earlier, we do not reject this style of learning under the direction of a master teacher. However, the dangers are evident. In the division example, the teacher's concern need not be mastery or even conceptual understanding, which can come later. If so concerned, the teacher would have to see to it that specific difficulties arose naturally in the chosen exercises. Two such difficulties are:

1. Divisors like 78 that make estimation of partial quotients more difficult and may lead to a need for correcting first trials

2. Partial quotients of zero

And in the sand-filled classroom problem, the teacher would have to remain alert to the wide range of conceptual and computational difficulties embedded in the task. Not least among the difficulties to look for would be the tendency of many students to recoil from such a task and give up.

A PROCESS HIERARCHY

In the division example of the previous section the student was learning an essentially meaningless trick. While the student could do long division, perhaps quite well, the teacher neither addressed the question of why the trick worked nor when to use it.[9] What the processes are about is a very important understanding that lies at the heart of the instructional program, but it is one that is often inadequately addressed. Several of our earlier examples illustrate this.

Robert Wirtz feels that remembering experiences, problem solving, and independent investigations form their own hierarchy and *that each* should be addressed in concrete, semiabstract, and abstract ways.[10] Wirtz has suggested a hierarchy that could be represented by the following figure:

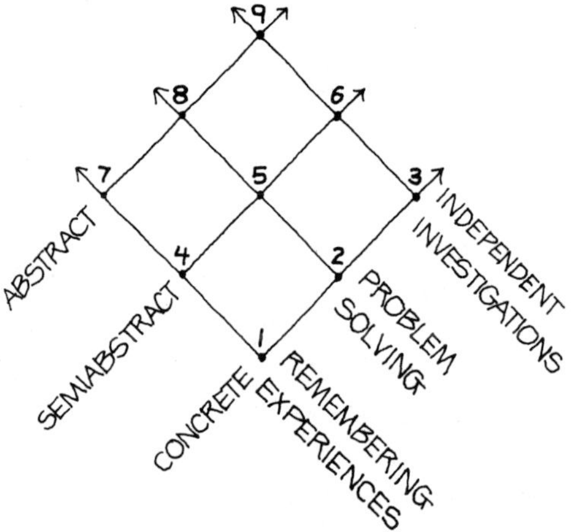

WIRTZ'S DEVELOPMENTAL LEARNING HIERARCHY MATRIX

---

[9]This is not meant to criticize the teacher, whose decision was that such questions were not then appropriate. In this regard there is a well-known saying: The beginning teacher teaches all he knows and more, the experienced teacher teaches just what he knows, but the master teacher selects from what he knows what is appropriate for the students.

[10]Materials by Wirtz in this and other sections are largely drawn from *CDA Math,* an elementary worktext series. For more on his learning theory and materials, see Robert Wirtz, *Mathematics for Everyone* (Curriculum Development Associates, Suite 414, 1211 Connecticut Avenue, N.W., Washington, D.C., 1974), pp. 36–74.

In order to illustrate further what is meant by this we have numbered the intersections on the matrix. Here are examples that relate these points to learning the concept of addition:

1. *Concrete: Remembering Experiences.* Counting physical objects and recording. The students are given some beans and a sheet of paper with many diagrams of the following form:

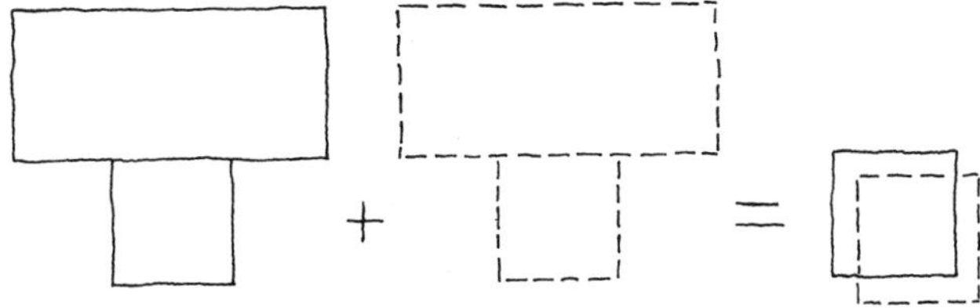

They are instructed to complete each exercise as follows:

(a) Put some beans in the large solid frame on the left.

(b) In the small box below the frame write the number of beans.

(c) Put some other beans in the large dotted frame on the right and record the number in the box below.

(d) Count all the beans used in both large frames and enter the number in the double-line box to the right.

2. *Concrete: Problem Solving.* Students are given six popsicle sticks on which beans have been glued, as in the figure. There are a

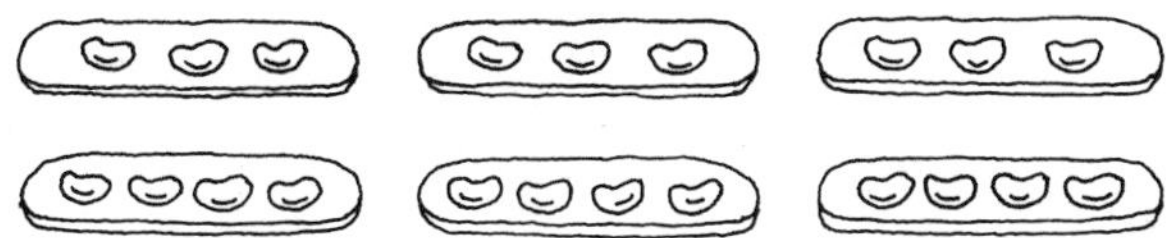

total of 21 beans. They are asked to indicate which numbers of beans, 0 through 21, they can pick up (circle those numbers) and which they cannot (cross them out).

0 1 2 3 4 5 6 7 8 9 10 11 . . . 18 19 20 21

3. *Concrete: Independent Investigations.* Students are provided beans and a figure like the following. They are instructed to place some

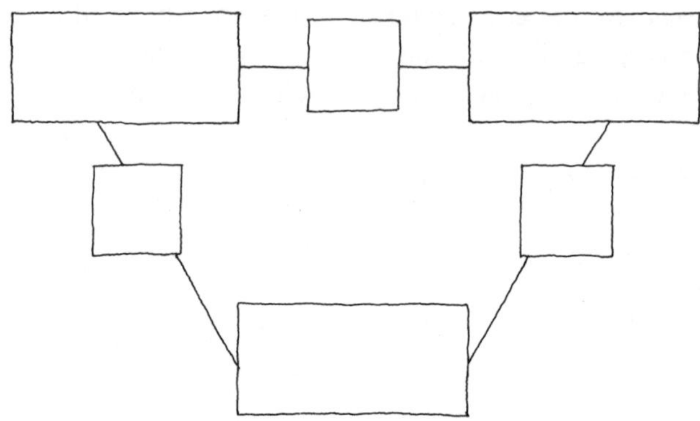

beans (or none) in each of the large rectangles and then to record the sums of beans in the interconnecting square boxes, as in the following reduced figure on the left:

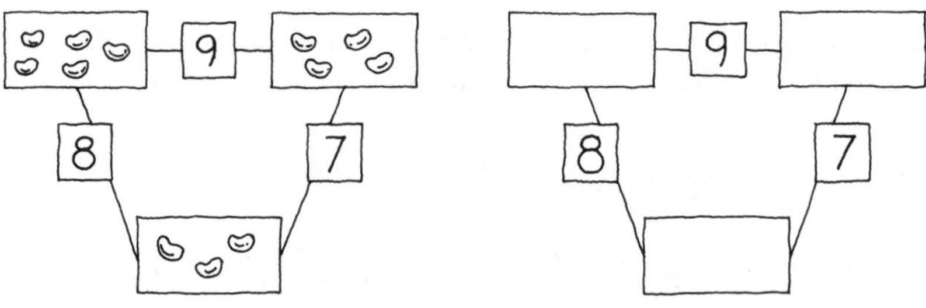

Now students sweep off the beans, leaving the figure on the right. This figure is passed to another student who tries to replace the beans in the original pattern.

4. *Semiabstract: Remembering Experiences.* Students are given a series of figures like the following:

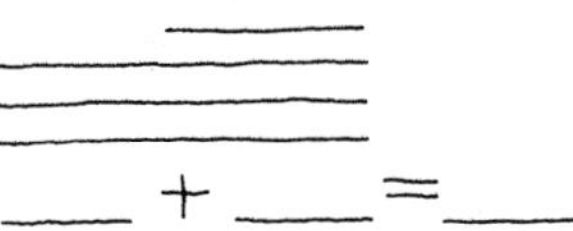

The task: draw vertical lines, count intersections, and record as in the following example:

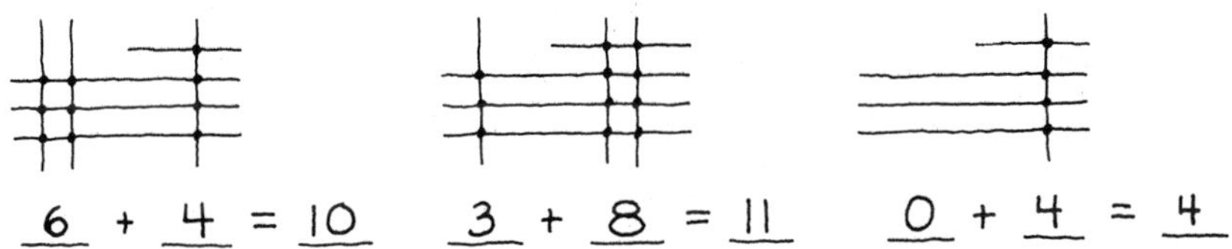

5. *Semiabstract: Problem Solving.* As in 4, but now students are invited to complete figures to make all the sums that are possible from 0 to 15.

6. *Semiabstract: Independent Investigations.* Try to make a figure (like that in 4 above) with a different number of horizontal lines for which the largest number that is not possible is 7. Can you make a figure with no upper limit of impossible numbers?

7. *Abstract: Remembering Experiences.* Standard textbook exercises fit this category:

$$\begin{array}{r} 3 \\ +\,4 \\ \hline \end{array} \qquad \begin{array}{r} 5 \\ +\,2 \\ \hline \end{array} \qquad \begin{array}{r} 6 \\ +\,1 \\ \hline \end{array} \qquad \begin{array}{r} 4 \\ +\,4 \\ \hline \end{array} \qquad \begin{array}{r} 2 \\ +\,7 \\ \hline \end{array}$$

A more interesting activity would be to form all the combinations with sum 13.

8. *Abstract: Problem Solving.*

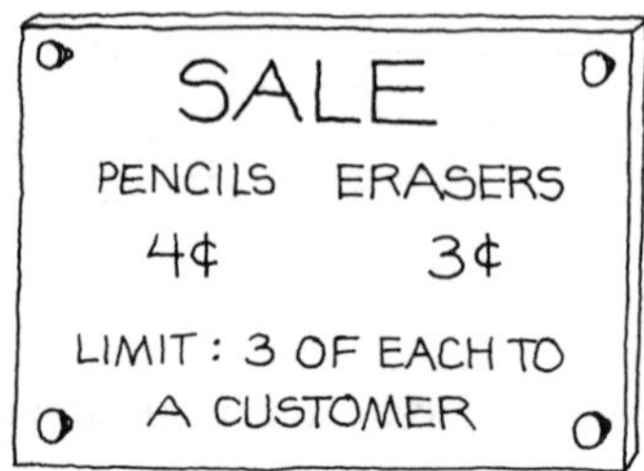

Which exact amounts can be spent at the sale?

9. *Abstract: Independent Investigations.* On the following figure, fence in numbers whose sum is 10.

PROBLEM

2	1	2	3
7	3	4	5
3	4	1	8
2	2	2	1

SOLUTION

2	1	2	3
7	3	4	5
3	4	1	8
2	2	2	1

Can you make up a problem with two different solutions?

Wirtz suggests that most classroom instruction focuses on points 1, 4, 7, and 8 of his matrix (page 116), with little attention given to independent investigations, and little opportunity for students to meet problem-solving activities at the concrete and semiabstract levels. He suggests specific patterns of development, diagrammed:

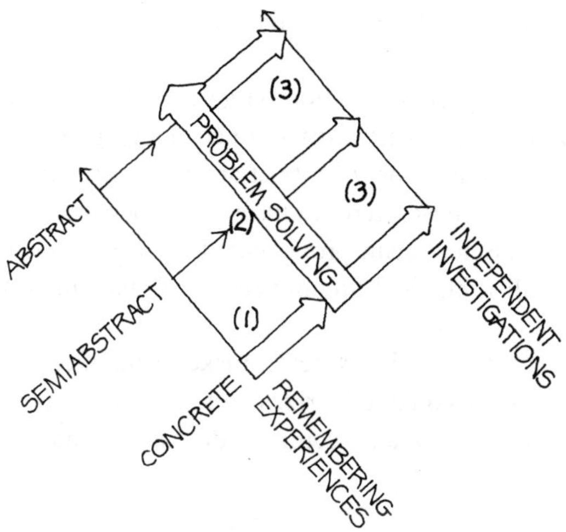

He describes the three basic elements in strategy.[11]

1. *To introduce the basic operations of arithmetic at the manipulative level (what we have called* concrete*),*
2. *To provide abundant "drill and practice at the problem solving level," and*
3. *To encourage learners who are inclined to make independent investigations.*

We support these reasonable suggestions, in addition to Wirtz's belief that too much classroom instruction and textbook presentation flows up the far left side of the diagram, and deals only with the intersections numbered 4, 7, and 8. This is a specific concern to which every classroom teacher should be sensitive. Those who agree with Wirtz feel it is essential to supplement textbook activities to make sure students receive an adequate conceptual basis for the arithmetic processes.

[11]Wirtz, *Mathematics for Everyone,* p. 50.

DRILL IN CHALLENGING SETTINGS

The examples of the previous section (largely modified from Wirtz's activities) show that drill and practice that are challenging and fun for students can be provided. You need only contrast any straightforward drill exercises with those of Wirtz, whose exercises have a deeper purpose. Such examples implement what the new math proponents have called for: replacement of both drill-for-drill's-sake and unmotivated drill with interesting drill that has a purpose.

Often the context of the exercises makes a significant difference. One final example, also attributed to Wirtz, should clarify this point. The following is a cross number puzzle, a common device in contemporary texts:

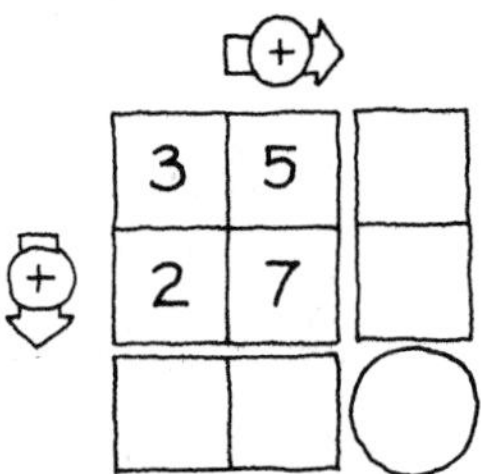

Students add across and down, placing sums in the appropriate boxes.[12] Finally they add the sums across, placing the result in the circle. This is checked against the sum of the vertical sum boxes:

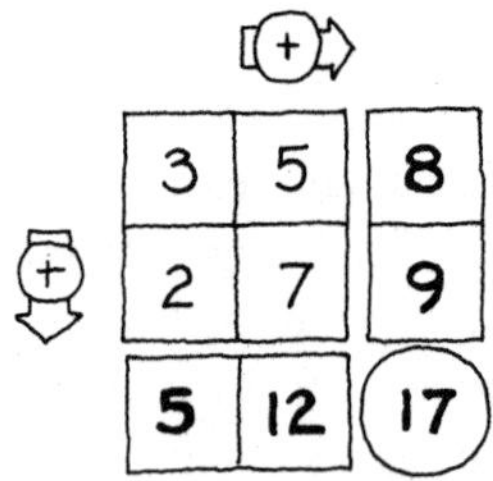

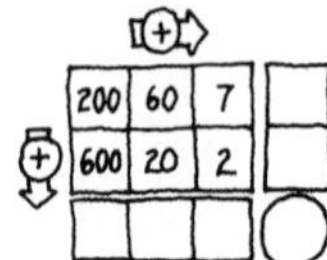

[12]The same form may be used for other operations, including mixed operations (for example, adding across and multiplying down). It also provides an interesting supplement to instruction in addition of higher decade numbers, as shown in the figure.

In this case the vertical and horizontal sums are *both* 17. These boxes provide a useful and unconventional drill format for students.

But now, suggests Wirtz, consider the following question: Can you make a cross number puzzle for which the loop number is *not* the same vertically and horizontally? (You may wish to stop here to try a few examples before reading ahead.) This question is pedagogically quite different. It is now a type 9 (Abstract: Independent Investigations) problem on which students can work at *their own levels of competence.* Weaker students can experiment with small numbers while stronger students extend themselves with larger addends. All will be practicing, drilling themselves in a setting that provides a partial check or feedback, as students search for cases where the vertical and horizontal sums differ. Some, but certainly not all, students will be able to answer the conceptual question they are attacking. Whether they do or not, they will have had drill in the context of an interesting exploration.

ARROW DIAGRAMS

In chapter 1 you were introduced to an arrow diagram in which the arrows represented the relation "is my sister." This device has been creatively developed and utilized by George and Frederique Papy in a wide range of settings. Originally used in a series of Belgian texts, arrow diagrams have been adapted by the Papys for the Comprehensive School Mathematics Program, a National Institute of Education experimental program in the United States. (See Appendix C.) In this section we suggest only a few of the many uses of this device for encouraging drill in challenging settings in the primary grades. Interested students will wish to explore this program in greater detail.

On any numerical arrow diagram, each dot represents a *different* number, just as each dot represented a different child in the example in chapter 1. Different colored arrows can be used to represent operations (like +3) or relations (like $<$). The following five exercises suggest some of the power of this device. In the following examples, arrows will be represented by different patterns (solid —>— and dotted --->--), each with a specific meaning for an exercise.

1. The largest dot represents 20. Label all the dots.

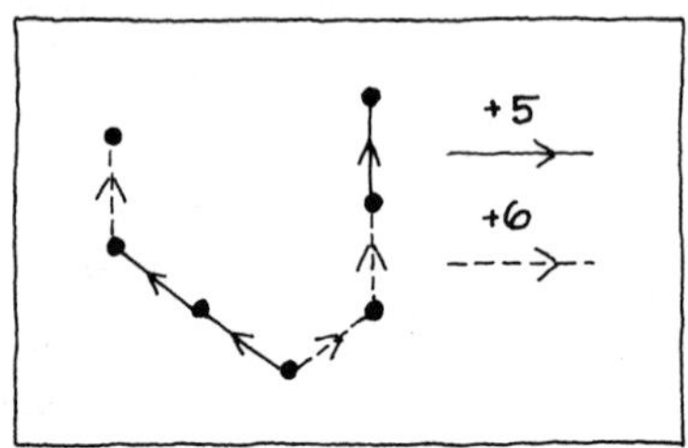

2. The dot labels are 17, 2, 12, 20, 9, and 27. Label them correctly.

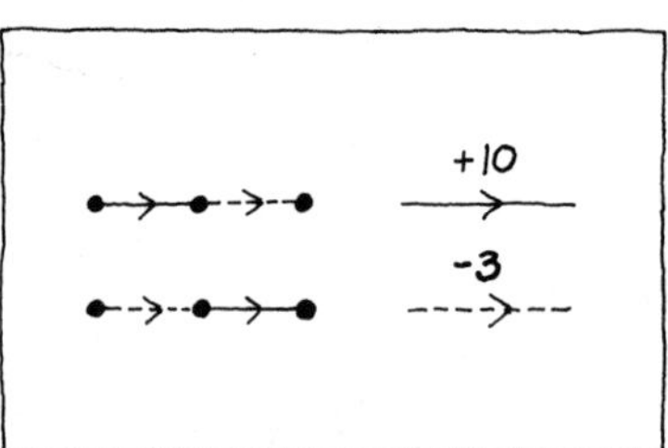

3. Use $\times$ 10 (→—) and + 1 (--→--) arrows to build a road joining the given points. (You may add dots.)

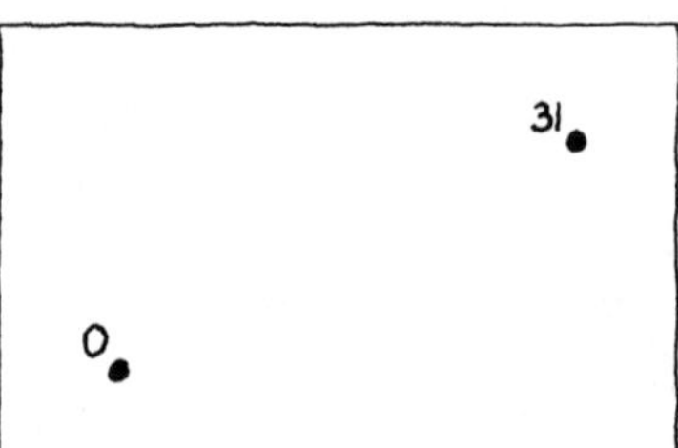

4. Label the other arrows and dots. Many answers are possible.

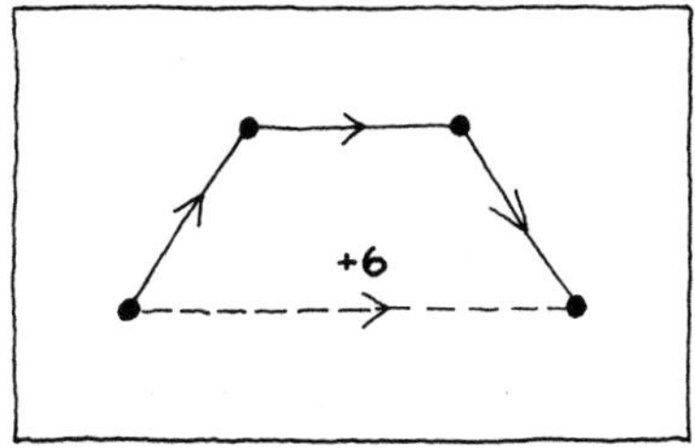

5. Identify Joe and Moe.

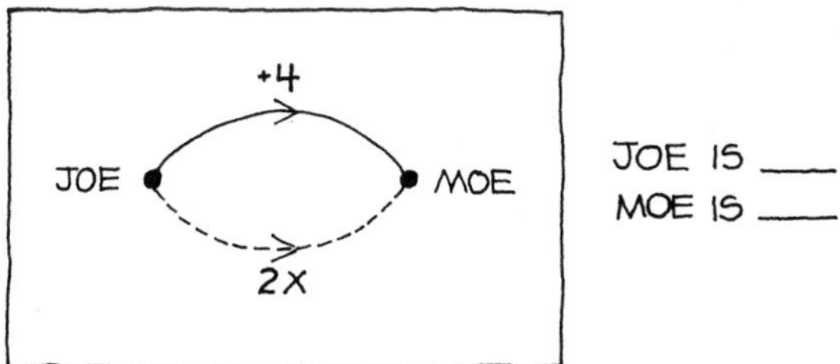

The range of applications of this device is almost boundless. You will be able to think of many additional exercises.

THE COMPUTER AND THE CALCULATOR

Both computers and calculators are slowly making their presence felt in the secondary and even in the elementary classroom. In the immediate future they will extend in many ways the kinds of activities that may be undertaken in elementary school classrooms. While we strongly recommend computer access for elementary schools, we recognize that it will be some time before a significant number of installations are available. We have therefore omitted consideration of sophisticated computers from this text.

Calculators are another matter. With the advent of the small, inexpensive, hand-held calculator (at this writing, already in the $5 to $10 range) major changes in mathematics instruction are already being incorporated. Not just a few, but almost all practices may change in the near future. Some people are even recommending elimination of instruction in basic algorithms. While we believe that the calculator has an important role to play in every classroom, we do not agree that the study of algorithms should be ignored. Algorithms, when carefully and rationally developed, provide deep insights into mathematical structure, insights we do not wish to lose.

But calculators will certainly open up the areas of exploration and application rapidly. Consider, for example, the problem: If we could fill this room completely with sand (we couldn't because the windows would probably break and the floor would probably collapse), what would the sand weigh? That problem is within the range of ability of fourth-grade students. The reasons that we don't ask them to solve it now are:

1. We don't believe that students are capable of the necessary data collection (weighing some sand and relating it to volume).

2. We know that they will get lost in the calculations.

The calculator responds to the second point, allowing us to focus student assistance on the first one.

We do not believe that calculators should be limited to the role of checking solutions. In fact we believe that they could be used for computation before algorithms are developed. In first grade, for example, once students are introduced to what addition is and before they learn their tables, they might use calculators to add cash register tapes from grocery stores. This would give them a feel for the power of addition, and if well presented could motivate them to learn how to do it on their own. The teacher might suggest: "If that little toy can add, surely we can," or "Let's see how the box works," or "I wonder if the calculator always gives the right answers. Let's see what it does so we can check it."

While it is true that calculators are capable of performing most everyday *calculations,* there are many mathematical concepts and problems that render the calculator almost useless. For example, in the following problem there is a great deal of calculation, but we cannot use the calculator: Use sums of two or more consecutive numbers to represent as many numbers as possible from 1 to 100.

1 = cannot do	8 = _____
2 = cannot do	9 = 4 + 5 or 2 + 3 + 4
3 = 1 + 2	10 = 1 + 2 + 3 + 4
4 = _____	11 = _____
5 = _____	12 = _____
6 = _____	13 = _____
7 = _____	14 = 2 + 3 + 4 + 5
	etc.

In this problem, there are many interesting conceptual questions that can be explored, where the calculator is of no use.

> Is there a pattern to those numbers that cannot be represented by the sum of two or more consecutive numbers?
>
> Find other numbers like 9 for which there is more than one possibility. Are these numbers related?
>
> Why are the odd numbers easier than the even numbers? Is there a pattern for them?

There are many other problems to which the calculator cannot contribute. Like any other tool it is most useful for certain tasks, not at all useful for others. But to fail to incorporate it in appropriate ways into the school curriculum is to fail to respond to the facts of contemporary life.

The calculator can be used as an immediate feedback device to encourage mental computation. Here is the kind of procedure we mean:

> Cover the calculator display.
>
> Enter 7.
>
> Multiply by 2.

Add 3.

Guess the answer and record your guess.

Check against the calculator display.

RECOMMENDATIONS FOR TEACHING ARITHMETIC

We conclude this chapter with some recommendations about instruction in arithmetic:

1. Arithmetic should continue to be the central but no longer exclusive part of mathematics in the elementary grades.

2. Serious attention should be given to the development of arithmetic concepts and skills. In particular, students should be provided concrete and semiabstract foundations for abstract computations. Procedures should always be delayed until conceptual groundwork is firm, and students should be encouraged to regress to concrete formulations when they experience difficulties.

3. Review and remediation should be a continuing part of the instructional program. Some teachers (and some textbooks) develop a series of "check ups," short three to five minute review quizzes that may be administered every three or four days. These short exercises not only provide practice and encourage faster work, but also help the teacher focus on individual and class difficulties related to computation errors. Some teachers allow a set time period for each test in the sequence, say five minutes, and then have students retake imperfect tests during subsequent periods until they achieve perfect scores. Many students enjoy the challenge of moving forward in such a sequence.

4. You will find that review of a topic, no matter how important and necessary it is, can be deadly. "We already did that," is the response to review most often heard from the students who need

it the most. For this reason your creativity is most challenged when you reteach. You must then seek out new and different ways of approaching the same ideas. Alternate textbooks are sometimes useful for this.

5. Since computation can be dull and routine for many students, you should be extra alert to inject life into these activities. The answer to this problem, however, is *never* avoidance. There are hard routines in arithmetic—like long division—that students should practice. Do not dismiss these routines, but rather seek to place them in interesting contexts.

6. You must consider it your continuing responsibility to seek out rich and creative exercises for students. Books, journal articles, other texts, and colleagues are all good sources, as is your own ingenuity.[13]

---

[13]Two excellent sources are *The Arithmetic Project Course for Teachers* and *Drill and Practice at the Problem Solving Level.* See Appendix C.

EXERCISES

1. Discuss each of the four examples on pages 101–103 in regard to the following:
   (a) The specific student difficulties, if any
   (b) Associated pedagogical problems
   (c) Possible remediation

2. In example 3 on page 118 explore the following question: Are there situations for which two different arrangements of beans can occur? If so, under what conditions? Would allowing fractions (of beans) change your answers?

3. Comment on your experience with exercise 2 in regard to the following:
   (a) Was the problem challenging to you?
   (b) Is it a problem a primary-grade child could answer? Why?
   (c) Is it a problem you would ask a primary-grade child? Why?

4. Answer the question posed in example 6 on page 119.

5. Make up some additional 4×4 fencing problems. Develop an easy way to construct problems that do have solutions. Can you suggest one with two different solutions?

6. How could fencing problems be presented at the concrete and semiabstract levels?

7. Explore the conceptual development of one of the following processes (not the algorithms), relating them to the Wirtz matrix (page 116), using a mathematics text:
   (a) Addition, grade one
   (b) Multiplication, grade two
   (c) Multiplication of fractions, grade five

8. Try to answer the problem on page 123 related to cross number puzzles.

9. Using a textbook for a grade level you plan to teach, trace the steps in the development of an algorithm.

10. Were the steps that you listed in exercise 9 the same as those that you followed when you learned this procedure? Is the procedure the same one you use? How do they differ?

11. Assume that the answers to the first two questions in exercise 10 were both no. How should this affect your teaching?

12. Answer the questions in the text about the representations of integers by sums of successive integers on page 127.

13. Consider the following: borrowing; equal additions; number line; 20 − 4 = _____ becomes 4 + _____ = 20.

(a) Which method works best for 3,275 − 1,999?

(b) Give an exercise for which each of the other methods works best.

(c) Is there a relationship between the four methods?

14. Some concrete materials, like Dienes blocks and Cuisenaire rods, are very useful for introducing place-value ideas. (Students who have access to these may utilize them in responding to the following question.) An alternate approach, somewhat weaker because it is two-dimensional rather than three-dimensional, is as follows:

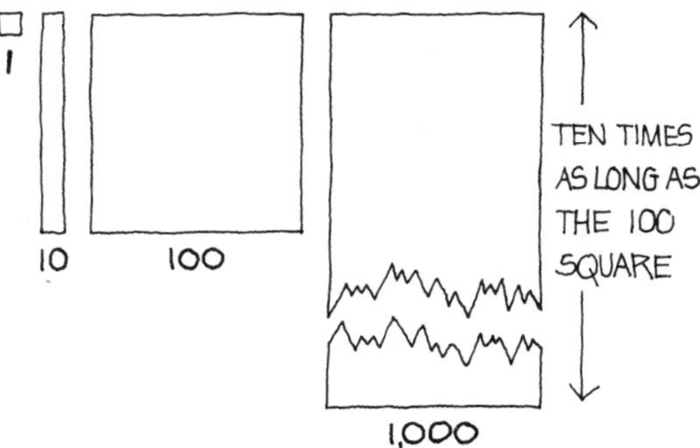

(a) Show how multiple copies of these concrete models could be used to communicate ideas about number structure. To do this, cut out models from squared pages and explain in terms of them the calculations:

3,782	2,163
+ 1,453	− 1,628

(b) Assuming the pattern square, rectangle, square, rectangle, how would you extend the model to display 10,000? .1? .01?

15. Respond to the following quotations about calculators by means of examples from this text:

The minicalculator will replace math instructors.

We won't need to teach any algorithms now that we have calculators.

The calculator keeps my child from learning mathematics.

16. Find some exercises in this text for which calculator access would be useful.

17. Examine a text for your grade level to estimate what proportion of the exercises would be easily answered by means of a calculator.

18. Consider the following situation: In a sixth-grade class, the teacher asks, "If I start with 3 and keep adding 3s, will I ever hit 6,234?" After a few minutes the teacher asks if students have found a short way to solve the problem, and then asks, "If I start with 4 and keep adding 3s, will I hit 6,769?"

   (a) In what way would the first solution be misleading in searching for a solution to the second problem?
   (b) Give two ways of finding a solution to the second problem.

19. Construct three problems that utilize arrow diagrams.

20. A problem for calculator solution. Recall the song "The Twelve Days of Christmas." In that song, gifts are received as follows:

> *Day 1: a partridge*
>
> *Day 2: 2 turtle doves and a partridge*
>
> . . .
>
> *Day 12: 12 lords, 11 ladies, 10 pipers, . . . , 2 turtle doves, and a partridge*

Suppose after a lover's quarrel the gifts are returned one each day starting the day after Christmas. On what date will the last gift be returned? (Assume one day for each turtle dove, for example.) The answer will surprise you.

CHAPTER FIVE

TEACHING FOUNDATIONS: STRUCTURE AND LOGIC

THE IMPORTANCE OF LOGIC AND STRUCTURE

The reader will recall from chapter 2 that the logical or "formal operations" stage of Piaget's cognitive development usually occurs at adolescence. This might seem to suggest that logic should be beyond the purview of this text. We think this view is shortsighted. This view would prevent us from developing mathematics beyond the barest rudiments in the elementary school, where so much material leans heavily on logic and structure. It is essential that teachers understand the rudimentary nature of students' logical development and the role of teachers in contributing to that development.

In this chapter we will first provide some background information about set theory and proof. Next we will introduce some exercises involving reasoning to show how structure is exposed. Finally, we will provide examples to suggest how the structure and logic of mathematics may be communicated.

SET THEORY

During the 1960s much use was made of sets in mathematics instruction. For deep understanding of mathematics, sets and function do play an important role. But the results of instruction in set theory in the elementary and secondary schools can at best be described as mixed. Sets do provide a useful way to explain basic ideas in a relatively concrete way. For example, a set of objects may be displayed:

$$\{\triangle, \square, \odot\}.$$

And the number of objects in the set may be named as a specific property of that set, in the same way that color is a property of certain sets:

$$N\{\triangle, \square, \odot\} = 3.$$

This provides the basis for a natural progression from the union ($\cup$) of sets, which combines their elements, to addition:

$$\{\triangle, \square\} \cup \{\odot\} = \{\triangle, \square, \odot\}$$

$$N\{\triangle, \square\} + N\{\odot\} = N\{\triangle, \square, \odot\}$$

$$2 + 1 = 3.$$

While this sequence makes perfect sense based on logic and the foundations of mathematics, in terms of children's understanding it fails. It overcomplicates with notation the basic concept that we can develop and check addition facts by counting groups of objects. During the 1960s, it unfortunately led teachers to spend too much energy teaching set processes that could have been better devoted to developing skill with related arithmetic processes.

The point here should not be missed. It *is* important that students at any grade level grasp the meaning of the procedures we present. But if we do not look to set theory for the underlying rationale for addition, where do we look? Our answer is that we *do* look to set theory, but that we do so in a much more informal and easily understood way. Given the addition exercise

$$2 + 1 = \_\_\_\_,$$

students should have more than a rote memorized response ready. They should be able to *prove* the answer. At primary-school age this means that computations can be based on ordinary counting, using concrete objects like beans:

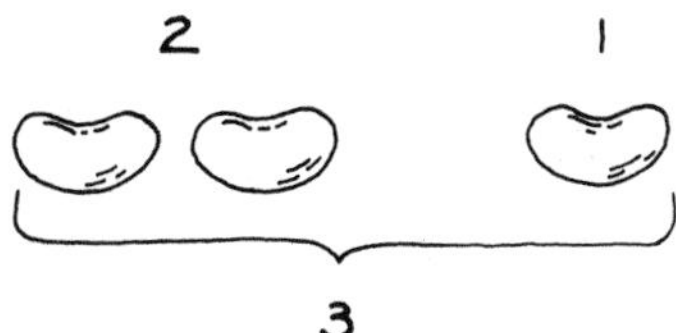

This process mirrors informally the more formal, notation-bound set theory approach. It provides a concrete and logical base for the abstract operation of addition. Given this procedure and the ability to count, students should be able to extend their knowledge, for example, to construct an addition table.

The reader should note that the preceding paragraph is not modern math. It is in fact the way thoughtful teachers have taught since the Middle

Ages, when our numeration system moved from symbols that had the number of objects pictured (semiabstract) to our present abstract notation:[1]

II		2
Roman numeral	→	Arabic numeral
(semiabstract)		(abstract)

WHAT IS PROOF?

Mathematician Robert Exner, who has been concerned with questions of logic in mathematics and mathematics instruction for many years, encourages teachers to think of proof like a practicing mathematician. To the mathematician a *proof is an argument that convinces.* Two mathematicians discussing a mathematical problem do not start every discussion from a logical foundation like *modus tolens* (implication). They merely provide what to them are convincing arguments. If either becomes dissatisfied at any point, he can always get more information by asking, Why? This simple question controls the level of the discussion, forcing the presenter to back up and fill in details or to provide additional support for his statements.

This definition of proof has an excellent pedagogical application to elementary school instruction. It suggests that proof in the classroom should be in clear terms that students can understand. It also suggests the obverse: that proof not in such terms will fail to carry any meaning. Armed with this definition and its pedagogical application, we return to Piaget. To convince a primary-grade student, we should deal most often with the concrete; as we move up through the grades more semiabstract proofs may be presented. The example with the beans applies this principle.

In the primary grades children should be asked to prove addition and subtraction computations by displaying blocks and, when appropriate, taking

[1]Some students work out their own methods to move from abstract to semiabstract. As noted in chapter 2, one author always counted the points in the symbol 3 (and the corners in 4), which effectively substituted for memorization but slowed down his computation.

opportunities for trading unit blocks for ten blocks and vice-versa, as in the figure. Such concrete demonstrations serve as quite satisfactory proofs.[2]

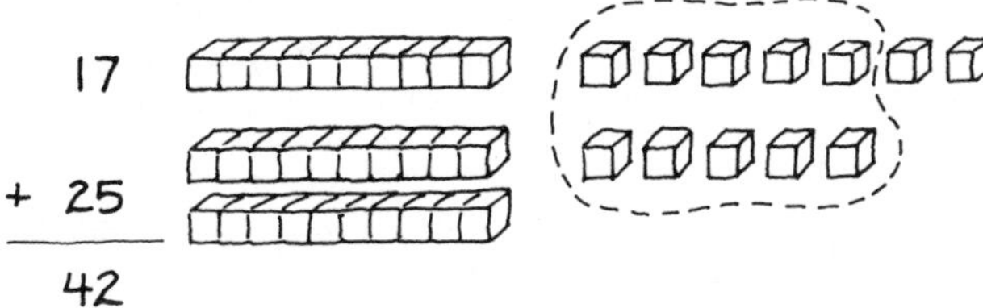

Even in higher grades, when concepts are being initially developed, it is well to return to concrete objects. Thus introductory lessons in fractions in intermediate grades should be based on objects cut into appropriate pieces, if possible by the students themselves. When students have difficulty, they should be given the opportunity to return to such concrete embodiments. This means that the initial concrete presentation should be careful and unhurried.

A good example of semiabstract proof is the Papy school-yard proof of chapter 1, where students identify the representations with their concrete counterparts. It is invariably those students who do not fully make that connection who fail to understand the proof. At all grade levels, the greatest pedagogical danger is too rapid progression to abstraction (including, of course, the failure to provide any concrete base at all). Every teacher should be alert to this danger.

SOME EXAMPLES OF PROOF

We now offer four examples of serious proofs, not with the intention of encouraging you to use these specific ones in the classroom, but rather to show what we mean by proof at concrete and semiabstract levels. Each responds in a certain way to a serious and sophisticated problem.

---

[2]Set theoreticians sometimes argue that such demonstrations are only specific examples, that the abstract number concept is distinct from the specific objects. They merely state this and give further specific examples that represent classes. No student is or should be concerned with such technicalities; we urge the same for teachers.

CHECKERBOARD AND DOMINOES

PROBLEM 1. Given a checkerboard with squares one inch on a side and a set of 32 1″×2″ dominoes, it is easy to see that the dominoes may be used to cover the checkerboard. The illustration shows one of the many possible coverings.[3] But

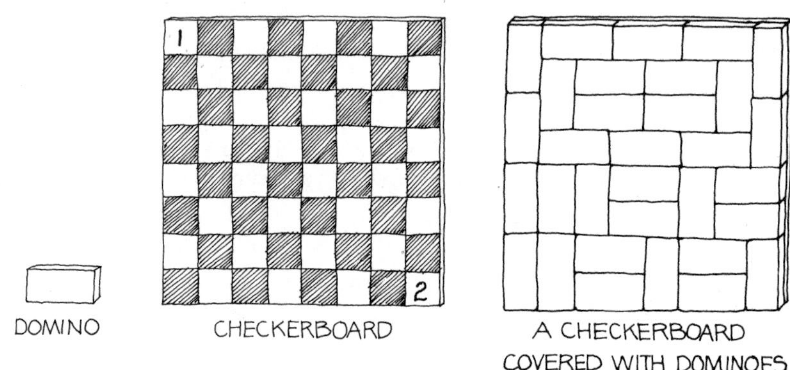

now we consider a checkerboard with the diagonally opposite corners removed (squares numbered 1 and 2 in the figure). The reduced checkerboard has 62 squares. Can 31 dominoes cover this board? (You may wish to try to answer before reading further, but don't spend too much time on it. This kind of question requires an insight that is almost a chance encounter for an inexperienced student.)

There are a variety of approaches to a problem like this. Most people would assume that the answer to the question is yes, and to try to display a covering, perhaps by setting out dominoes to accomplish the feat. One possible attempt might lead to the following partial covering; notice that this time it cannot be completed. It turns out in fact that this approach will always lead to such an impasse. The answer to the original question is no; the reduced board cannot be covered.

---

[3]The example should make explicit the distinction between *cover* and *covering*.

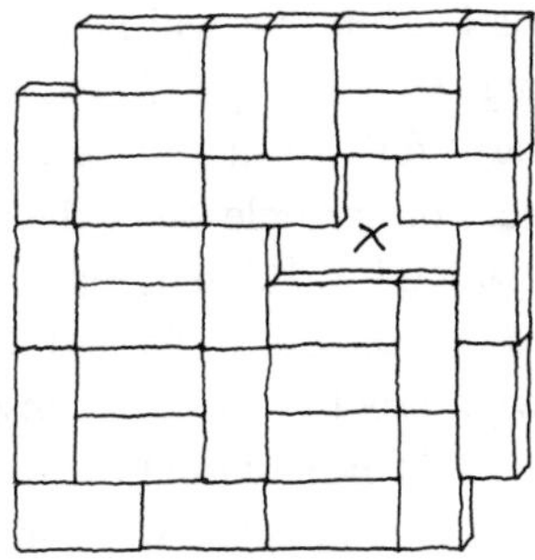

Both of the last two dominoes cannot fit in space *x*.

The following is a proof of that fact that is concrete enough to be clear to *you* and to *elementary school students.*[4] Return to the original colored checkerboard. Notice that every domino placement covers both a dark and a light square. For the full board, 32 dominoes cover 32 dark and 32 light squares.) Now note how the board is reduced: opposite corners are necessarily the same color. In the example, two light squares are removed leaving 32 dark and 30 light squares. But since the 31 dominoes can cover only 31 dark and 31 light squares, it is impossible to succeed.

A DOMINO FENCE

PROBLEM 2.

This problem also involves 1'' × 2'' dominoes. We seek a relationship that will help us to tell how many different patterns are possible in building a 2'' × *n*'' fence, where *n* is the number of dominoes. For example, the 4-domino fence has the following 5 possible patterns:

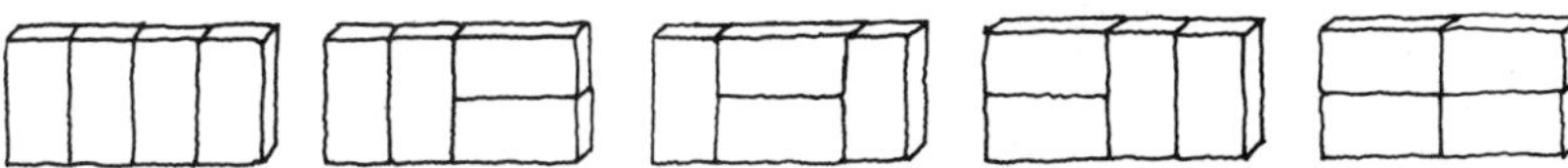

(You may wish to make a table of values for various length fences and seek a pattern before reading further.)

---

[4]This is based on the concrete, semiabstract, abstract scale.

We claim that a relationship that will help to determine the number of patterns is the following: $P_n + P_{n+1} = P_{n+2}$. In other words, when we know the number of patterns for two successive values of n, we merely add them to get the next value. For example, since the number of patterns for a 2" × 9" fence is 55 and for a 2" × 10" fence is 89, the number of patterns for a 2" × 11" fence is 144 (the sum of 55 and 89).

Consider the following proof of this relationship, which we construct by looking at a 2" × (n + 2)" fence. Start at the left end of the fence, using a domino. There are only two possible ways of starting—with either a

vertical domino or two horizontal dominoes. (Be sure you see that this exhausts the possibilities.) Now what is left? In case 1 (with a vertical domino first) the figure is reduced to a 2" × (n + 1)" fence, which would require

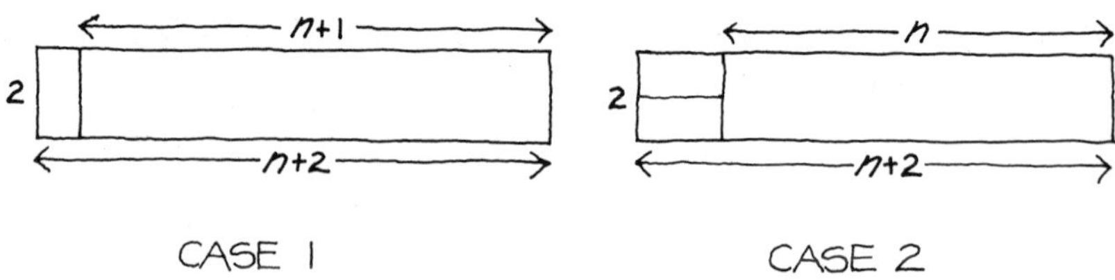

P_{n+1} patterns. In case 2, it reduces to a 2" × n" fence, requiring P_n patterns. Since those are the only possibilities, the patterns sum and we have

$$P_{n+2} = P_n + P_{n+1}.$$

A DIAGONAL PROBLEM

PROBLEM 3. A rectangle with integer values for length and width is separated into interior squares and one diagonal is drawn. We want to prove that the number of squares through which the diagonal passes is $w + l - 1$ when the diagonal does not pass through an interior corner. For example, for the 3×5 rectangle the diagonal passes through 7 squares ($3 + 5 - 1$ by the formula).

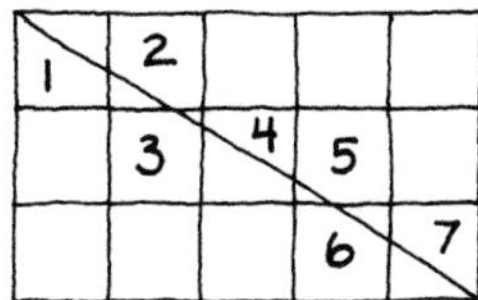

Consider the following proof of this fact. Assume that you are drawing the diagonal starting from the upper-left corner. As you enter the first square

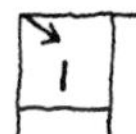

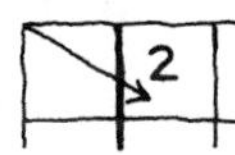

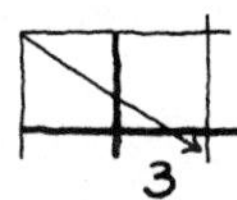

you count 1. It should be evident that you add to that count each time you cross an interior line. This continues until you finally enter the last square in the lower-right corner. Now how many lines must you cross? You should see that you cross all the lines (once each) except the outside edges of the

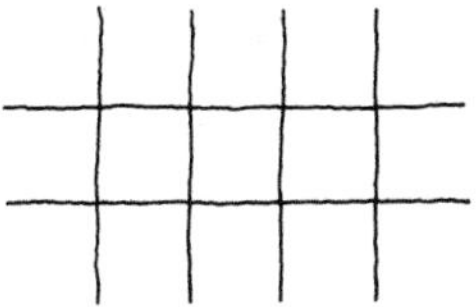

rectangle. How many of these are there? Examination reveals that there are $w - 1$ horizontal lines and $l - 1$ vertical lines. So we have counted:

1	$+$	$w - 1$	$+$	$l - 1$
THE FIRST SQUARE		HORIZONTAL LINES		VERTICAL LINES

This reduces to $w + l - 1$ squares in all.

GETTING OUT OF WORK

PROBLEM 4. You and a friend agree to cut the lawn of your jointly owned rectangular property using the following odd scheme. Your friend will choose a point on the property and you will draw a line of your choosing through that point and also choose either part of the rectangle to cut. Your friend will cut the rest. The

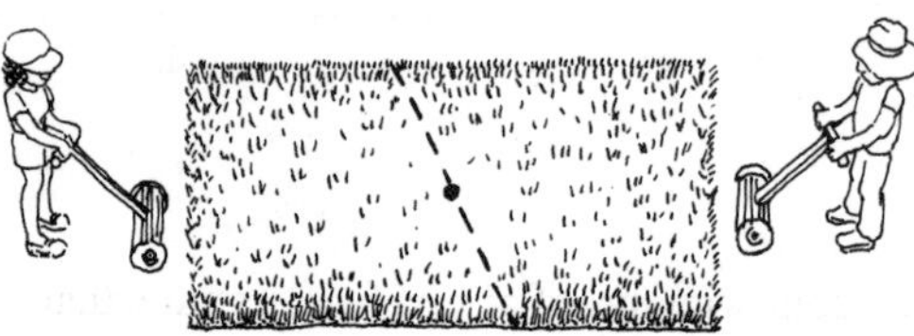

friend should obviously choose the center of the rectangle to protect his in-

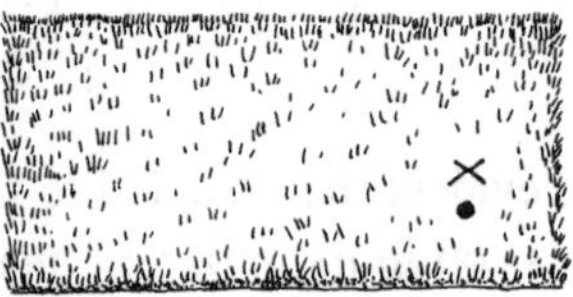

terest, since any line you draw would then divide the rectangle into two equal areas.[5] But suppose he foolishly chooses another point, say x in the following diagram, how can you assure yourself the least possible amount to mow?

We suggest the following procedure. Within the larger rectangle make a new, small rectangle with x at its center. A diagonal of that rectangle should be your line. You can prove that $\triangle ABC$ is the smallest possible

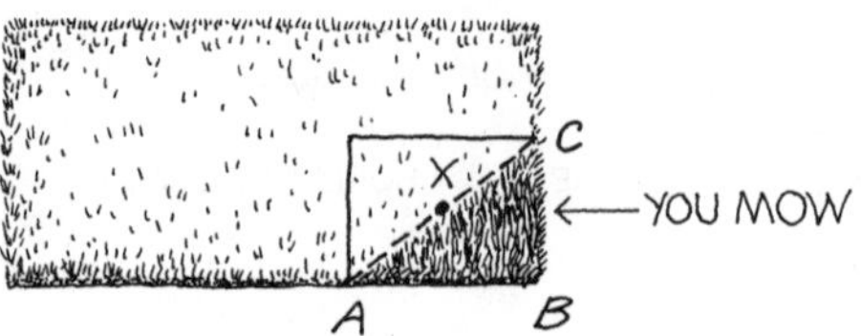

[5]The center is the point at which the diagonals intersect.

region by the following reasoning. Draw any other line through x, say $\overline{PQ}$. Now $\overline{PQ}$ must also divide the small rectangle into two equal parts so

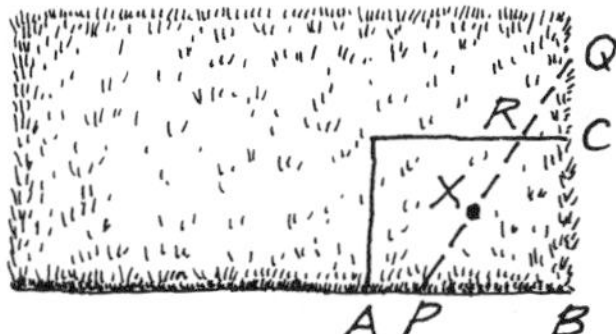

the part of that rectangle it bisects is equal in area to $\triangle ABC$. (In other words, the shaded part of the smaller rectangle, like $\triangle ABC$, is half the area of that rectangle.) But this would mean that we have half of the rectangle and the additional area of $\triangle QRC$ to mow. Since any line other than $\overline{AC}$ will delineate such an extra triangle, $\overline{AC}$ is the best line to choose.

SYSTEMS THAT ENCOURAGE LOGICAL DEVELOPMENT

The problems of the preceding section illustrate kinds of logical thinking that are accessible to your students. They could understand the reasoning behind each solution, but only rare students could develop the ideas on their own. We need to provide students with the opportunity to develop their own answers and to generate their own reasons for those answers.

We have already suggested that the question *Why?* is the key to this. This should be the classroom teacher's most common pedagogical tool to unlock students' thinking processes. You should help students to understand that a single instance, or even a number of instances are not sufficient proof of a more general statement. For example, students may claim that since

$$\frac{1\not{6}}{\not{6}4} = \frac{1}{4} \quad \text{and} \quad \frac{1\not{9}}{\not{9}5} = \frac{1}{5} \quad \text{and} \quad \frac{2\not{6}}{\not{6}5} = \frac{2}{5} \quad \text{and} \quad \frac{4\not{9}}{\not{9}8} = \frac{4}{8}$$

they can cancel digits to reduce fractions. Students should not only receive assistance in resolving this mathematical problem, but the teacher should stress that rules with exceptions aren't often useful in mathematics.

While opportunities for developing the basic ideas of structure and proof occur throughout elementary mathematics, teachers may wish to assist their students by more direct techniques. We describe now three such activities. Although they progress in complexity, each may be suitably modified for almost any grade level. This claim is based not so much on our classroom experience as on our experiences playing complex games with young children, like "Clue," a Milton-Bradley game in which complicated clues eventually lead to the discovery of a criminal.

HIGH-LOW

In the game "high-low," the teacher divides the classroom into two teams (sometimes geographically, sometimes by sex, and so on).[6] "I have chosen a number between 1 and 1,000," the teacher explains. "I'm going to call on a member of Mary's team, then one from Tom's team, and so on. When I call on you, you can ask exactly one question about my number, or you can guess what my number is. Remember, you can do only one of those. I will answer only yes or no or right or wrong. The winning team is the one that guesses my number. Sally, you go first."

When students first play this game they merely guess, so the dialogue might be:

Teacher: Sally.

Sally: I guess 673.

Teacher: Wrong. Jimmy.

Jimmy: 411?

But here the teacher could shape the game a bit:

Teacher: Wrong. Notice that so far no one has asked a question about the number. Everyone has guessed. For the next four people I will only allow questions, not guesses. Sarah.

[6]See John Holt, *How Children Fail* for many comments and examples relating to this game. See Appendix B.

Sarah: Does the number have a 9 in it?

Teacher: That's better. But no. Hank.

Hank: Is the number bigger than 500?

Teacher: Excellent question. Yes. Polly.

Polly: Is the number 789?

Teacher: Polly, that's a guess, not a question. Can anyone tell Polly if her guess is a good one? [*Pause*] Yes, Polly.

Polly: I remember. There's no 9.

Teacher: That's better. Now, Paul.

As the game progresses, students soon realize that a good question is one that divides the remaining numbers into two equal or nearly equal parts. A very efficient game might go:

Teacher: My number is between 1 and 1,000. Sally.

Sally: Is the number more than 500?

Teacher: No. Jimmy.

Jimmy: Is the number more than 250?

Teacher: Yes. Sarah.

Sarah: Is the number more than 375?

Teacher: Yes. Hank.

Hank: Is the number more than 440?[7]

[7]The "best" number is actually 438 or 439.

Teacher: Yes. Polly.

Polly: Is the number larger than 470?

Teacher: No. Will.

Will: Is the number larger than 455?

Teacher: No. Nancy.

Note that in six questions the students have reduced the number of possibilities from 1,000 to 15. Guessing would probably only have reduced the number from 1,000 to 994.

There is more to the game than this. Students will soon find that efficiency is not always the only strategy. Nancy might now ask the question, "Is the number even?" This adds a new dimension to the game. If the teacher answers yes, the remaining possible numbers are 442, 444, 446, 448, 450, 452, and 454. All students must now pay closer attention, since remembering a range is no longer adequate.

This simple game has within it basic logical elements that not only contribute to student growth, but also provide the teacher with insights into student thinking. The teacher learns much, for example, about students who guess every turn no matter how far they are from the answer. A variation on this game, where each team has a different number, will discourage random guessing even more. (Although some teachers keep their number choices fluid in order to avoid rewarding a lucky guess too often, we believe this is unnecessary.)

GENERATING AND PROVING THEOREMS

Parity is a property of counting numbers (and integers) that designates numbers as even or odd. One way of developing an early idea of proof is to generate and prove theorems using a restructured system. Parity offers this opportunity. Here are the axioms or given statements for the system:[8]

---

[8]The properties of order and rearrangement for addition (the commutative and associative laws) are also assumed here.

AXIOM 1. $1 + 1 = 2$.

AXIOM 2. 2 is even.

AXIOM 3. Even + 1 = odd.

AXIOM 4. Even + even = even.

AXIOM 4½. Every integer is even or odd.

These axioms provide basic reasons for proofs.

Here is a list of theorems that a fifth-grade class made up and proved. This list represents the order that they appeared on the list the children used, not the sequence in which they were proved in class:

THEOREM 1. Even + even + odd = odd (Bob)

THEOREM 2. Odd + even + odd = even (Diane)

THEOREM 3. Odd + odd = even (Class)

THEOREM 4. Odd + even = odd (Class)

THEOREM 5. 17 odds = odd (Sandy)

THEOREM 6. Odd + odd + odd = odd (Casey)

THEOREM 7. Even + even + even + odd = odd (Casey)

THEOREM 8. Even + even + odd + odd = even (Bill)

THEOREM 9. 16 odds = even (Charles B.)

THEOREM 10. Even + even + even + even + odd + odd + odd = odd (Jeff)

THEOREM 11. Odd + even + odd + even + odd + even = odd (Ginny)

THEOREM 12. Even + even + even + even + odd = odd (Janet)

THEOREM 13. Odd + odd + odd + even + even + odd + odd + odd + odd = odd (Charles)

THEOREM 14. Even + even + even + odd + odd + odd + odd = even (Mike)

THEOREM 15. Even + odd + odd + even + even = even (Brian)

THEOREM 16. Even + 0 = even (Sandy)

THEOREM 17. 0 is even (Class)

THEOREM 18. Odd + 0 = odd (Sandy)

THEOREM 19. 1 is odd (Mike)

Examples of the format the class used to prove most of the theorems are shown at the top of the next page. The numbers in parentheses refer to the axioms listed above.

Only theorems like the last four in the list pose new problems. Theorems 16 and 18 are resolved by utilizing the property of zero for addition. Theorems 17 and 19 call for indirect proof, the kind used in the Papy playground problem in chapter 1. Students led through the following proof for theorem 17 will be able to construct their own for Mike's theorem 19:

THEOREM 17. We assume 0 is odd and show that this leads to a contradiction. By theorem 16, even + 0 = even. Now, assuming 0 is odd, even + odd = even.

BOB'S THEOREM 1

EVEN + EVEN + ODD
(4) (3)
= EVEN + EVEN + 1
(4)
= EVEN + 1
(3)
= ODD

DIANE'S THEOREM 2

ODD + EVEN + ODD
(3)
= EVEN + 1 + EVEN + ODD
(4) (3)
= EVEN + 1 + EVEN + 1
(4) (1)
= EVEN + 2
(2)
= EVEN + EVEN
(4)
= EVEN

This contradicts axiom 4½. Since "0 is odd" led to a contradiction, and since axiom 4½ states that all numbers are either even or odd, 0 must be even. (Compare this with the argument about the boys on the playground in chapter 1.)

If these last four theorems cause extra problems, you can easily avoid them by not accepting them on the class theorem list. In that case, axiom 4½ is not necessary.

CLUES

Like high-low, the game of "clues" is played by two teams. In this game the class seeks a number or numbers hidden among the clues, but they must do so by locating logical contradictions in the list so far.

The teacher has a list of clues for a specific game written on an overhead projector transparency. Alternately they could be written one at a time on the chalkboard. Either way the clues are displayed to the class in order, one new clue for each turn. When it is a team's turn, the member called on may either: (1) pass, (2) guess the final answer, or (3) name a contradiction among statements on the list so far. Scoring is as follows: pass is 0 points, a correct answer is 5 points, a wrong answer counts 5 points off, a contradiction counts 1 point for each statement used in the contradiction, and an incorrect contradiction counts 1 point off. As each contradiction is named correctly, the teacher marks the statements involved true or false (based on a master list). You will understand the game best by following this example:

Display

_____1. All of the numbers are odd.

Teacher: This game is about whole numbers. Here is the first clue. Team A. John.

John: Pass.

Display

_____1. All of the numbers are odd.

_____2. The sum of the numbers is less than 25.

Teacher: Team B. Mary.

Mary: Pass.

Display

_____1. All of the numbers are odd.

_____2. The sum of the numbers is less than 25.

_____3. There are 5 numbers.

Teacher: Team A. Bill.

Bill: Pass.

Display

_____1. All of the numbers are odd.

_____2. The sum of the numbers is less than 25.

_____3. There are 5 numbers.

_____4. All of the numbers are greater than 5.

Teacher: Team B. Patty.

Patty: Contradiction. Statements 2 and 4.

Teacher: No. That's −1 for Team B. [*Records score: A: 0, B: −1*] Team A. Roscoe.

Roscoe: Contradiction. Statements 2, 3, and 4.

Teacher: All right. That's 3 for Team A. [*Records score: A: 3, B: −1. Marks 2, 3, and 4 true or false, T or F, on the master list beside the appropriate numbers. Then adds statement 5.*]

Display

_____1. All of the numbers are odd.

__F__2. The sum of the numbers is less than 25.

__T__3. There are 5 numbers.

__F__4. All of the numbers are greater than 5.

_____5. All of the numbers are even.

Teacher: Team B. Sally.

Sally: Contradiction. Statements 1 and 5.

Teacher: Good. That's 2 for Team B. [*Changes score*] Now it is A: 3, B: 1. [*Notes answers to 1 and 5, and adds statement 6*]

Display

_F_1. All of the numbers are odd.

_F_2. The sum of the numbers is less than 25.

_T_3. There are 5 numbers.

_F_4. All of the numbers are greater than 5.

_F_5. All of the numbers are even.

____6. The largest number is 8.

Teacher: Let's see. It's Team A. Mark.

Mark: Contradiction. Statements 1 and 6.

Teacher: No. One off. [*Changes score*] A: 2, B: 1. Remember class, as soon as statement 1 is marked F, we know that not all of the numbers are odd. Therefore there is no contradiction with 6.

The game continues in this fashion, as students analyze the statements in preparation for upcoming turns.

Here is the full list of clues for this game with their true-false entries:

_F_1. All of the numbers are odd.

_F_2. The sum of the numbers is less than 25.

_T_3. There are 5 numbers.

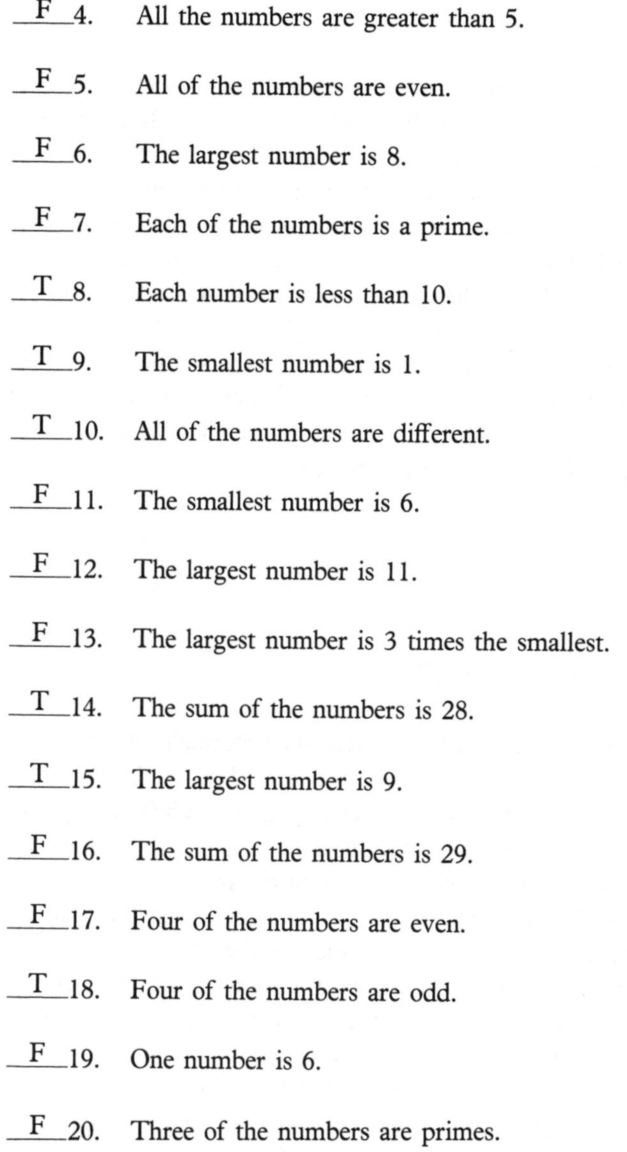

F 4. All the numbers are greater than 5.

F 5. All of the numbers are even.

F 6. The largest number is 8.

F 7. Each of the numbers is a prime.

T 8. Each number is less than 10.

T 9. The smallest number is 1.

T 10. All of the numbers are different.

F 11. The smallest number is 6.

F 12. The largest number is 11.

F 13. The largest number is 3 times the smallest.

T 14. The sum of the numbers is 28.

T 15. The largest number is 9.

F 16. The sum of the numbers is 29.

F 17. Four of the numbers are even.

T 18. Four of the numbers are odd.

F 19. One number is 6.

F 20. Three of the numbers are primes.

If, when the list is completed, the numbers have not been guessed and some statements are not yet designated true or false, the entries are made one at a time, giving teams alternate turns. The game ends when the correct answer is given. At that point, the team with the highest score wins. Since you will be asked to determine the answer to this game in the exercises, we do not give it here.

COMMENTS ON THE GAMES

These games invite children to think logically and carefully. By its very precision, mathematics brings this kind of thinking within the range of most children. The game format, especially when it is in the form of team play, encourages students to think deeply about their answers. This extra effort calls forth excellent thinking on the part of many students. Each of the games suggested may be modified to suit specific circumstances. Some teachers who have played the "clues" game have even had students prepare their own lists.

In the exercises that follow, you will be asked to reexamine these problems and games to provide further insights into logic and mathematical foundations. When thinking about these questions, you should gain insight into the reasoning problems of younger students.

STRINGS: AN APPROPRIATE USE OF INFORMAL SET THEORY

At the beginning of this chapter we displayed an overformalized application of the theory of sets. We discourage such activities. But set theory has an extremely important role to play even in primary grades in helping students to carry out the fundamental act of *classification.*

Frederique and George Papy and Burt Kaufman of the Comprehensive School Mathematics Program (CSMP) have developed what they call the "language of strings," in which set theory and modified Venn diagrams are used to pose interesting logical problems in a form young children can understand. The strings are loops separating numbers with a given property (inside) from those without that property (outside).

The following examples, most suitable for primary grades, suggest only a few of the many uses of this device. Further information may be obtained from the program itself. (See Appendix C.)

1. Draw a dot and label it for each of these numbers: 0, 3, 7, 8, 35, 40, 43. (44 is done for you.)

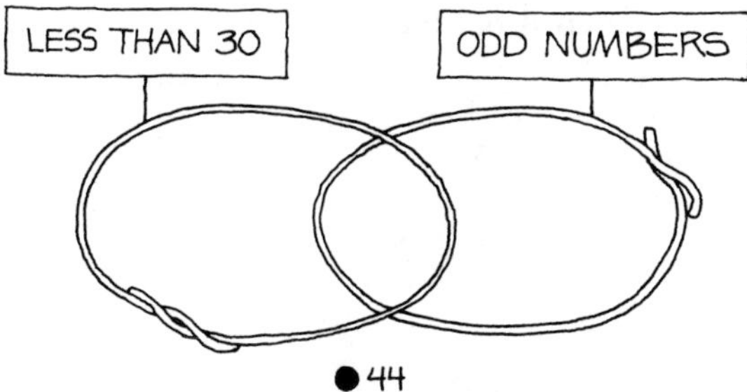

2. Bill is one of these numbers: 20, 21, 23, 24, 40, 41, 60, 63. Bill is in this string picture. Who is Bill?[9] ____

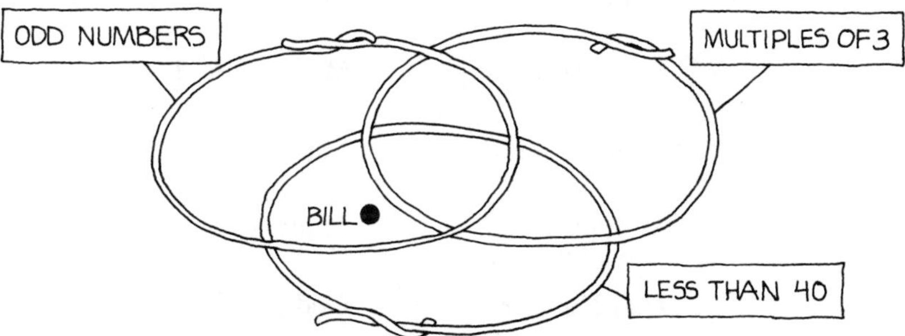

3. Greg is a secret number. Greg is in this string picture and in this arrow picture.[10] Who is Greg? ____

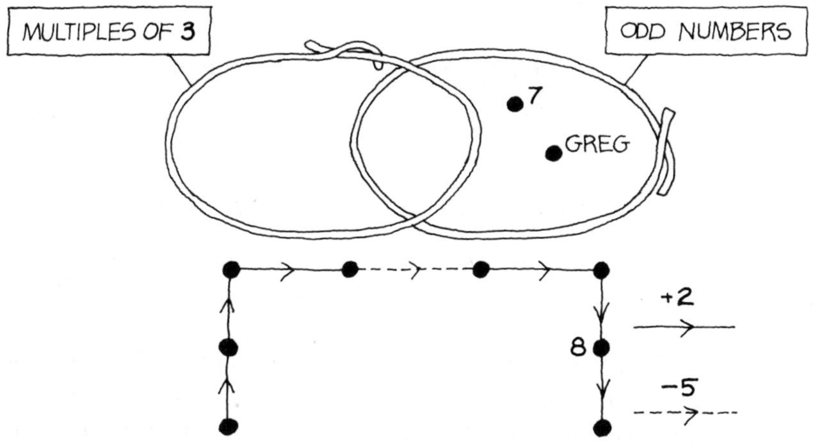

[9]Bill is a number. For readers who—unlike children—balk at anthropomorphization of numbers, rephrase this question: "Which number is designated Bill?"

[10]See chapter 4.

4. Use the clues to cross out the labels that the strings *cannot* have.

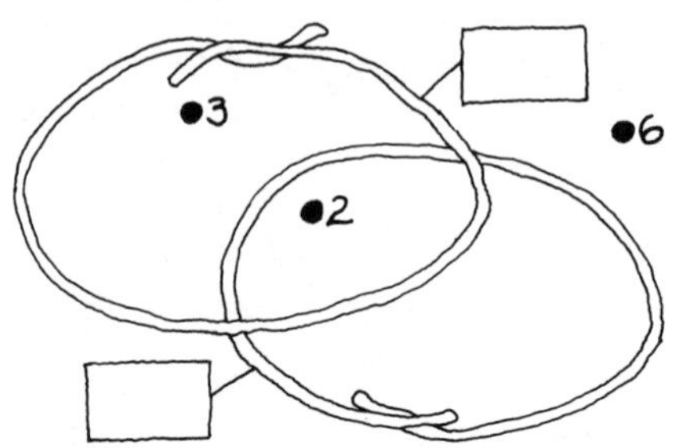

Upper string	Lower string
Multiples of 2	Multiples of 2
Multiples of 3	Multiples of 3
Multiples of 4	Multiples of 4
Odd Numbers	Odd Numbers
Prime Numbers	Prime Numbers
Divisors of 12	Divisors of 12
Divisors of 18	Divisors of 18
Divisors of 20	Divisors of 20
Divisors of 24	Divisors of 24

If the labels of the strings are in the lists, the upper string is ____, and the lower string is ____.

In the CSMP program a game format like that for the "clues" game is often used. In such a game a list of the possible labels (as in the previous question) and a set of point values are provided. Students take turns attempting to place individual points in the strings. A correct guess merits one additional turn. The winning team is the team that correctly places the last point *and* correctly names the labels. Remarkable reasoning is forthcoming even from primary-grade children.

EXERCISES

1. Examine carefully the four examples on pages 138–143. Do you find the arguments convincing? Explain.

2. Do you think of yourself as a logical or an emotional person or both? Comment on how this affects your thinking about mathematics.

3. Use the recurrence relationship established in the domino fence problem and the facts that $P_1 = 1$ and $P_2 = 2$ to generate the number of fence patterns up to $n = 15$. How does this kind of relationship differ from formulas you have used before? (*Hint:* Consider determining P_{100}.)

4. Which of the four problems is most abstract? Which proof is most difficult for you to understand? Comment.

5. Geometry has traditionally been the vehicle for teaching about logic. Based on what you have studied in this chapter, give a rationale for this. Do you agree or disagree? Why?

6. Develop and prove a formula for the number of interior cubes the diagonal of a rectangular solid with integral dimensions (l, w, h) passes, when it does not pass through an interior edge or corner. (*Hint:* Extend the technique of problem 3 on pages 140–141.)

7. Examine a chapter of a text at your level of interest and comment on the logical basis provided to students in the development of material.

8. Choose one of the logic examples and develop it into a lesson about proof for sixth-graders. (The lesson need not aim at having the children prove anything.)

9. Devise a logical explanation (proof) for the cross number problem of chapter 4.

10. What are the numbers that satisfy the "clues" games presented in the text?

11. Here is a set of clues, most without designation as true or false. Make up a compatible (noncontradictory) set of true-false values. In this game we seek 2 different counting numbers.

____	1.	The numbers are of the same parity (both odd or both even).
T	2.	The numbers are each less than 8.
____	3.	The sum of the numbers is odd.
____	4.	The product of the numbers is even.
____	5.	The sum of the numbers is 8.

12. Adjust your answer in exercise 11 until you reduce the possible solutions to one.

13. Try the "clues" game of the text in a fifth-grade classroom. Describe your experience. How would you adjust your lesson another time?

14. Make up your own clues for a "clues" game. (*Hint:* Start with an answer of 3 or 4 numbers.)

15. In this game we seek four different counting numbers:

T	1.	Their total is 8 times one of the numbers.
F	2.	The sum is an odd number.
T	3.	One of the numbers divided by another number equals one of the numbers.
F	4.	Seven is a factor of the sum.
F	5.	The largest number is 10.
T	6.	The sum is equal to ⅙ of a gross.
F	7.	Three of the numbers added together equal 25.
T	8.	The sum of two numbers is equal to the sum of two others.
T	9.	All are odd numbers.
T	10.	The sum of two numbers equals half of the sum of the other two numbers.

By covering later steps, see how many steps it takes to discover the answer. Can you prove your claim?

16. For the "high-low" game on pages 144–146, pose five *new* questions that could be asked in order to help pinpoint a number.

17. Consider the following situation: a student makes the mathematical error: $5 + 6 = 12$. Give three ways to "prove" to him that he is mistaken.

18. How does primary-grade student achievement with the "language of strings" fit Piaget's stages?

19. Make up five string game exercises suitable for your grade level.

PART 3

AS EACH SHEEP LEFT THE FOLD,
UGBOO PUT ONE PEBBLE IN THE BAG.

PEDAGOGICAL STYLES

In earlier chapters we surveyed the mathematical content of the elementary school and considered some of the psychological theories that relate to the ways young children learn. Now in this section we turn to the classroom itself. How does a teacher bring together these two strands—mathematical content and psychological theory—to communicate mathematics to students?

First, we must warn you that in discussing the following methods we somewhat artificially isolate teaching techniques in order to highlight them. No one technique is recommended as best for all situations. Each has special virtues for specific topics or specific goals. In selecting the most appropriate teaching technique, good teachers will consider how that style fits: (1) the content to be taught, (2) the particular educational goals, (3) the students, and (4) the teachers themselves. The fourth point is fully as important as the other three considerations. All teachers should consider their instructional programs in relation to their own skills. They should incorporate their own skills into their teaching programs. Of course, this does not mean that teachers should reject procedures that are new or difficult for them, but rather that they should be alert to such problems and exercise caution.

CHAPTER SIX

TEACHING FROM CONCRETE EXPERIENCE: THE LABORATORY METHOD

Much recent attention has been focused on mathematics laboratories as centers for hands-on learning of mathematics. We fully support this as *one* of the best ways to approach mathematics. Few teachers in this country have had experience with this method or been exposed to it. For that reason, we turn here to examples to illustrate our ideas and to provide teachers with a variety of activities with which to experiment. Only with experimentation, both with peers and children, will the values of this technique become clear.

SOME CLASSROOM EXAMPLES OF THE LABORATORY METHOD

Consider the following classrooms:

EXAMPLE 1. In a second-grade classroom, students have collected information from a class survey and are now working in small groups of three or four students. Each group is assigned the task of representing certain data "in the best way possible."

One group has been given slips of paper, each stating the birthdate of a fellow student. One slip reads "June 23, 1971," for example. The four members of each group are working together to organize information to graph on a large sheet of posterboard. As they discuss the graphing possibilities, one student suggests graphing the birthdays by month; another wants a representation by years "so it will show their ages." The students address their question to the teacher, who suggests that they cut the slips into two parts; thus the two slips "June 23" and "1971" replace the single slip. Having made this suggestion, the teacher answers questions from other groups. The group members decide to make two separate graphs, and pair off to do so. Their final representations appear in the figure on the following page. Later, when their charts are presented to the entire class, one team member says, "We could have also graphed the information by day of the month."

Some representations that other groups are working on are favorite colors, numbers of brothers and sisters, types of pets, heights, and arm spans.

EXAMPLE 2. Each student in a fifth-grade class has a geoboard and a supply of rubber bands. (The geoboard was described in chapter 2.) Students are working, alone or in pairs, on tasks assigned to them on cardboard work cards.

Some of the questions on the various cards are:

1. How many different shape triangles can you form on the geoboard? Keep a record on graph paper.

BIRTHDAYS BY MONTH

									NOV 30	
							SEPT 20		NOV 20	
JAN 31							SEPT 16		NOV 10	
JAN 20	FEB 20	MAR 30			JULY 9	AUG 25	SEPT 9		NOV 7	DEC 24
JAN 5	FEB 15	MAR 8	APR 26	JUNE 7	JULY 7	AUG 9	SEPT 9	OCT 25	NOV 3	DEC 13
JAN 2	FEB 1	MAR 1	APR 1	JUNE 3	JULY 4	AUG 6	SEPT 6	OCT 20	NOV 1	DEC 1

BIRTHDAYS BY YEAR

	1970		
	1970	1971	
	1970	1971	
	1970	1971	
	1970	1971	
	1970	1971	
	1970	1971	
	1970	1971	
	1970	1971	
	1970	1971	
1969	1970	1971	
1969	1970	1971	
1969	1970	1971	
1969	1970	1971	1972
1969	1970	1971	1972

EXAMPLE 2. (continued)

2. How many different size squares can you form whose sides are parallel to the side of the geoboard? Record their side lengths and areas.

3. For the squares in exercise 2, how many of each can be located on the geoboard?

4. How many different size tilted squares can you form on the geoboard? (Refer to the following figure.)

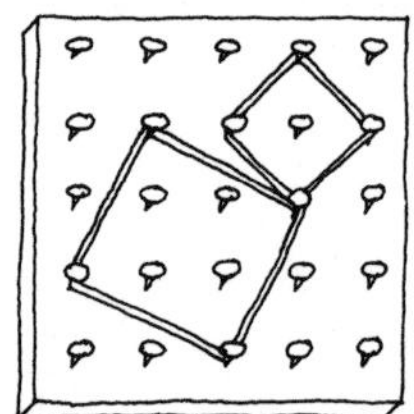

TWO "TILTED" SQUARES ON A GEOBOARD

5. For the squares in exercise 4, how many of each can be located on the geoboard?

6. What is the total number of squares that can be located on the geoboard?[1]

As each project is completed, students review their work with the teacher, who checks their reports and occasionally asks them further questions.

EXAMPLE 3. A team of three sixth-grade students is measuring the dimensions of the school building and play area in preparation for drawing a map of the school grounds. A bicycle is used as a measuring tool; it has an adhesive tape marker on the front tire so that wheel revolutions can be counted. One student carefully wheels the bike, while a second counts revolutions, and a third records the data on a rough sketch. Together they determine which measurements to take.

[1]Note that questions 2–6 would be on the same card or on an identified series of cards.

Now the team returns to the classroom to translate their data into an accurate map. In the process they will use proportions first to convert wheel revolutions into standard units and then, after determining an appropriate scale, into map lengths.

EXAMPLE 4.

In a first-grade classroom students are working at tables, five or six children at each. At one table the teacher has made a tower of blocks of various sizes and colors. The children are building duplicate towers. At another table children are playing a simple version of dominoes with large size tiles. At another they are playing with a variety of balancing scales. (Later in the year they will use these scales for more serious activities. Now they are merely balancing various objects.)

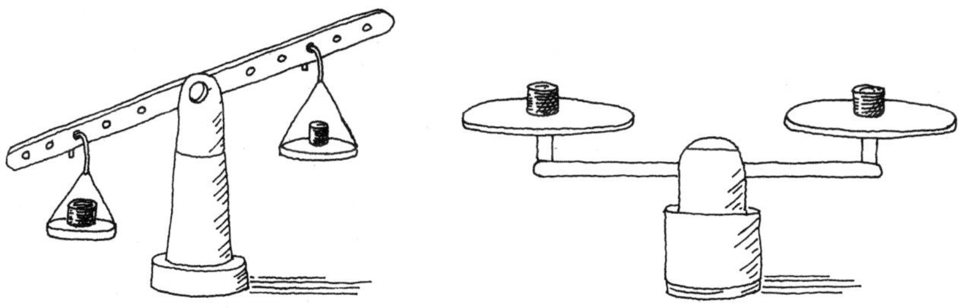

At still another table two children are filling in the sums on an addition table using addition slide rules—number lines or rulers—that they manipulate to add lengths. Another pair at the same table is constructing an addition table by counting blocks. There is an element of competition as each pair attempts to finish before the others. An alert observer would note that they are already beginning to use patterned shortcuts to save time.

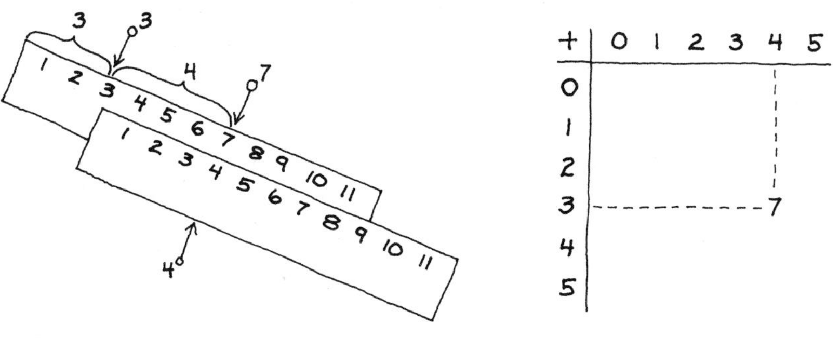

Finding and entering the addition fact 3 + 4 = 7 by means of number line addition.

EXAMPLE 5. A group of four sixth-graders is discussing how to approach a problem that has been given to them on a task card. Here is that card:

TASK CARD

When asked about the two blocks on the table, Mary said that the cube was best and Pam said that the other solid was best. Each was able to justify her answer by measurement.

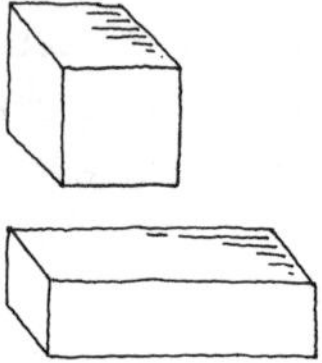

Find out what they might have done.

WHAT IS THE LABORATORY APPROACH?

The preceding section should have provided you with a basis for understanding the laboratory method of teaching. Let us examine what was common to the examples.

1. *The laboratory approach utilizes concrete materials.* It is therefore strongly oriented toward measurement and geometry. But of course it does not stop there. Data are recorded and arithmetical skills come into play.

2. *The laboratory method is active.* Students have responsibilities that take them away from assigned seats in the classroom. In some cases they may even go outside the school into the community. The problems they set out to solve often require manipulation of objects and other physical activities.

3. *The laboratory method involves student interaction.* Students often work in groups on problems, but even when they work individually

the laboratory method encourages interaction. When students move about a classroom they are bound to come in contact with more of their peers (and in the process to generate more noise, something that bothers many teachers and administrators). Students compare notes, work out procedures together, share data collecting and recording roles, and even help friends with difficulties.

The laboratory approach then is an activity-oriented classroom reorganization, which encourages individuals or small groups of students to work together. They usually work with concrete materials, which provide them with data for mathematical problems, and from which they derive mathematical relationships and concepts.

AN EXAMPLE OF AN ORGANIZED LABORATORY APPROACH

The previous examples of laboratory activities helped to encourage thinking in an activity framework, but were not organized in a way that focuses on a larger topic. In this section we suggest a series of related activities that give students an experiential base for understanding mathematical functions.

AN EXTENDED UNIT ON FUNCTIONS

Functions pervade all of mathematics and science. Since they play a role as prominent as that of numbers, they are now becoming an important part of the elementary school mathematics curriculum. Functions and numbers are, so to speak, the "bread and butter" of mathematics.

Functions give us a way of relating sets of numerical or physical objects to each other. Before exploring some examples of numerical functions, consider briefly the development of this concept. Embodiments, or experiences that realize theoretical concepts, provide an experiential base on which to build the abstract concept of a function. These provide a way of interpreting a concept. Some of the embodiments that follow occur in a discovery setting, and lead to the formation of a rule or function. Others simply require that we formulate rules to accompany previously identified geometric equivalents of the function. We now turn to a series of such examples that would aid intermediate-grade students to grasp this important idea.

1. Blocks versus height of column:[2]

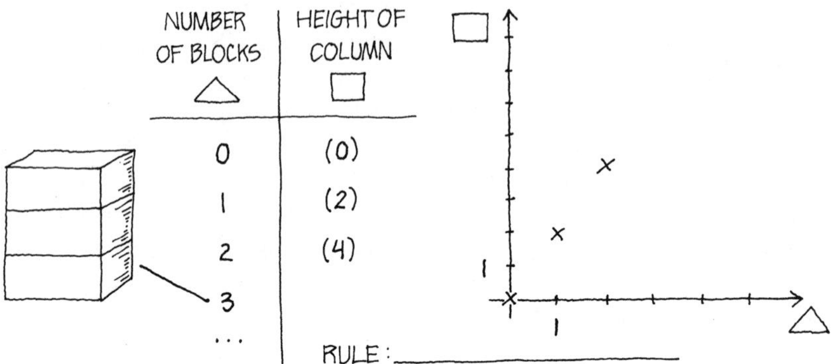

2. Number of rods versus exposed surface area:

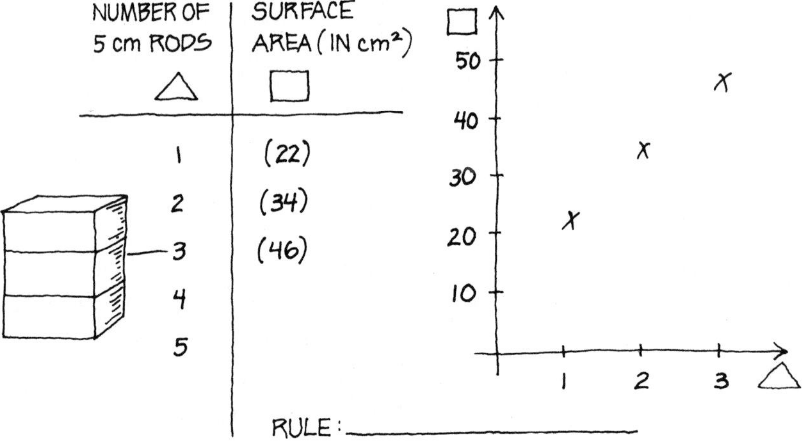

[2]The columns on the right in the following figures would be filled in by students. We have entered data in parentheses.

3. Number of rods versus volume of rods:

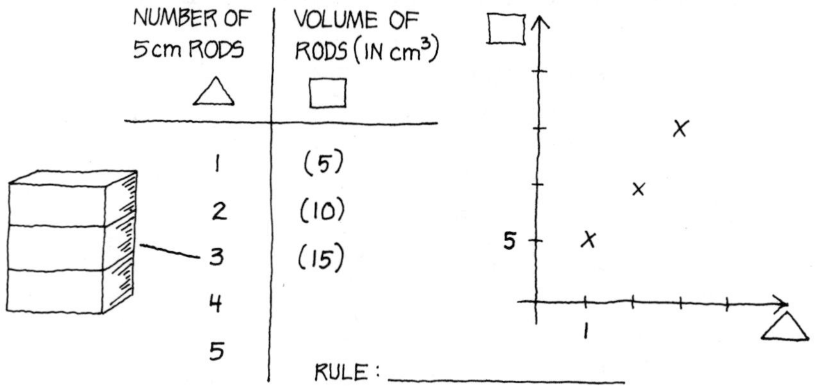

4. Number of sides of a polygon versus number of triangles formed by diagonals coming from the same vertex:

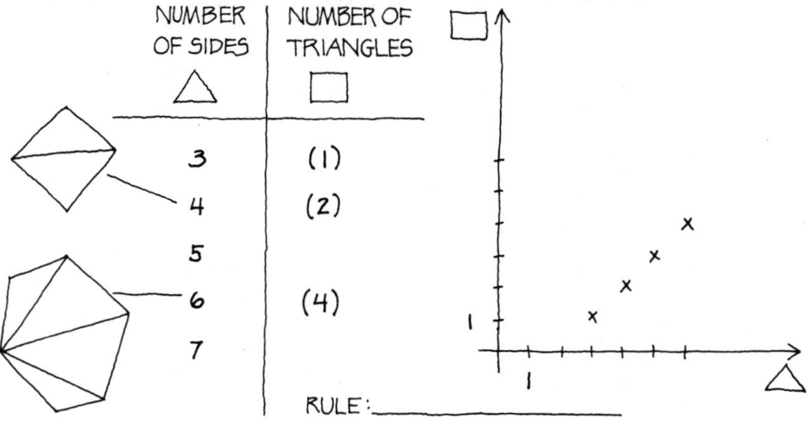

5. Number of sides of a polygon versus sum of the interior angles of the polygon (students would attempt this exploration after learning that the sum of the interior angles of any triangle is 180°):

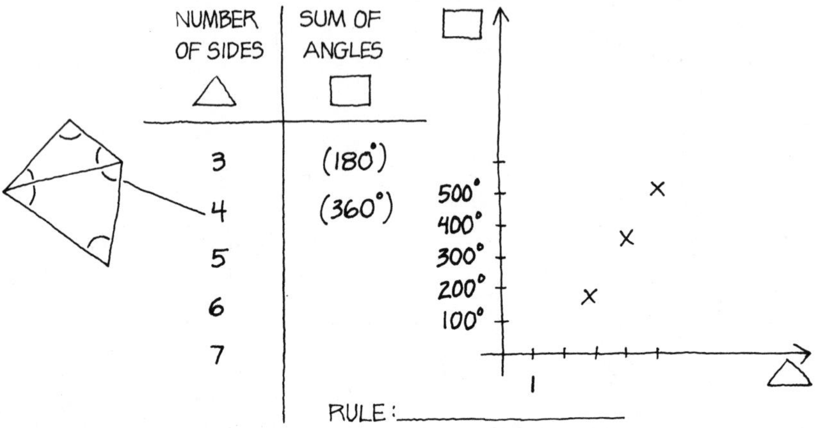

6. Length versus width of a rectangle with fixed perimeter (20 cm):

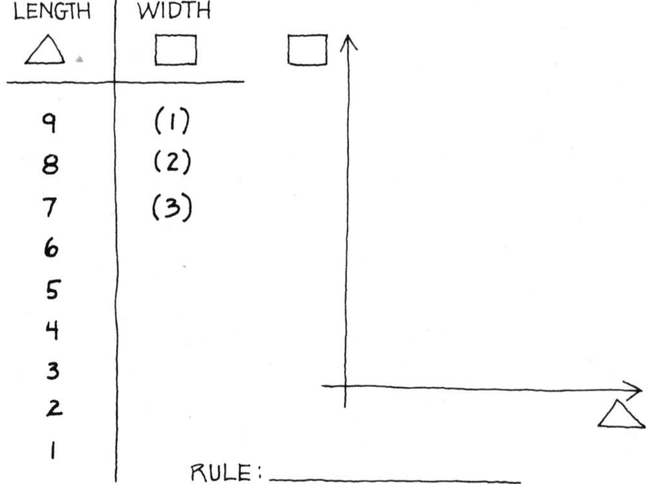

7. Length of rectangle versus area with fixed width (4 cm):

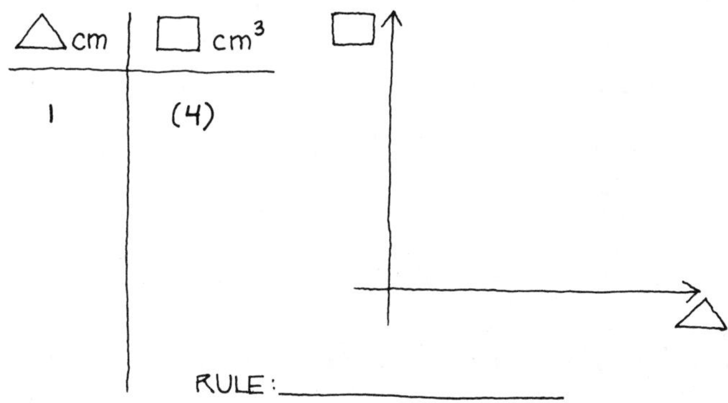

8. Length of side of square versus area (collect and represent your own data).

RULE: ____________

Now the rules become more complex. Students should be encouraged to gain partial insights into relationships even when they are not able to produce the specified rule.

9. Number of points on a circle versus number of chords:

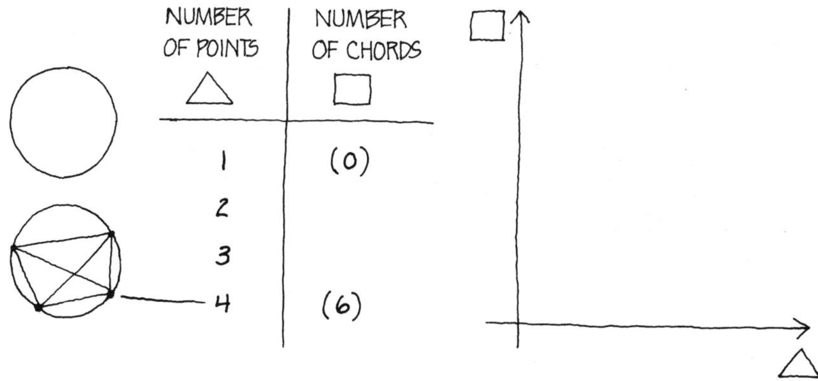

Find the differences between entries in the second column. Use what you notice to predict the following entries *before* drawing figures to check.

△	□
5	
6	
7	

RULE: __________

10. Number of intersecting chords of a circle versus maximum number of regions:

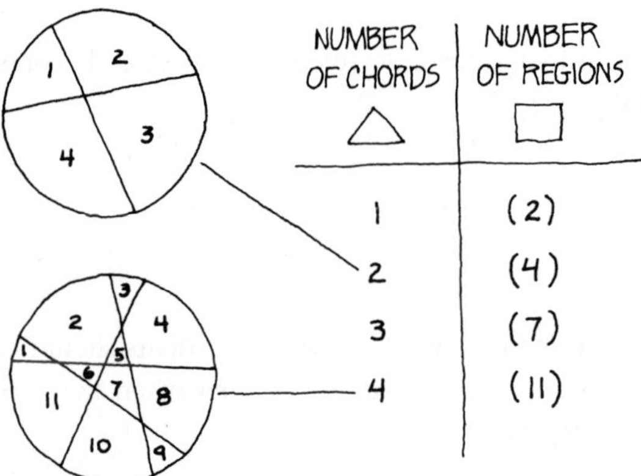

Predict other entries before checking.

△	□
5	
6	
7	
8	
9	
10	

RULE: $\square = \dfrac{(\triangle \times \triangle) + \triangle + \_\_}{2}$

11. The peg game: Materials needed include eight pegs or golf tees, four each of two different colors; and a flat board with nine holes.

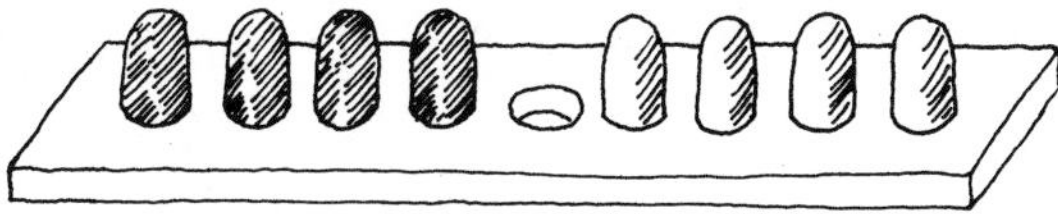

Object: Make minimum moves to interchange the yellow and white pegs.

Playing the game: Pegs are placed in the holes as in the figure, leaving the middle hole empty. They must move in the direction stated. No backward moves. Move only to a vacant adjacent hole or jump over one peg of an opposite color only.

Data:

NUMBER OF PEGS ON ONE SIDE △	NUMBER OF MOVES TO INTERCHANGE (MINIMUM) □
1	
2	
3	
4	

Predict the value for 5 pegs of each color and check.

RULE: ________________

12. The tower puzzle: Materials needed are six tiers (discs) with openings in the center of each and a three-tower board.[3]

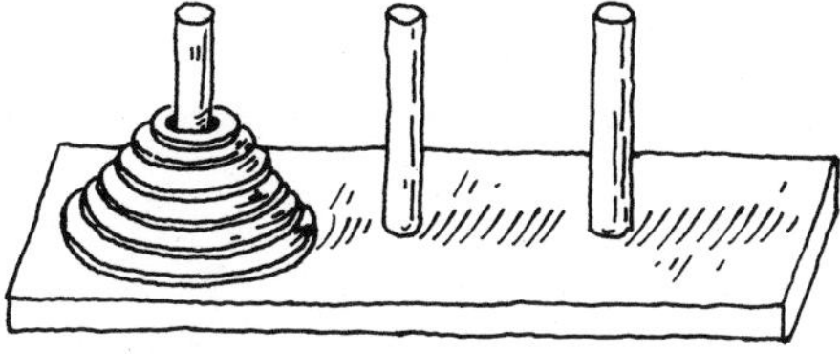

[3]Coins of differing size (for example, a quarter, a nickel, a penny, and a dime) and a paper with three loops to represent tower bases will do as a substitute.

Object: Transfer tiers from one tower to another in a minimum number of moves.

Playing the game: Move one disc at a time. A larger disc must never be placed on a smaller disc.

Data:

NUMBER OF RINGS △	NUMBER OF MOVES TO TRANSFER (MINIMUM) □
1	(1)
2	(3)
3	
4	
5	

Predict the number of moves to transfer 10 rings.

RULE: ________________

13. Pick's formula: This experience is constructed for you to discover Pick's formula for the area of a simple closed polygon.[4] Pick's formula is an embodiment of a two-place function within the scope of elementary school mathematics.

First, consider the following twelve problems. Adjacent to each problem are the placeholders □ and △. The instructions at the top of the figure require you to count the grid points that lie on the simple, closed polygon and record the number in the

[4]This exercise can be done with the use of the geoboard.

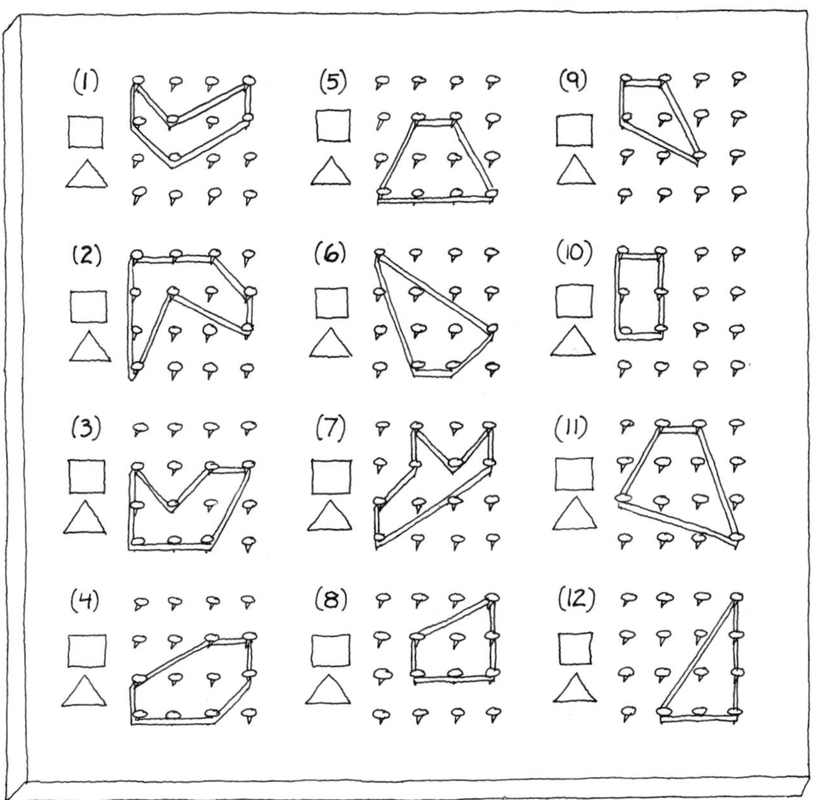

□. The number of points in the interior of the simple closed polygon is recorded in the △.

After finishing this counting chore, proceed to the partially completed table. While filling in the missing entries, probe for a pattern and formulate it as a rule. This rule should tell you how to combine the □ and △ points to calculate the area *S*, of any simple closed polygon.

There are empty spaces provided at the bottom of the table. If a pattern doesn't emerge in the twelve problems provided, create more problems and record more data.

a. Fill in the missing numbers from the figure.

b. Find a rule for *S* (area of a simple, closed polygon) using □ and △.

	boundary points	*interior points*	*area of simple, closed polygon*
1	6	1	3
2	9	1	9/2
3	8	1	
4	7	2	
5	6	2	
6	4		4
7	7		7/2
8		1	3
9		1	2
10	6		
11	4		
12		1	3

VALUE OF THE LABORATORY APPROACH

Referring back to the examples of math labs in action, it is easy to see some of the values that result from this approach. Some of the important ones are:

1. *Students work directly with concrete materials in relatively unpressured circumstances.* One aspect of this is observed in many math labs: Students return to play with the materials during free time. Similarly games and contests introduced within the lab program are continued after class.

2. *Students see mathematics as closely associated with the real world, since it is derived from nonabstract activities.* The opportunity for transfer of learning is evident in this approach.

3. *Students learn to take individual responsibility.* The classroom is no longer teacher-centered. Students cannot drift and daydream while the teacher carries their responsibilities. Even when working in groups, each student is encouraged to contribute. It is one thing to let the teacher down; it is quite another to let down one's peers. See pages 207–208.

4. *Mathematics itself is extended.* Important aspects of mathematics (such as data collection) that are often omitted completely from standard programs play an important role in the laboratory method.

5. *Quite sophisticated problems are brought within the range of students,* since they are introduced through use of concrete materials. You need only restate many laboratory activities without concrete materials to see how difficult the problems can become.

6. *Good math labs tend to generate positive student reactions toward mathematics.*

DANGERS ASSOCIATED WITH THE LABORATORY APPROACH

As is often the case with essentially good teaching techniques, the math lab presents certain dangers:

1. *When it is not carefully organized, the math lab can be a disaster.* Too often beginning teachers trying to organize a math lab are so shocked by their failure that they turn against the technique. Teachers should realize that:

   (a) There is always some difficulty associated with *any* change in classroom organization. One or two days is never a fair test of a teaching program as it takes students at least that long to adjust.

(b) Extra dimensions of planning and classroom management are associated with the laboratory method. Failure to account for them, combined with the freedom of the laboratory program, can be a volatile mixture.

2. *Some teachers let this method become more important than the mathematics program itself.* It should be quite evident that the laboratory approach emphasizes the process of learning rather than the product. This is, of course, exactly the opposite of traditional instruction, where the teacher focuses directly on the product or content of mathematics. Process is of course an important dimension of mathematics, but so too is the mathematical content and the sequence in which it is developed. It requires an especially sensitive teacher to see that both content development and sequencing are well managed in the mathematics laboratory.

3. *Individual and small-group learning exacerbates the problem* of point 2. The teacher must be assured that all students are advancing their understanding of mathematics in a reasonable way. Otherwise, individual students may easily miss key prerequisites for later mathematical development.

ORGANIZING THE MATHEMATICS LABORATORY

We have stressed the dangers inherent in a poorly organized mathematics laboratory. As in all teaching, careful planning is the key to success here. Such planning includes not only specific mathematical activities but also management procedures such as how students are assigned to tasks, how their work will be monitored, and how they will be routed to new tasks. Some on-the-spot adjustments usually need to be made, but there is no good response to students who have completed all your tasks and have nothing to do.

Classroom problems arise most often at transition points between activities. Busy students cause little trouble, but students waiting for the teacher to check their work or for their next task are inevitably a source of difficulty. If you are alert to this, you can seek ways to head off these transition problems by shortening the change periods.

Here are some steps you should follow in organizing laboratory activities:

1. *Establish in your own mind the goals you seek to attain in your lessons.* Your goals may range from general problems, such as exposing students to mathematical applications, to specific goals, like establishing a concrete basis for a specific operation with fractions. Keep these in mind as you develop the various activities.

2. *Develop clear statements of the tasks you wish your students to undertake.* This does not mean that you seek to mechanize student work. You should leave the tasks as open as possible. For example, you might ask a first-grade student to measure his height in centimeters. He would then know the task. To ask him to measure his height in centimeters by marking his height on the wall, obtaining the teacher's meter stick, and so on would drain away any creative aspects of the task.

3. *Identify and provide all materials needed for each task.* This may include not only the materials for manipulation but also graph or drawing paper and drawing instruments where necessary.

4. *Develop a careful plan for assigning students to tasks.* Suppose, for example, you have seven groups of students, four to each group, and you plan to have them move through a series of unordered tasks. Then it would be unwise to provide only seven different task stations. If you did that, one group might finish before the others and would then be forced to wait. Additional task stations, as in the figure, respond to this kind of problem. In the figure, the circles represent task stations and the letters A–G the seven groups.[5] If group A finishes first they may work on task 8. The

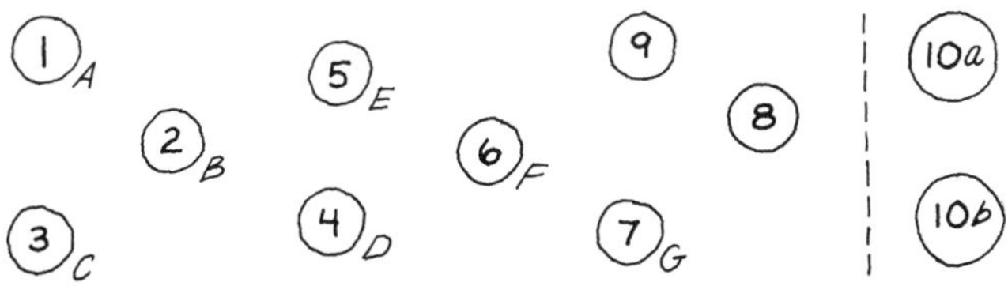

[5]The circles in no way imply circular tables. Classroom facilities will determine this. If the work is individual, a student's desk may be the work base; if it is assigned to groups, students may merely cluster their chairs and desks. The diagram also suggests that groups move to the various tasks; this may be necessary if much apparatus is involved. Otherwise students might instead take the tasks to their own desks.

next group finishing could work on task 1 (*A*'s completed task). Tasks 10*a* and 10*b* could involve the same task at two stations, providing a larger open-ended enrichment task on which only groups that finish early would work.

5. *Prepare your students for the work.* Students should be fully informed about the procedures, their responsibilities, and your expectations.

TYPES OF LABORATORY ACTIVITIES

Here are some different kinds of laboratory activities:

1. *Measure objects to determine relationships.*

WORK CARD (Grade 6)

Equipment: none[6]

Locate and carefully measure in centimeters circumference (C) and diameter (d) of five different circular objects. Complete the following table (all entries to tenths). Note any regularities.

object	*circumference* (C)	*diameter* (d)	$C + d$	$C - d$	$C \times d$	$C \div d$
1.						
2.						
3.						
4.						
5.						

[6]Note: Students must find the circular objects. Later the teacher may wish to pool class results. The more different circles the better.

WORK CARD
(Grade 3)

Equipment: 30 or more cubes of the same size

The drawing is a rectangular solid (or prism) formed by 12 unit cubes. Marked on this drawing are its width (w), length (l), and height (h).

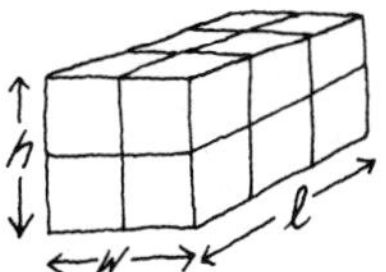

Use the blocks provided to build 10 different rectangular solids. Record the dimensions and the volume (total number of cubes) for each in a table (v represents volume).

	w	l	h	v
1.	2	3	2	12
2.				
3.				
4.				
5.				

Look at your table. Do you see a pattern? Describe the pattern in a sentence.

2. *Find a pattern by manipulating concrete objects or by drawing figures.*

WORK CARD
(Grade 2 and up)

Equipment: 7 red Cuisenaire rods

Use red (Cuisenaire) rods to build a wall like this.[7] The wall is the height of the red rod.

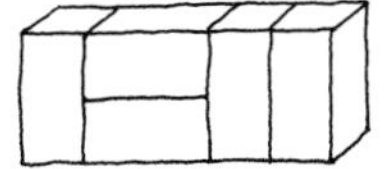

[7]Any $1 \times 1 \times 2$ rectangular solids will do.

WORK CARD (continued)

Here is a different wall with the same number of blocks. How many different walls can you make with 5 red rods? (Be sure they are the height of a red rod.)

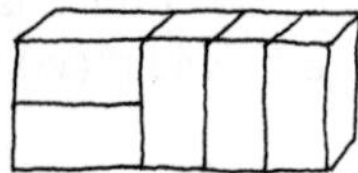

Make a table for different length walls and the number of possible patterns:

Length of red wall	1	2	3	4	5	6	7
Number of patterns							

Can you see a pattern so that you can tell the number of patterns for a red wall with 8 rods? 9 rods?

WORK CARD (Grade 3 and up)

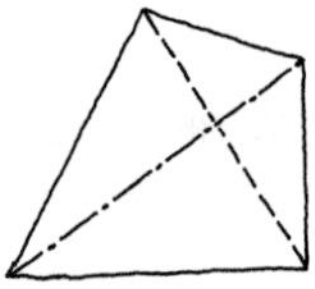

Equipment: none

This figure has 4 sides and 2 (dotted) diagonals.

Draw figures to fill the table.

Number of sides	3	4	5	6	7
Number of diagonals					

Can you see a pattern so that you can tell the number of diagonals for an 8-sided figure? 9-sided?

3. *Collect and summarize survey data.*

Equipment: none Find out how far from school each student in your class lives. Who lives farthest? Who lives closest? What is the average distance? Present this information and any other you wish to add in a news article or on a poster.	WORK CARD (Grades 5 or 6)

4. *Build or duplicate a model.*

Equipment: blocks Build a block house exactly like the one on the worktable.	WORK CARD (Grade 2)

Equipment: cardboard Build a scale model of this classroom.	WORK CARD (Grades 7 or 8)

A MINICOMPUTER EXPERIENCE VIA TASK CARDS

Here is an ordered set of forty-five task cards developed to teach primary- or intermediate-grade children how to use the Papy minicomputer. It is advisable to work with primary children on the first twenty-three cards to familiarize them with the mechanics of the computer. Red, blue, and green chips are useful to represent different numbers. The colors play no essential role in addition and multiplication operations other than aiding the teacher in checking the accuracy of the initial representation of numbers by the students. (Here, we have used different kinds of circles.)

After successful completion of the addition task cards, subtraction, multiplication, and division can be introduced via the discovery method. It is alternately possible to design equivalent sets of task cards for these operations.

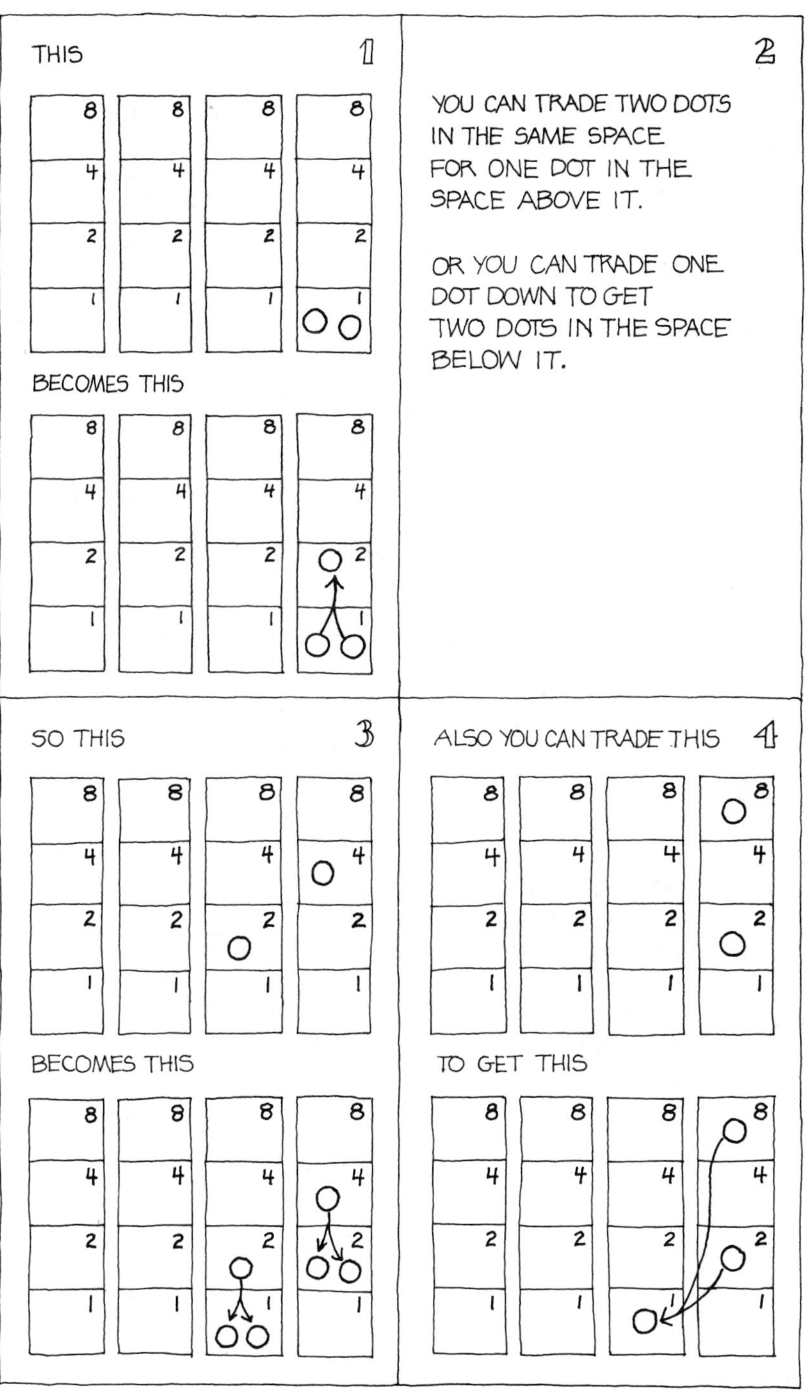
THIS
1
8
4
2
1
BECOMES THIS
2
YOU CAN TRADE TWO DOTS
IN THE SAME SPACE
FOR ONE DOT IN THE
SPACE ABOVE IT.
OR YOU CAN TRADE ONE
DOT DOWN TO GET
TWO DOTS IN THE SPACE
BELOW IT.
SO THIS
3
BECOMES THIS
ALSO YOU CAN TRADE THIS
4
TO GET THIS

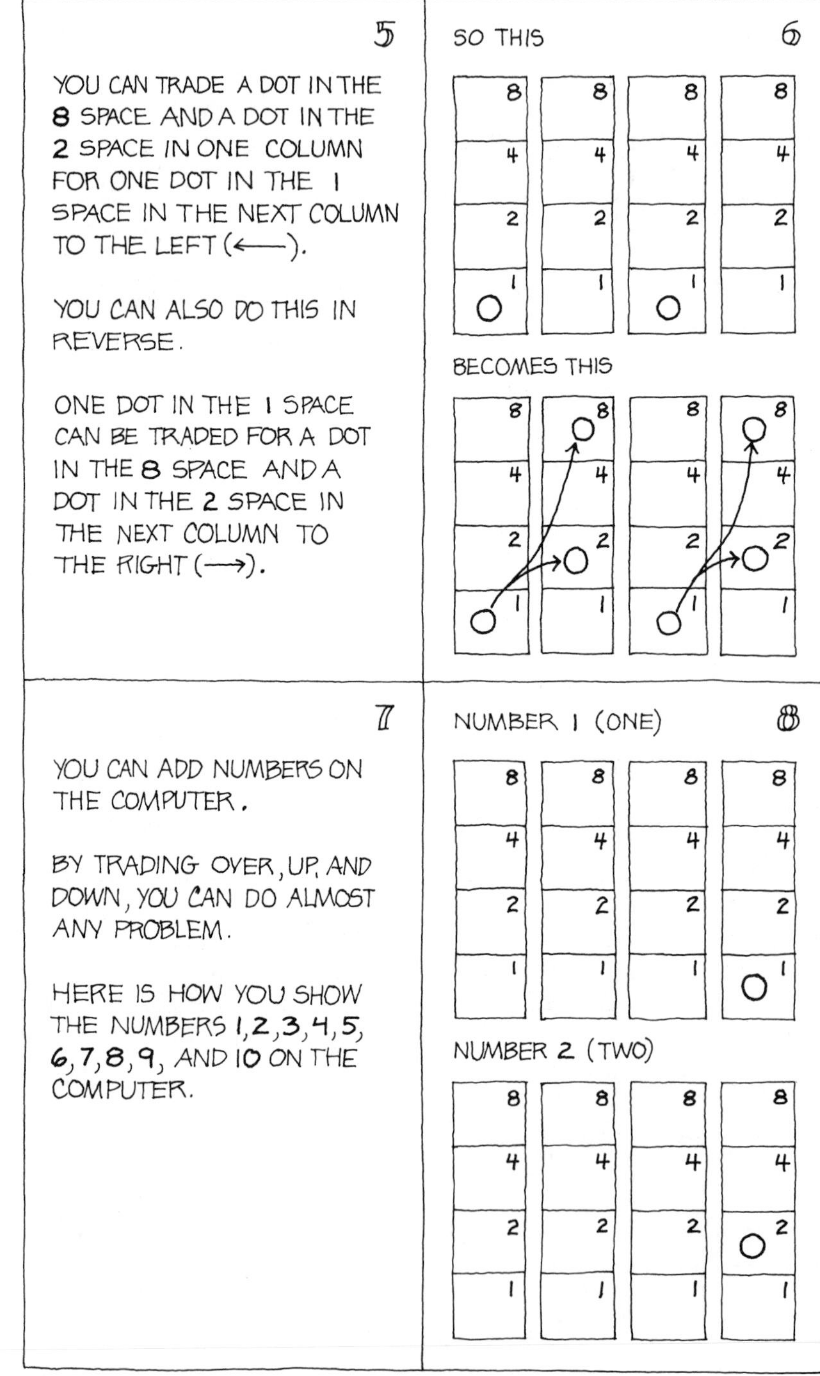
5
YOU CAN TRADE A DOT IN THE 8 SPACE AND A DOT IN THE 2 SPACE IN ONE COLUMN FOR ONE DOT IN THE 1 SPACE IN THE NEXT COLUMN TO THE LEFT (⟵).
YOU CAN ALSO DO THIS IN REVERSE.
ONE DOT IN THE 1 SPACE CAN BE TRADED FOR A DOT IN THE 8 SPACE AND A DOT IN THE 2 SPACE IN THE NEXT COLUMN TO THE RIGHT (⟶).
SO THIS
6
BECOMES THIS
7
YOU CAN ADD NUMBERS ON THE COMPUTER.
BY TRADING OVER, UP, AND DOWN, YOU CAN DO ALMOST ANY PROBLEM.
HERE IS HOW YOU SHOW THE NUMBERS 1, 2, 3, 4, 5, 6, 7, 8, 9, AND 10 ON THE COMPUTER.
NUMBER 1 (ONE)
8
NUMBER 2 (TWO)

9

NUMBER 3 (THREE)

8	8	8	8
4	4	4	4
2	2	2	O 2
1	1	1	O 1

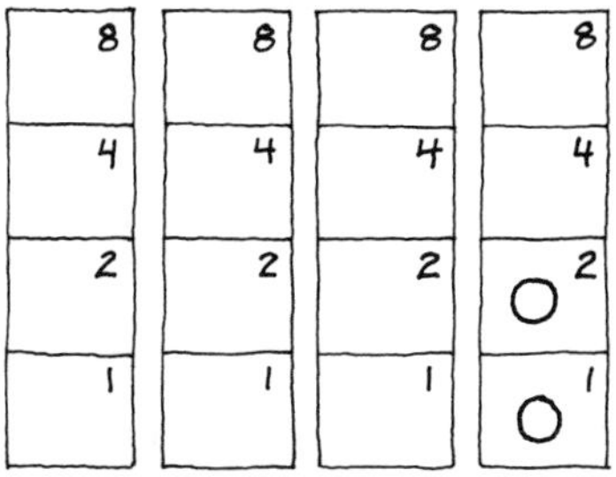

NUMBER 4 (FOUR)

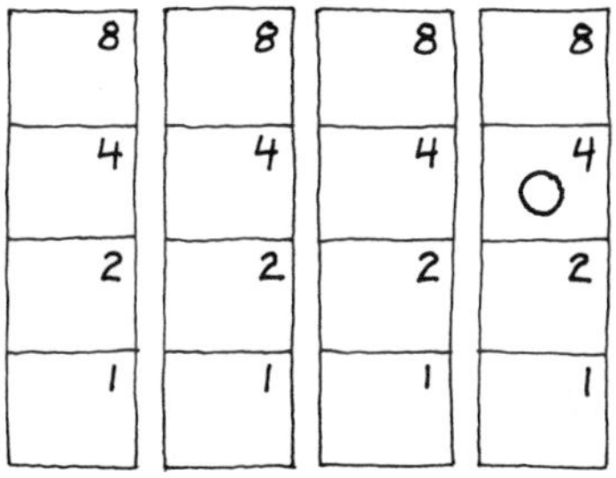

8	8	8	8
4	4	4	O 4
2	2	2	2
1	1	1	1

10

NUMBER 5 (FIVE)

8	8	8	8
4	4	4	O 4
2	2	2	2
1	1	1	O 1

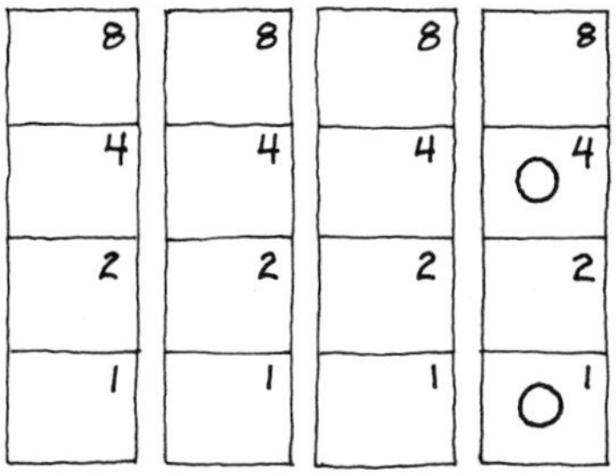

NUMBER 6 (SIX)

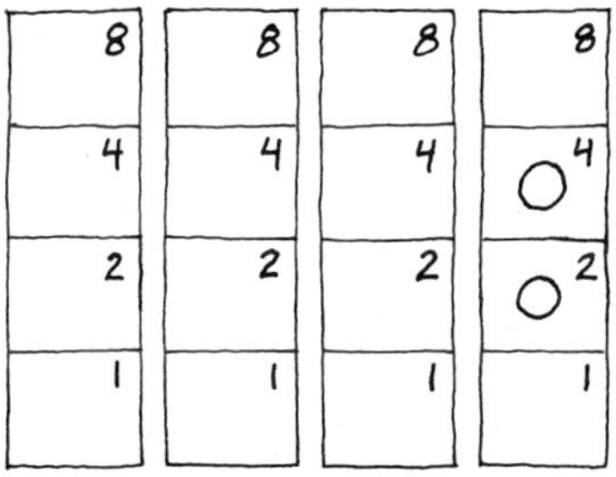

8	8	8	8
4	4	4	O 4
2	2	2	O 2
1	1	1	1

11

NUMBER 7 (SEVEN)

8	8	8	8
4	4	4	O 4
2	2	2	O 2
1	1	1	O 1

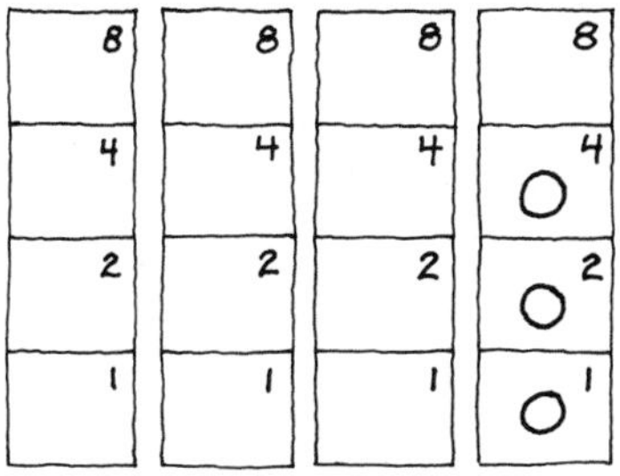

NUMBER 8 (EIGHT)

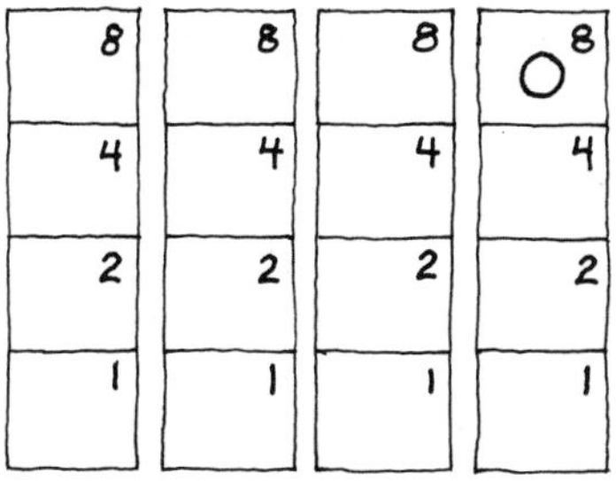

8	8	8	O 8
4	4	4	4
2	2	2	2
1	1	1	1

12

NUMBER 9 (NINE)

8	8	8	O 8
4	4	4	4
2	2	2	2
1	1	1	O 1

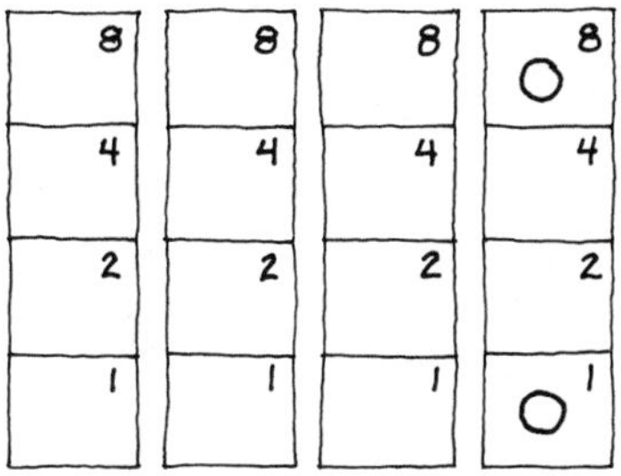

NUMBER 10 (TEN)

8	8	8	O 8
4	4	4	4
2	2	2	O 2
1	1	1	1

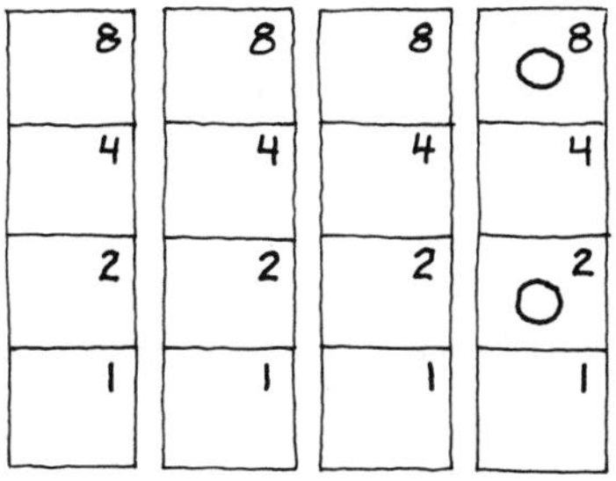

13

NOW LET'S ADD 3 + 2 = ☐

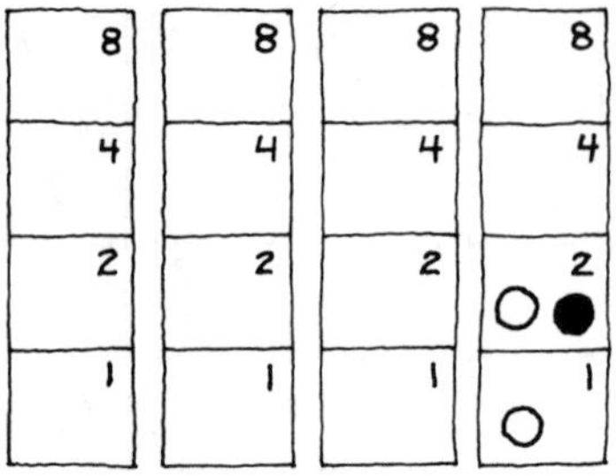

8	8	8	8
4	4	4	4
2	2	2	2 ○ ●
1	1	1	1 ○

THE HOLLOW DOTS SHOW THE NUMBER 3. THE SOLID DOT SHOWS THE NUMBER 2.

NOW YOU CAN USE TRADING TO FIND THE ANSWER.

TRADE UP ↑.
WHAT'S YOUR ANSWER ?

14

DOES IT LOOK LIKE THIS ?

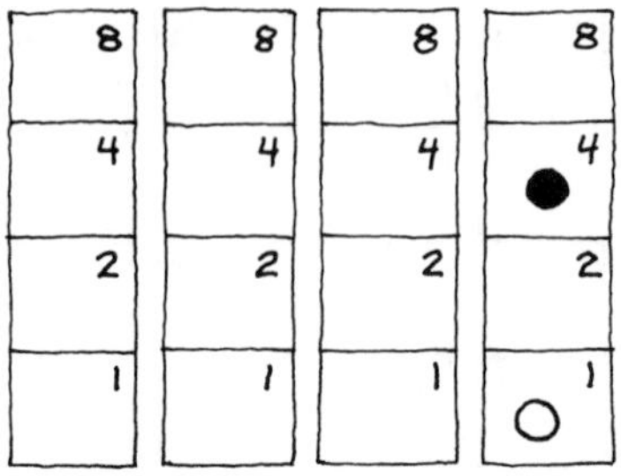

8	8	8	8
4	4	4	4 ●
2	2	2	2
1	1	1	1 ○

YOU TRADED THE TWO DOTS IN SPACE 2 FOR ONE DOT IN THE 4 SPACE.

IT DOESN'T MATTER IF YOU USE THE SOLID DOT OR THE HOLLOW DOTS FOR YOUR ANSWER WHEN YOU ADD. SO 3 + 2 = [5]

15

HERE ARE SOME PROBLEMS FOR YOU TO TRY:

1. 7 + 3 = ☐
2. 4 + 5 = ☐
3. 8 + 2 = ☐
4. 2 + 4 = ☐
5. 1 + 1 = ☐
6. 6 + 2 = ☐
7. 3 + 4 = ☐
8. 5 + 3 = ☐

AFTER YOU DO EACH PROBLEM CHECK YOUR ANSWER WITH THE CARD THAT HAS THE SAME PROBLEM ON THE TOP.

16

7 + 3 = [10]
DID YOU START LIKE THIS?

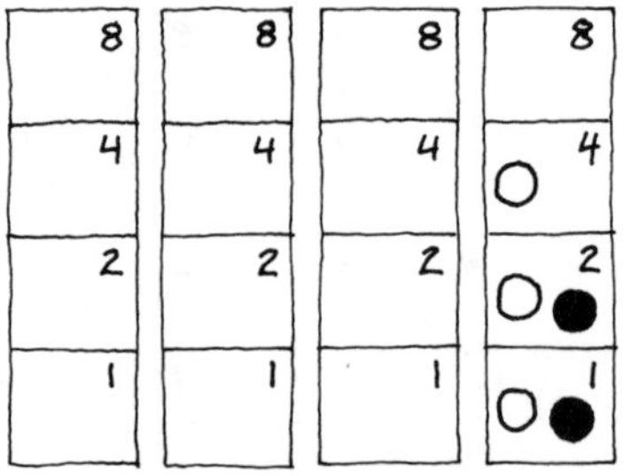

8	8	8	8
4	4	4	4 ○
2	2	2	2 ○ ●
1	1	1	1 ○ ●

DOES YOUR ANSWER LOOK LIKE THIS?

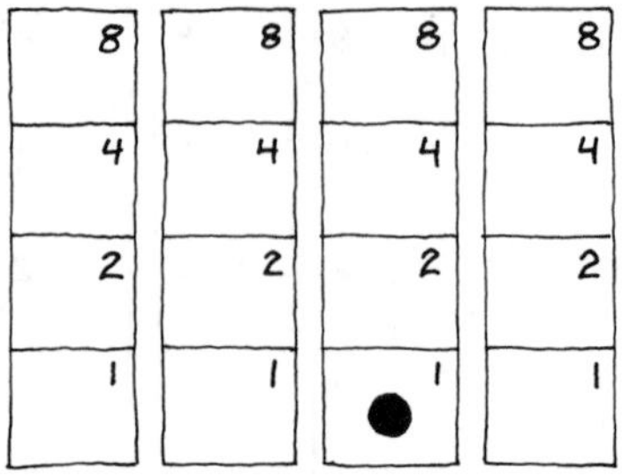

8	8	8	8
4	4	4	4
2	2	2	2
1	1	1 ●	1

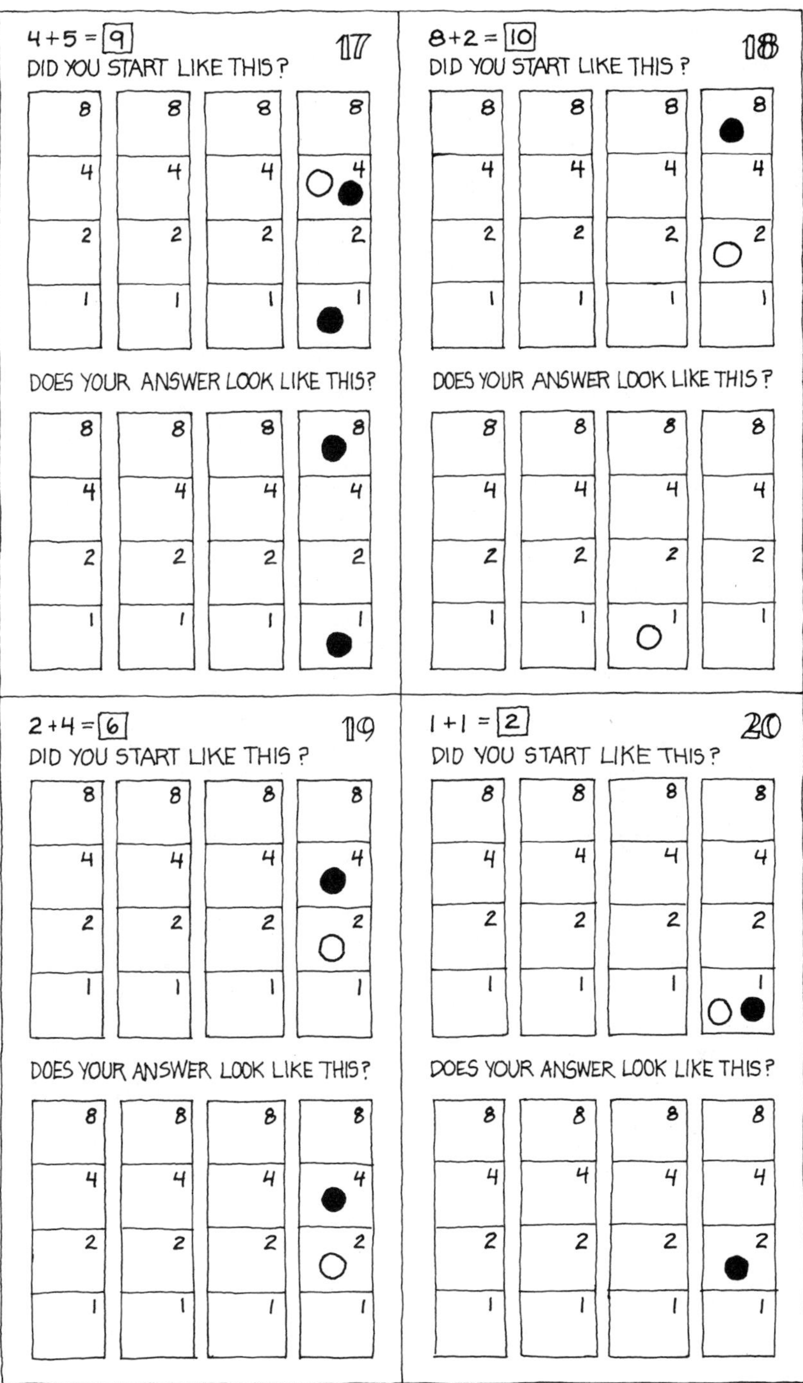
4+5 = 9
17
DID YOU START LIKE THIS?
8 8 8 8
4 4 4 4
2 2 2 2
1 1 1 1
DOES YOUR ANSWER LOOK LIKE THIS?
8 8 8 8
4 4 4 4
2 2 2 2
1 1 1 1
8+2 = 10
18
DID YOU START LIKE THIS?
8 8 8 8
4 4 4 4
2 2 2 2
1 1 1 1
DOES YOUR ANSWER LOOK LIKE THIS?
8 8 8 8
4 4 4 4
2 2 2 2
1 1 1 1
2+4 = 6
19
DID YOU START LIKE THIS?
8 8 8 8
4 4 4 4
2 2 2 2
1 1 1 1
DOES YOUR ANSWER LOOK LIKE THIS?
8 8 8 8
4 4 4 4
2 2 2 2
1 1 1 1
1+1 = 2
20
DID YOU START LIKE THIS?
8 8 8 8
4 4 4 4
2 2 2 2
1 1 1 1
DOES YOUR ANSWER LOOK LIKE THIS?
8 8 8 8
4 4 4 4
2 2 2 2
1 1 1 1

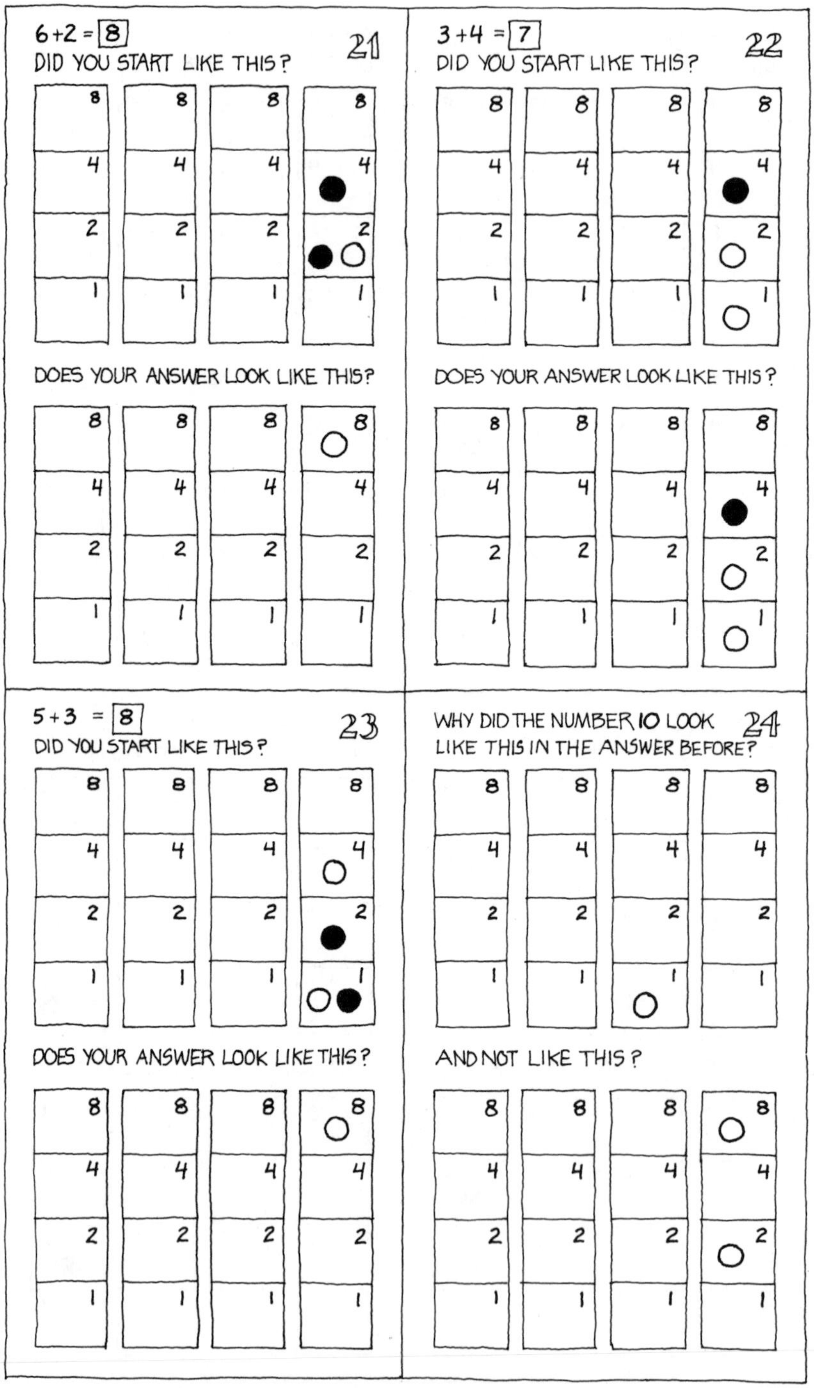

21

6 + 2 = 8

DID YOU START LIKE THIS?

DOES YOUR ANSWER LOOK LIKE THIS?

22

3 + 4 = 7

DID YOU START LIKE THIS?

DOES YOUR ANSWER LOOK LIKE THIS?

23

5 + 3 = 8

DID YOU START LIKE THIS?

DOES YOUR ANSWER LOOK LIKE THIS?

24

WHY DID THE NUMBER **10** LOOK LIKE THIS IN THE ANSWER BEFORE?

AND NOT LIKE THIS?

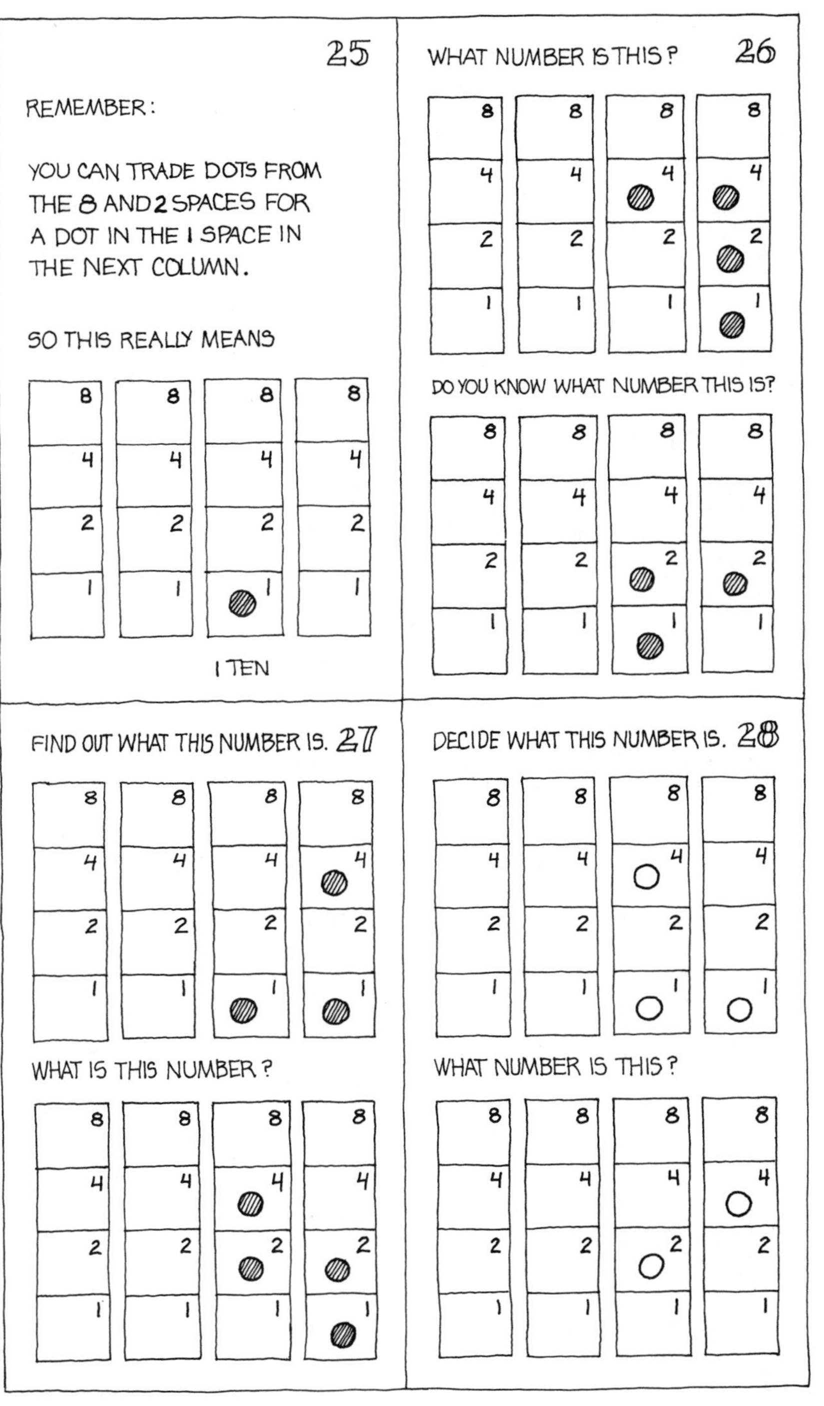
25
REMEMBER:
YOU CAN TRADE DOTS FROM THE 8 AND 2 SPACES FOR A DOT IN THE 1 SPACE IN THE NEXT COLUMN.
SO THIS REALLY MEANS
8 4 2 1
1 TEN
WHAT NUMBER IS THIS? 26
DO YOU KNOW WHAT NUMBER THIS IS?
FIND OUT WHAT THIS NUMBER IS. 27
WHAT IS THIS NUMBER?
DECIDE WHAT THIS NUMBER IS. 28
WHAT NUMBER IS THIS?

29

NOW THAT YOU CAN USE TWO-DIGIT NUMBERS ON THE COMPUTER, TRY THESE:

1. 51 + 24 = □
2. 47 + 32 = □
3. 15 + 63 = □
4. 47 + 51 = □
5. 24 + 15 = □
6. 63 + 32 = □
7. 24 + 63 = □
8. 51 + 32 = □

REMEMBER:

USE A DIFFERENT KIND OF DOT EACH TIME YOU PUT ANOTHER NUMBER ON THE COMPUTER. CHECK TO SEE IF YOU STARTED WITH THE RIGHT NUMBERS.

30

WAS THIS YOUR ANSWER FOR 51 + 24 = 75 ?

8	8	8	8
4	4	4 ○	4 ●
2	2	2 ○	2
1	1	1 ○	1 ○

DID YOU GET THIS NUMBER FOR 47 + 32 = 79 ?

8	8	8	8 ●
4	4	4 ●	4
2	2	2 ○	2
1	1	1 ●	1 ○

31

WAS THIS YOUR ANSWER FOR 15 + 63 = 78 ?

8	8	8	8 ●
4	4	4 ○	4
2	2	2 ○	2
1	1	1 ○	1

DID YOU GET THIS ANSWER FOR 47 + 51 = 98 ?

8	8	8 ●	8 ●
4	4	4	4
2	2	2	2
1	1	1 ●	1

32

WAS THIS YOUR ANSWER FOR 24 + 15 = 39 ?

8	8	8	8 ○
4	4	4	4
2	2	2 ○	2
1	1	1 ○	1 ○

DID YOU GET THIS ANSWER FOR 63 + 32 = 95 ?

8	8	8 ○	8
4	4	4	4 ●
2	2	2	2
1	1	1 ●	1 ○

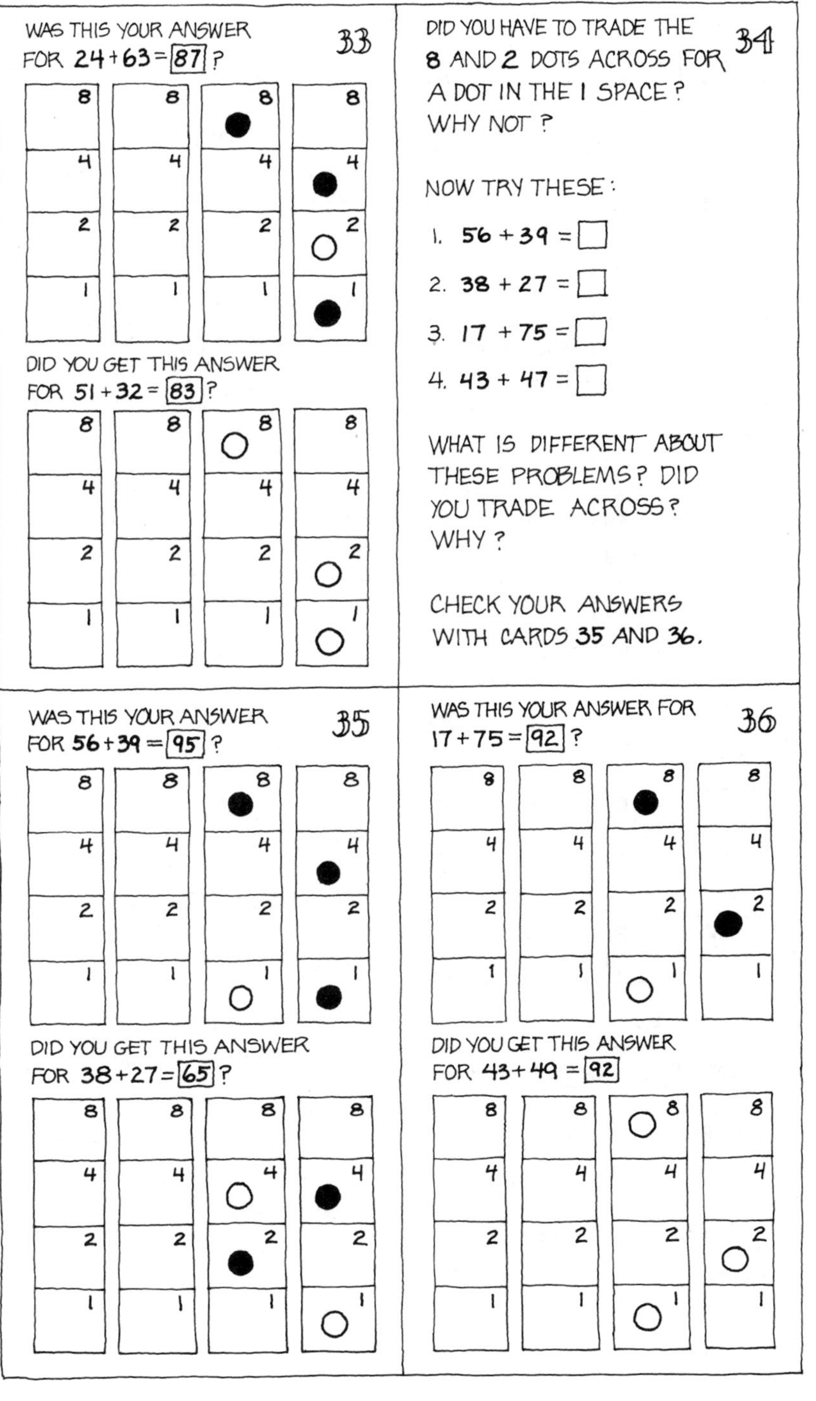

33
WAS THIS YOUR ANSWER FOR 24 + 63 = 87 ?
8 4 2 1
DID YOU GET THIS ANSWER FOR 51 + 32 = 83 ?
8 4 2 1
34
DID YOU HAVE TO TRADE THE 8 AND 2 DOTS ACROSS FOR A DOT IN THE 1 SPACE? WHY NOT?
NOW TRY THESE:
1. 56 + 39 = □
2. 38 + 27 = □
3. 17 + 75 = □
4. 43 + 47 = □
WHAT IS DIFFERENT ABOUT THESE PROBLEMS? DID YOU TRADE ACROSS? WHY?
CHECK YOUR ANSWERS WITH CARDS 35 AND 36.
35
WAS THIS YOUR ANSWER FOR 56 + 39 = 95 ?
8 4 2 1
DID YOU GET THIS ANSWER FOR 38 + 27 = 65 ?
8 4 2 1
36
WAS THIS YOUR ANSWER FOR 17 + 75 = 92 ?
8 4 2 1
DID YOU GET THIS ANSWER FOR 43 + 49 = 92
8 4 2 1

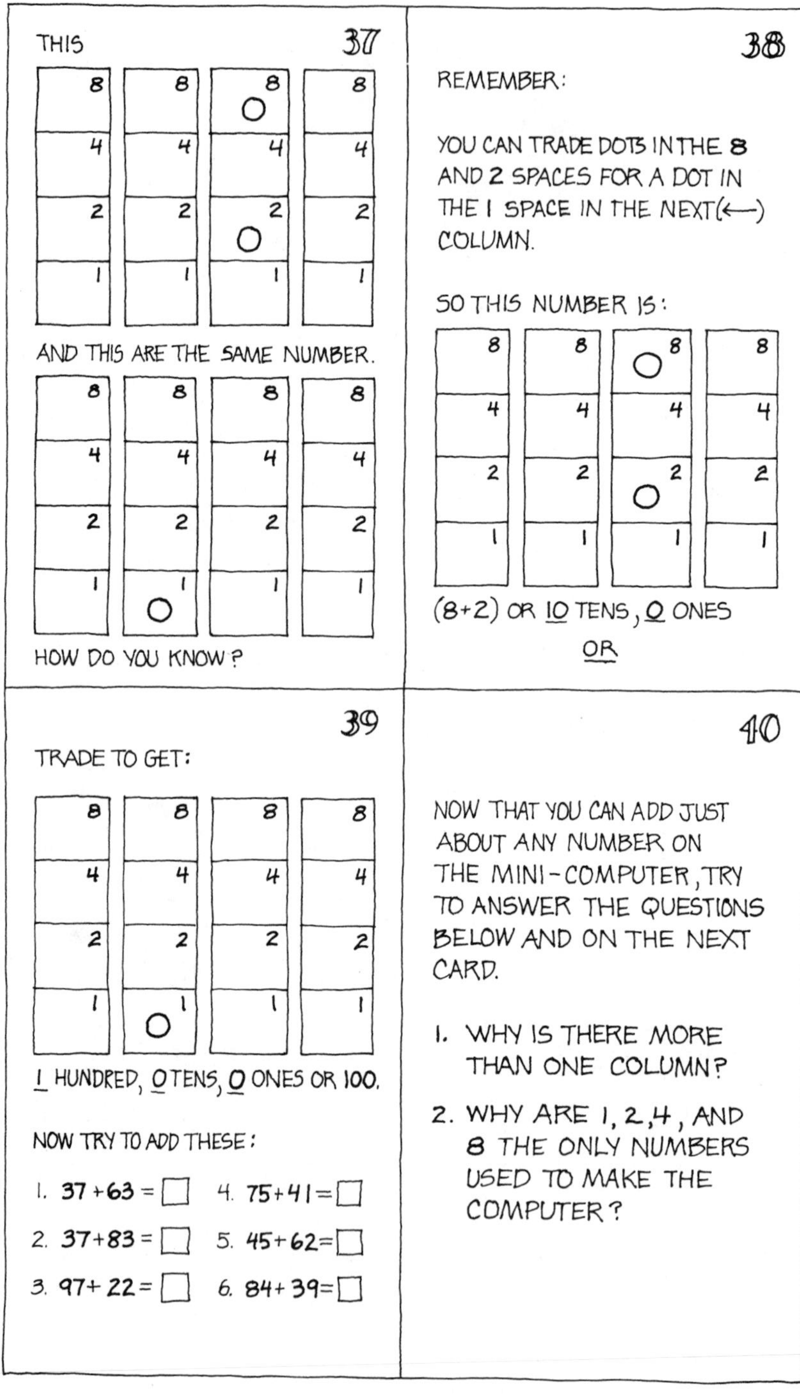
37
THIS
8 8 8 8
4 4 4 4
2 2 2 2
1 1 1 1
AND THIS ARE THE SAME NUMBER.
8 8 8 8
4 4 4 4
2 2 2 2
1 1 1 1
HOW DO YOU KNOW?
38
REMEMBER:
YOU CAN TRADE DOTS IN THE 8 AND 2 SPACES FOR A DOT IN THE 1 SPACE IN THE NEXT (←) COLUMN.
SO THIS NUMBER IS:
8 8 8 8
4 4 4 4
2 2 2 2
1 1 1 1
(8+2) OR 10 TENS, 0 ONES
OR
39
TRADE TO GET:
8 8 8 8
4 4 4 4
2 2 2 2
1 1 1 1
1 HUNDRED, 0 TENS, 0 ONES OR 100.
NOW TRY TO ADD THESE:
1. 37+63=□ 4. 75+41=□
2. 37+83=□ 5. 45+62=□
3. 97+22=□ 6. 84+39=□
40
NOW THAT YOU CAN ADD JUST ABOUT ANY NUMBER ON THE MINI-COMPUTER, TRY TO ANSWER THE QUESTIONS BELOW AND ON THE NEXT CARD.
1. WHY IS THERE MORE THAN ONE COLUMN?
2. WHY ARE 1, 2, 4, AND 8 THE ONLY NUMBERS USED TO MAKE THE COMPUTER?

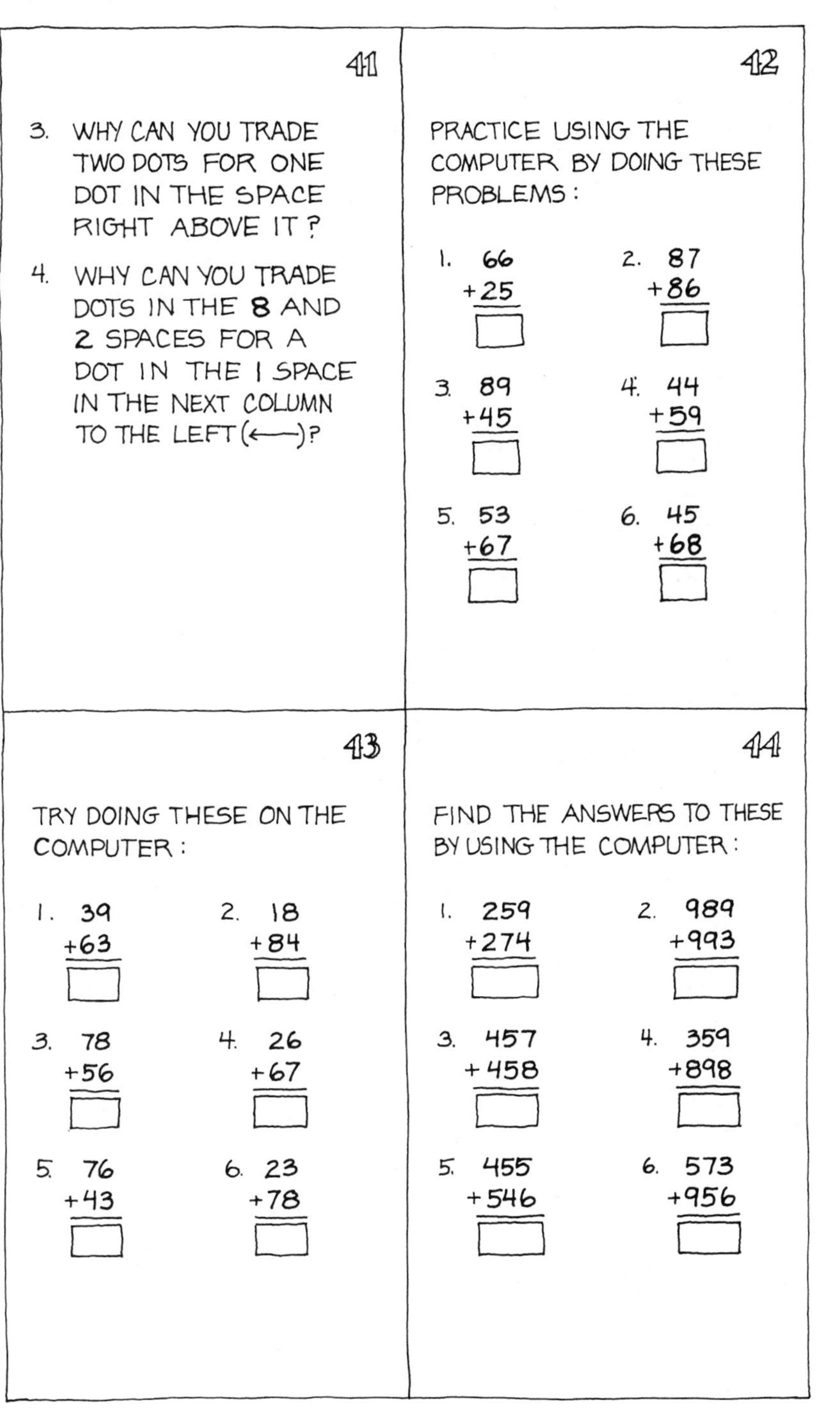
41
3. WHY CAN YOU TRADE TWO DOTS FOR ONE DOT IN THE SPACE RIGHT ABOVE IT?
4. WHY CAN YOU TRADE DOTS IN THE 8 AND 2 SPACES FOR A DOT IN THE 1 SPACE IN THE NEXT COLUMN TO THE LEFT (⟵)?
42
PRACTICE USING THE COMPUTER BY DOING THESE PROBLEMS:
1. 66 +25
2. 87 +86
3. 89 +45
4. 44 +59
5. 53 +67
6. 45 +68
43
TRY DOING THESE ON THE COMPUTER:
1. 39 +63
2. 18 +84
3. 78 +56
4. 26 +67
5. 76 +43
6. 23 +78
44
FIND THE ANSWERS TO THESE BY USING THE COMPUTER:
1. 259 +274
2. 989 +993
3. 457 +458
4. 359 +898
5. 455 +546
6. 573 +956

IDEAS FOR LAB ACTIVITIES

Today sets of task or work cards and laboratory equipment are available from many commercial firms. (Ten years ago, when this was not the case, teachers were on their own.) You will want to seek these out, but at the same time you should be prepared to generate your own ideas. Here are some tasks that could be developed into laboratory activities:

Build nomographs for computation.

Make Napier's bones out of cardboard.

Construct magic squares.

Play mathematics-oriented card games.

Develop mathematics-based codes and ciphers.

Carry out simple probability experiments.

Develop mathematical relationships related to toys such as electric trains. (Is the weight of the engine in scale?)

Experiment with apparatus such as a pendulum or spring.

Duplicate geometric patterns such as tangram forms.

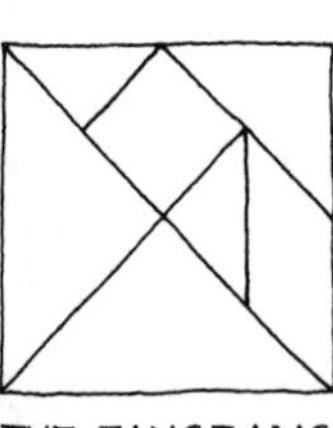

THE TANGRAMS

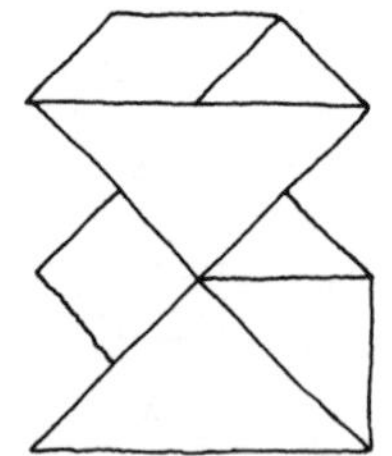
ANOTHER TANGRAM PATTERN

Develop various geometric forms by paper-folding.

Measure angles and sides of polygons to detect regularities.

Carry out a school or community survey related to scoring records (in athletics), school attendance, lunchroom or bookstore sales, television viewing, student physical characteristics (be careful to avoid embarrassment), reading habits, school grades, preferred courses, local taxes, or traffic patterns (on highways or in school hallways).

Develop a proposal for a playground or park in your town or city, including costs and method of financing.

HISTORY OF THE LABORATORY APPROACH

The laboratory approach has its antecedents in the work of Pestalozzi, Montessori, Cuisenaire, Gattegno, Dienes, and others, but its recent spectacular growth is due to a movement in the British primary schools. Supported by the Nuffield Foundation and led by HMI Edith Biggs,[8] this movement has spread rapidly, and developed important concepts, including the idea of a teacher center where teachers of a region meet to develop and share ideas. In the United States and Canada, Kenneth Kidd, William Fitzgerald, and David Clarkson have been major contributors to this movement.

[8]HMI refers to Her Majesty's Inspector of Schools, an important figure in English education. A well-known HMI was the poet Matthew Arnold.

EXERCISES

1. Using a cup or saucer for a template, draw a circle on a sheet of paper and cut it out. Determine a procedure to fold this disc into the largest possible equilateral (equal-sided) triangle. Describe the procedure in words.

2. Consider exercise 1 as a laboratory exercise that you have now performed.
   - (a) Describe your experience in carrying it out, noting especially anything you learned in the process about mathematics or about yourself.
   - (b) For what grade(s) would this activity be appropriate? Inappropriate? Justify your answers.
   - (c) Could the exercise be assigned to a group? If so, how large a group? Indicate what you think would be the advantages and disadvantages of a group attack on this and other problems.
   - (d) How is exercise 1 related to the following high school geometry exercise: Inscribe an equilateral triangle in a circle. (Answer only if you studied high school geometry.)

3. Develop a work card related to the area of a rectangle, similar to the volume card on page 183, and designed for second grade. Be careful of vocabulary.

4. Develop five task cards that are specific to the grade level you are interested in teaching. If possible, try them with individual students and report on your results.

5. Visit a class in which the teacher employs the laboratory method. Try to determine student and teacher reaction. Report on your visit.

6. Summarize what you believe to be the advantages and disadvantages of the laboratory method as it relates to the psychological theories of chapter 2.

7. In chapter 4 we discussed algorithms and their use. Choose an algorithm in an elementary text for the grade level of your choice, and devise a laboratory approach for teaching that algorithm or some part of it.

8. For which field of mathematics (geometry, algebra, etc.) do you feel the laboratory approach is best suited? Discuss your answer.

9. Identify three topics you would *not* teach by the laboratory method. What is it about these topics that makes them less suited to this approach? Do they all have the same characteristics?

CHAPTER SEVEN

TEACHING FOR INDEPENDENCE: THE DISCOVERY METHOD

DISCOVERY IN TODAY'S CLASSROOMS

It would be hard to find an educator today who would oppose having students discover concepts for themselves. Discovery teaching was perhaps the most readily accepted aspect of the new math movement of the 1950s and 1960s. Since then it has faced little serious criticism. And yet in contemporary classrooms discovery teaching is like an exotic wildflower, rare and bordering on extinction.

Why is discovery teaching so rare? The answer is simple: It requires the most sensitive teaching. The teacher must be adroit at setting the stage, asking exactly the right questions at the right time, encouraging students to think, identifying what students mean when they respond, and rewarding creativity. For discovery is that quantum leap of the gestalt diagram (on page 46). It is the point at which students are able to put together the pieces for themselves to provide a significant problem solution and in the process a significant increment in understanding. Proponents of discovery teaching have said that it so involves the students in the learning process that they embrace the content discovered, making it their own. In other words, it is much more difficult to forget cognitive schema that you have constructed yourself.

PATTERNS IN DISCOVERY TEACHING

There is a second reason that discovery teaching is uncommon. Many teachers who sincerely believe that they employ this technique so trivialize it that it is not only no longer discovery teaching, but is actually bad teaching. Discovery is often associated with patterns in the elementary school. By recognizing patterns students are indeed conceptualizing, but even conceptualization may take place at a trivial level. Consider in this regard two examples of searches for patterns. Continue the sequences:

1, 2, 3, 4, 5, ____, ____, ____, ____, ____, . . .

2, 3, 5, 6, 8, ____, ____, ____, ____, ____, . . .

Pattern recognition is so firmly embedded in school instruction today that virtually every student would extend the first sequence: 6, 7, 8, 9, 10. For two reasons, that is not discovery: The student has seen it before, and it is a trivial response. There is no leap up the conceptual ladder here; there is not even a step up.

Suppose we asked instead to give a different pattern for that first sequence. Many students would respond 4, 3, 2, 1, 2, starting an up and down sequence that is at least a step forward, but surely not a discovery. The usual answer to the second pattern question (above) is at about this same level. (Be sure that you have answered before you read ahead.) Most students and teachers would answer 9, 11, 12, 14, 15, and justify their sequence as skipping every third number.

But suppose now we provide the additional information that the next two terms in the second sequence are 9, 10, instead of 9, 11. Many responders would continue to focus on the same idea and would produce a sequence that skips the third number twice, the fourth number twice, and so on. That is a little bigger step perhaps, but not much, especially since it doesn't fit our sequence. Now we reach the level of a real challenge and the possible opportunity for discovery learning.

Here is the second pattern extended:

2, 3, 5, 6, 8, 9, 10, 12, 13, 15, 16, 18, 19, 20, 21, 22, 23, 24, 25, 26, 27, 28, 29, 30, 31, 32, . . .

Can you see the pattern now? What is the next number? What are the next dozen numbers?

To see the pattern, you might change your focus to the numbers skipped. We omitted 1, 4, 7, 11, 14, 17, and then will omit 41, 44, 47, and 71. Viewed in this way some of you (and some students) would see the pattern. Here are two possible descriptions:

1. The sequence of counting numbers containing any of the digits 2, 3, 5, 6, 8, 9, or 0

2. The sequence of counting numbers not made up exclusively of 1s, 4s, and 7s

Why those digits? Can you see something about the first list that is different from the second? That was the basis for our description:

3. The sequence of counting numbers containing at least one "curved" digit, that is, a digit not drawn entirely with straight segments.

WHAT IS AND WHAT IS NOT DISCOVERY?

Our example may suggest to you the beginning of an understanding of discovery learning. A discovery involves a substantial *reorganization* of thinking. Every science student knows the story of Archimedes leaping from his bath and crying, "Eureka!" ("I have found it!") when the idea came to him of the principle of buoyancy.[1] That is indeed the seminal example of discovery, probably challenged only by the fall of Newton's apple. These stories are remembered because they are tied to major discoveries in our intellectual history. We need not expect the same in our classrooms.

For students, a discovery should be based on what is appropriate for them in their own intellectual milieux. Discovery must involve *their* putting things together in ways that are significant to *them.* In other words a discovery for a bright student is quite different from one for a less able child; it is different for a sixth-grader from what it would be for a primary-grade student.

Consider one more famous historical example, one that is often used as an example of a discovery exercise appropriate for the elementary school. When the famous mathematician Gauss was a child, his schoolmaster set a task for his class.[2] He asked the students to add the numbers from 1 to 100. Teachers should recognize that this kind of exercise is used to keep students busy while the teacher turns attention elsewhere. Gauss spoiled the teacher's plan by bringing forward his slate immediately. On it he had recorded the correct answer. How did he do this so quickly?

Before we discuss this example, be sure that you try to answer the question Gauss's teacher posed:

$$1 + 2 + 3 + \ldots\ldots\ldots\ldots + 98 + 99 + 100 = \_\_\_\_$$

It seems evident that Gauss did not proceed: $1 + 2 = 3, 3 + 3 = 6, 6 + 4 = 10$, and so on, adding the series term by term. We suspect a shortcut, a reorganization of the information in a significantly different way. To use a mathematician's term, we seek an *elegant* solution. There are several, one of which is the following:

---

[1]A floating object displaces its weight of the liquid in which it is immersed. Archimedes is said to have used this discovery to catch goldsmiths who substituted base minerals for some of the gold in his king's crown.

[2]Our examples have included the three greatest mathematicians of history: Archimedes, Newton, and Gauss. The only modern mathematician occasionally classed with them is Albert Einstein.

1. Notice that as the problem is displayed

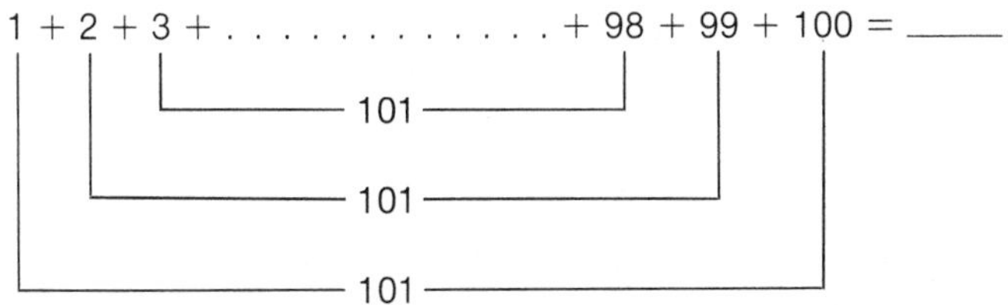

the first and last terms total 101. So do 2 + 99 and 3 + 98.

2. There are exactly 50 such pairs, so the sum is 50(101) = 5,050.

For you, if you had never seen the problem before, and for intermediate-grade students, this would indeed be a discovery exercise. If you solved it in a reasonable way (not necessarily the way given), you have experienced a "personal discovery." You did not experience this, of course, if you merely read the answer.

Consider this experience of discovery. The learner builds up frustration as he confronts the magnitude of the problem, but at the same time recognizes the considerable challenge this poses to him. Now if he is able to solve the problem, he receives strong positive reinforcement. His self-assurance rises substantially—much more, for example, than after solving an information recall exercise. Compare in this regard the sense of accomplishment you would get from extending the first sequence on page 202 with that gained from the second. A sense of accomplishment gives the discoverer a strong incentive to attack and solve further problems. Gestalt psychologists rightly claim that this incentive is more significant than the stimulus the behaviorist psychologists realized from small increments of learning. The positive reinforcement of discovery moves the student into the left cycle of the figure, while failure places him in the right cycle. In this way success breeds success and failure breeds failure.

SUCCESS
EFFORT
ENJOYMENT

FAILURE
AVOIDANCE
DISCOMFORT

OBSTACLES TO DISCOVERY IN THE CLASSROOM

The discovery examples should make clear why discovery learning is so difficult to produce in the classroom. Some of the problems associated directly with discovery learning are:

1. Students too often give up before they give themselves a chance to discover anything. (One corollary of this is the fact that much homework is done by parents, who then wonder why the classroom teacher doesn't teach how to do the exercises.) Few students will spend more than five or ten seconds thinking about a problem if left to their own resources. Unless the teacher is sensitive to this pedagogical problem and responds to it with skill, discovery learning cannot take place.

2. Many class discovery exercises are what we refer to as Magellan exercises. One student (or sometimes the teacher) plays Magellan and discovers, while the rest play oarsmen and not only do not discover, but in their roles as oarsmen may even face the wrong way. In such situations, the teacher asks a challenging question, and a bright student invariably gives the answer. Having heard the correct answer, the others are no longer confronted with even the possibility of discovery. This format can also result in class dislike for the problem-solver, which, if it involves a sensitive child, can lead to withdrawal.[3]

3. Developing discovery exercises that are right for students is a most difficult pedagogical problem. Posing any discovery question is a creative pedagogical exercise; posing one just right for students demands considerable skill.

In the following sections we offer some partial responses to these difficulties.

---

[3]Perhaps the extreme of this kind of thinking was displayed on television at the time the first Russian space flight made us aware that we must encourage better learning of school science and math. Questioned about her reasons for not studying these subjects, a junior-high cheerleader replied: "My mother won't let me. She says the boys wouldn't like me and I'd never get married."

A RESPONSE TO PROBLEM ONE: GETTING STUDENTS TO TRY

In many cases students do not attempt problems because they have no self-confidence. "I'm no Einstein" is a common response. We seek then a way to address this negative self-image, one of the most significant problems of all schooling.

William Bailey, Sherman Stein, and others have proposed having students work in small groups as a way to attack this teaching problem. Bailey's research on this technique showed the following: Students working in groups of four solved many problems that they could not solve individually, and, more important, after the group experience students made greater progress solving problems when working individually.

Since this appears to offer an answer to the problem of increasing student effort, let us explore the dynamics of small-group learning. First, it is evident that the group operates as a team of peers in much the same way an athletic team does. Athletic coaches tell us, and teams display in a variety of ways, how the whole team is more than the sum of its individual members. In his important book, *The Adolescent Society,* James Coleman has made a case for translating this into classroom practice. A group provides both peer pressure to achieve and peer support for achievement.

Consider a group at work. There is some intergroup competitive pressure since other groups appear to be making progress (even though the other group may be having the same difficulties). One student suggests a method of attack. Another explains why that won't work. They agree. Another direction is suggested. That appears productive so the group moves ahead. They compare results, share tasks, and interact in useful ways. Anyone observing such group classroom situations is struck by the way one team member usually assumes leadership responsibilities. He or she is often but not always the brightest. It is seldom that a team member fails to participate.

What is it about group situations that lengthens the period students are willing to work on a problem? There are several answers to this:

1. There is team pressure to succeed.

2. Four have a better chance than one to hit on a good lead.

3. Even wrong trials by team members provide opportunities for interaction and extend the period of effort.

4. Each good idea extends the period of attention. Four heads are better than one; indeed four heads together are far better than four working individually.

As an example, here is a partial record of a sixth-grade team working on the following difficult problem.

PROBLEM

In the 3×4 rectangle the unit squares and the diagonal are drawn. The diagonal passes through 6 of the squares. Similarly, for the 2×4 rectangle the diagonal passes through 4 squares. Find a general rule for a $w \times l$ rectangle.[4]

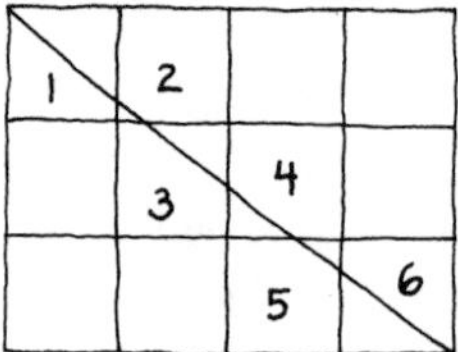

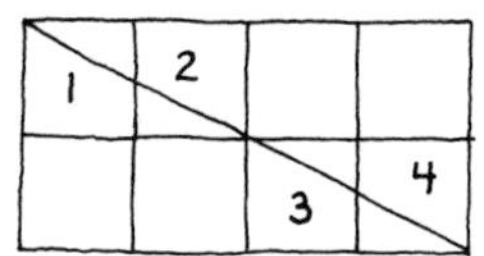

The group quickly decides that they must try other rectangles to see what happens. They locate squared paper and each group member draws some rectangles. Soon one student sees a pattern: "If the rectangle is one unit wide the diagonal passes through all the squares." (This is already more progress than most students would make on this problem working alone!)

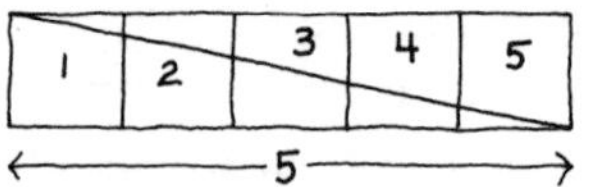

One student now suggests that they pool their information for rectangles of width 2. They make the following charts.

[4]This is the same problem discussed on pages 140–141 from a quite different perspective. We assume here, of course, that students have not seen the other approach. In addition this attack on the problem considers a more general case.

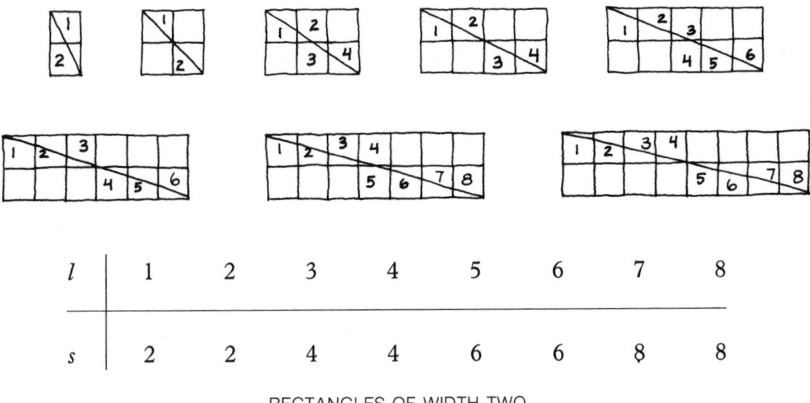

l	1	2	3	4	5	6	7	8
s	2	2	4	4	6	6	8	8

RECTANGLES OF WIDTH TWO

(s indicates the number of squares through which the diagonal passes.) They note the obvious pattern and how it extends: For even numbers it remains the same; for odd numbers, add 1. Now they try rectangles of width 3.

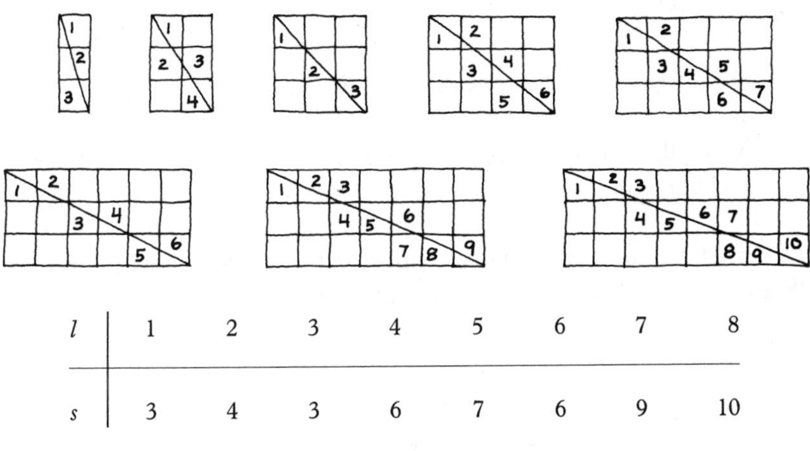

l	1	2	3	4	5	6	7	8
s	3	4	3	6	7	6	9	10

RECTANGLES OF WIDTH THREE

This time the pattern is more difficult, and they soon realize that this approach will lead to many different patterns instead of the one requested in the problem. At this critical point one student notes that it is when the diagonal goes through a corner that "trouble" is generated. They reexamine their tables to see when this happens.

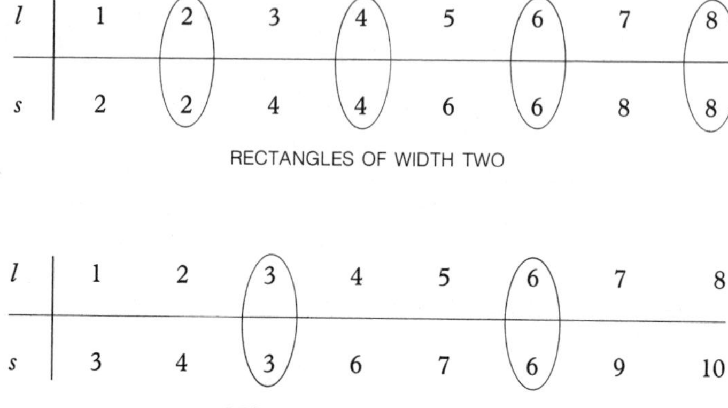

l	1	2	3	4	5	6	7	8
s	2	2	4	4	6	6	8	8

RECTANGLES OF WIDTH TWO

l	1	2	3	4	5	6	7	8
s	3	4	3	6	7	6	9	10

RECTANGLES OF WIDTH THREE

Looping the cases when the diagonals pass through corners, the students notice two things:

1. When the diagonal passes through the corners, $s = l$.

2. When the diagonal doesn't pass through a corner, $s = l + 1$ for width 2 and $s = l + 2$ for width 3.

The first conjecture appears to be simpler, so the students check it for other rectangles. They soon find counterexamples: for a 4×6 rectangle, $s = 8$.

After trying unsuccessfully to adjust this conjecture for some time, they return to their second observation. They check it for rectangles of width 4 and 5.

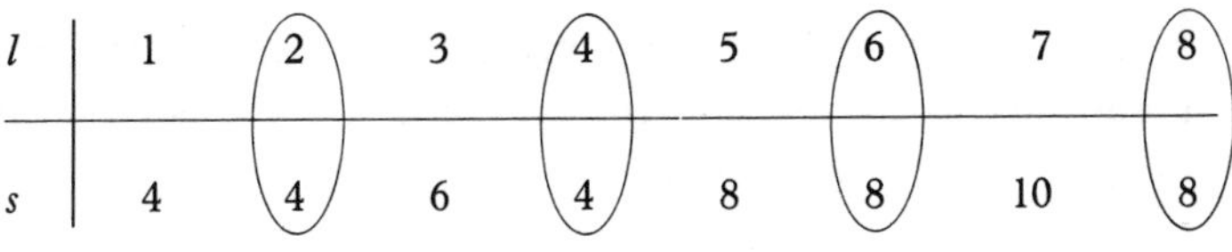

l	1	2	3	4	5	6	7	8
s	4	4	6	4	8	8	10	8

RECTANGLES OF WIDTH FOUR

l	1	2	3	4	5	6	7	8
s	5	6	7	8	5	10	11	12

RECTANGLES OF WIDTH FIVE

The students see a new pattern for the cases when diagonals do not pass through a corner:

For width 2: $s = l + 1$

For width 3: $s = l + 2$

For width 4: $s = l + 3$

For width 5: $s = l + 4$

A student predicts that for width 6, $s = l + 5$. They try and it does. Another suggests that s is just one less than the sum of l and w. Proud of this discovery, they call the teacher, who asks if they can express this in an equation. A student responds:

$$v = l + w - 1.$$

The teacher remarks on this excellent result and tells the group members they can be proud of their accomplishment. Now, the teacher suggests, they can explore the more difficult problem of how to adjust the 1 in the formula to include the other cases.[5] The students return to work.

[5]Notice here how the teacher gives a hint that doesn't provide a solution, but does suggest a focus for further search.

This real example took place in a mixed-ability sixth-grade classroom. All six groups in this class made significant progress on this problem, five going beyond the described episode.

A RESPONSE TO PROBLEM TWO: PROTECTING THE DISCOVERY FOR ALL STUDENTS

Discovery proponents have developed a delightful classroom game, which may be used at any grade level, called "What's My Rule?" In the game, the teacher makes up a rule but doesn't tell the class what it is. Instead he calls upon students to give him numbers. To each student number, he responds with the number his rule generates. For example, a first-grade dialogue might be:

Teacher: Sarah.

Sarah: Two.

Teacher: Four. Billy.

Billy: Five. [*Sarah and Billy have picked numbers at random.*]

Teacher: Seven.

At this point several hands would go up because students think they know the rule. As soon as this happens, the teacher checks them by reversing roles as follows:

Teacher: [*Pointing to a third student with a hand up*] Okay, Jimmy, fourteen.

Jimmy: Sixteen.

Teacher: Six.

Jimmy: Eight.

Teacher: You've got it. Now Cynthia, twenty.

And so on.

Note the key to this game. The teacher *does not ask:* How did you get that? By delaying this question he does not give away the secret. The students who have guessed the rule show that they know by applying it. This generates additional cases for weaker students who have not yet found the solution.

The following dialogue might transpire if a student incorrectly guesses the rule:

Teacher: Sam, twelve.

Sam: Eleven.

Teacher: No, Sam, you haven't got it yet. Listen carefully. Eileen.

Now students know that 12 doesn't generate 11 by the rule. Negative as well as positive results help them to zero in on the rule.

Only when it is apparent that many students have found the rule should the teacher let students describe it. Here is a possible dialogue:

Teacher: What was your rule, Paul?

Paul: Add two.

Teacher: That works. Did anyone have another rule? Laura.

Laura: Skip a number.

Teacher: That's good too. Any others? Helen.

Helen: (*The class show-off*) I added three and then subtracted one.

Teacher: Fine. Now let's try a new rule.

A variant of the game is to let a student make up a rule, whisper it to the teacher (so any misplays can be corrected if they occur), and then play the teacher role in the game.

We have illustrated the game with a first-grade example. To illustrate the wide range of sophistication, consider the following four examples, each of which is generated by a different secret rule. Before reading beyond them, try to guess the teacher's rule for each.

RULE 1		RULE 2		RULE 3		RULE 4	
student	*teacher*	*student*	*teacher*	*student*	*teacher*	*student*	*teacher*
11	32	3	18	17	24	5	4
4	11	10	900	10	7	7	5
7	20	5	100	3	24	1	3
10	29	1	0	7	24	11	6
2	5	7	294	4	7	27	11
1	2	4	48	5	24	30	6

Some possible rules that fit the given data are:

RULE 1. Multiply by three and subtract one: $3x - 1$

RULE 2. Multiply by itself and then by one less: $x^2(x - 1)$, or subtract the number squared from the number cubed: $x^3 - x^2$

RULE 3. Odd → 24; even → 7

RULE 4. The number of letters in the word for the number; for example, 3 → three → 5 (letters numbered 1 2 3 4 5)

Students familiar with this game can "guess" the rules for quite challenging relationships. The types of rules devised are limited only by your creativity. Here then is one way that discovery can be protected for all students.

A RESPONSE TO PROBLEM THREE: DEVELOPING DISCOVERY EXERCISES

There is no simple solution to the difficult problem of developing appropriate exercises. Perhaps the best response a teacher can make is to collect a pool of problems from which to draw those appropriate for your class or for individual students. Sources for such problems are textbooks, workbooks, laboratory cards, problem books, and—last but far from least—your fellow teachers. You cannot start too soon to collect and retain such problems. In order to avoid forgetting them it is useful to form a card file of problems. Here are a few examples:

Find a strategy to win at one-pile Nim. TEACHER'S FILE

RULES: Fifteen toothpicks or other counters are placed on the table. Two players take turns taking 1, 2, or 3 toothpicks from the pile. The winner is the player who takes the last toothpick(s).[6]

Harry claims that he has a way of generating primes. Choose any number, he says, and put it in each of the boxes. Do the arithmetic, and the result will be a prime. TEACHER'S FILE

$$(\square \times \square) - \square + 17$$

For example: $(3 \times 3) - 3 + 17 = 23$, a prime.

Is Harry right? Does his method always work?

---

[6]A variant of this game is to declare the loser to be the player who takes the last toothpick. Many new games are generated by this rule reversal, so well known to game players as to be given the name, miseré. Tic-tac-toe and checkers are two games that may be played in miseré form.

TEACHER'S FILE

Find a shortcut way to solve the following:

1. $\frac{2}{7} + \frac{1}{3} + \frac{2}{3}$
2. $3\frac{1}{4} + 7\frac{1}{5} + 2\frac{4}{5}$
3. $231 + 764 + 236$
4. $947 + 821 + 179$
5. $2\frac{4}{5} + 3\frac{6}{7} + 1\frac{1}{7}$
6. $36 \times 25 \times 4$
7. $47 \times 1\frac{1}{4} \times 8$
8. $\frac{5}{7} \times \frac{2}{3} \times 1\frac{1}{2}$
9. $327 \times 12.5 \times 8$
10. $66 \times \frac{1}{14} \times 7$

TEACHER'S FILE

Each of the following is an *Ooglie:*

Which of the following are *Ooglies?* Why?

A WARNING ABOUT PATTERNS

The search for patterns or regularity is an important component of mathematical and scientific development. It is an important activity that students should be involved in from the earliest grades. But pattern development is only part of the problem. We must be assured in some way that the pattern chosen is the correct one, and the only route to such assurance is proof. We have already seen that more than one answer may be justified as the following entry in a sequence, which suggests the danger we face here.

1, 2, 3, 4, 5, ____

Mathematicians would tell us that *any* number can be justified by formula for the next and subsequent terms! So we must balance pattern-generation with reality.

One way to make our point about the necessity of proof is with concrete materials that allow generation of additional data. But even this is not always enough. Consider in this regard the following examples:

EXAMPLE 1.

How many chords are determined by n points on a circle? We address the problem by generating data.

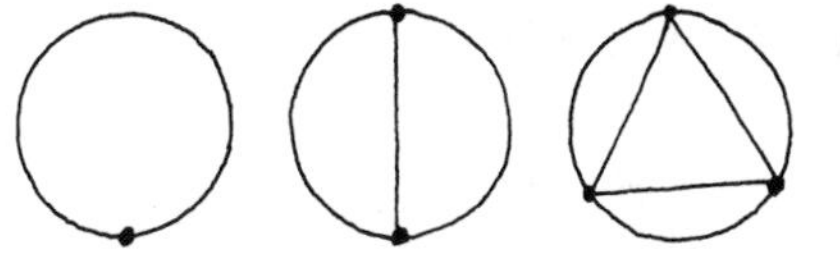
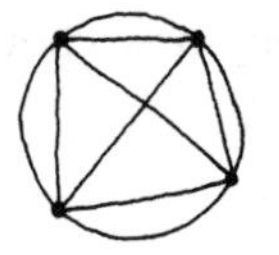

We can record our results in a table (where P represents the number of points and c the number of chords):

P	1	2	3	4	5	6
c	0	1	3	6	10	15

By analyzing the data we can see that the number of chords increases by one each time. We would expect 7 points to determine 21 chords.

EXAMPLE 2. Into what maximum number of regions do n chords separate the interior of a circle?

We can see from the diagrams above that our early data will be (assuming r is the number of regions):

P	1	2	3	4
r	1	2	4	8

The number of regions appears to double each time. But explore the cases for 5 and then 6 points to see what happens.

Now return to example 1 to see how it is different from example 2. The difference is that we can justify our partial answer in the first example. Suppose we have 4 points on a circle with the chords drawn and we put on the fifth. How many new chords are formed?

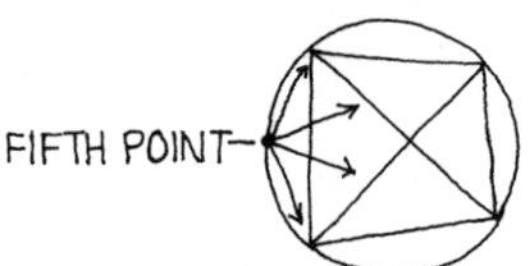

It is evident that there are exactly 4 new chords, one for each of the old points. *We have a logical explanation for our correct formulation.* For example 2 we can find no such logical basis, and we cannot justify our answer by more than hope: hope that is not fulfilled.

Where then does this leave the teacher? Should you ignore patterns except where they can be proved? We counsel you to continue to use patterns and to encourage their recognition, even when no proof can be found. But we suggest that, especially with older students, you do the following:

1. Encourage students to find *alternate correct* patterns. Even though they are mathematically equivalent, they will encourage students not to fix on one possible answer.

2. Encourage students to give reasons, when those reasons are within their range.

3. Use counterexample exercises like the second example card on page 215.

4. Show examples like the chord-region problem, where expected patterns occasionally do break down. Use them as justification for proof. (See chapter 5.)

DISCOVERY BY BRAINSTORMING

Most of the discovery exercises we have discussed in this chapter are based on a single type of discovery exercise, specifically one that searches for patterns or formulas. In many cases, we want students to make the discovery of a formula that will solve problems similar to the one presented in the "What's My Rule?" game discussed on pages 212–214. There is, however, another type of discovery exercise that can be used as an effective tool in the classroom: brainstorming. In this type of discovery the children pose their own questions about a mathematical phenomenon. For example, consider the sequence 5, 6, 8, 9, 11, 12, 14, 15, ... Instead of asking questions that deal specifically with the missing numbers in the sequence, questions may arise such as:

1. What will happen if we add 3 to every number of that sequence? How would the sequence change?

5, 6, 8, 9, 11, 12, 14, 15, . . .	original sequence
↓ ↓ ↓ ↓ ↓ ↓ ↓ ↓	
8, 9, 11, 12, 14, 15, 17, 18, . . .	new sequence (by adding 3)

2. What will happen to the sequence if we subtract 2 from every number? When 3 was added, the new sequence was made up of the same numbers as the old (except 5 and 6). Is that true when 2 is subtracted?

A major advantage of this approach is that there is something here for everyone. Both slow and above-average students will be encouraged to ask questions at *their own* levels of sophistication. In this way each can enjoy discovering new and different mathematical ideas at his own level.

PLANNING FOR DISCOVERY

When you think about it, the title "Planning for Discovery" seems a contradiction in terms. Obviously it is not possible to program your own discoveries. That would be like Columbus setting out the itinerary for his first westward voyage. In the classroom, however, most "discoveries" are actually rediscoveries. Very seldom if ever will a child discover a mathematical relationship not previously known. What he will discover—in the true sense of that word—will be mathematics that is new *to him.* Planning for discovery, then, means setting up situations in which opportunities for personal discovery abound.

We have already suggested that organizing students in small groups to work on significant problems is a way of promoting the sort of concentration that encourages discovery opportunities. And we have suggested some specific activities for discovery lessons. The teacher should also be sensitive to opportunities for discovery that arise within the day-to-day classroom regimen.

While we will stress in chapter 12 a balanced program in the classroom, it is well that we suggest now that discovery teaching should not be separated from other teaching. Teachers who try to set aside "a day for discovery" are foredoomed to failure for two reasons:

1. Since students will view discovery as somehow distinct from "the regular math," the derived motivation will not carry over.

2. The quality of other lessons will be reduced by the separation.

We find from our own teaching that it is unsatisfactory merely to rely on one's spontaneity to take advantage of "opportunities that arise" to promote discovery. More often than not you will find yourself thinking after class about chances you missed. Instead you should carefully review every lesson for discovery opportunities before instruction. Often the most straightforward lessons will provide interesting possibilities for a discovery approach.

EXERCISES

1. State the problem asked of Gauss carefully, as you might offer it to a class. Refine your statement so that you give enough information to place the problem in its historical context, but not so much that you remove the challenge.

2. The first step of the solution of Gauss's problem was the observation of the pairs 1 + 100, 2 + 99, 3 + 98, and so on, each of whose sum is 101. Explain why this pattern continues.

3. Give two shortcut methods of solving Gauss's problem *different* from that of this text. Rank the three solutions (your two and that in the text) as to your subjective judgment of elegance. Defend your ranking.

4. Comment on the problem of bright students generating dislike in the classroom. How would you try to help such a student? (Be careful that you do not suggest ways that will impair learning.)

5. Comment on discovery teaching and laboratory teaching. How are the two similar or different?

6. Try to complete the solution to the discovery exercise on pages 208–211. If you have difficulty, consider the hint given at the end of these exercises.

7. Devise and describe another technique for encouraging classroom discovery while avoiding the Magellan syndrome.

8. *A problem suitable for group attack for grade 5 to adult.* Dominoes are 1×2 rectangular tiles on which two groups of dots are etched. For example:

These are the 1-6, 3-4, and 0-5 dominoes. There are 28 dominoes in a set that runs from 0-0 through 6-6, with one of each type. In the following array the 28 dominoes have been randomly placed so that they form a 7×8 rectangle.

4	1	3	4	3	5	3	3
5	0	4	1	1	5	0	2
0	1	2	0	2	1	6	2
2	5	1	0	6	4	0	0
5	3	5	6	6	6	5	3
6	4	3	0	2	1	5	6
6	2	3	2	4	1	4	4

Your challenge: Find the positions of the individual dominoes in the array. For example, you must decide if the domino in the upper-left corner is a 4-5 or a 4-1. Try solving this problem in a group of four. Comment on the group experience. (*Note:* Additional problems of this type may be generated merely by mixing up a set of dominoes, laying them out, and copying the numbers as above or in other patterns.)

9. Utilize any sources (including your own creativity) to collect five problems you feel are suitable for discovery exercises appropriate to the grade level you plan to teach.

10. Choose one of the discovery activities of this chapter that is suitable to a grade you plan to teach. Discuss strategies you would employ if students were not able to make progress with the problems.

11. Give Gauss's problem to two children (in grades 4–8) and to one adult. Observe how they deal with the problem. Discuss their responses to the problem and their methods of attack. How do they differ? How are they similar?

12. Give Gauss's problem to a group of middle-grade children. Observe their group response to the problem. How does the group respond differently from the individuals in exercise 11?

13. How might the following exercises be extended by the method of brainstorming discovery?

(a) Fifth-grade students have been representing integers by four 4s

$$1 = 44/44$$

$$2 = (4 \times 4)/(4 + 4)$$

$$3 = (4 + 4 + 4)/4$$

(b) Third-grade students have constructed a 3×3 magic square. (The sums of rows, columns, and diagonals are all equal.)

8	1	6
3	5	7
4	9	2

(c) First-grade students have recorded all the "total beans" that could result from the following bean sticks.

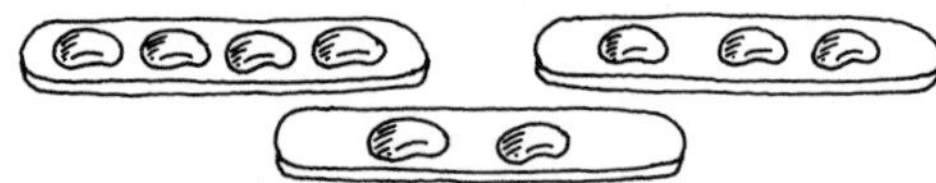

(d) Seventh-grade students have discovered the generating law for the Fibonacci numbers (add two terms to get the next) 1, 1, 2, 3, 5, 8, 13, ...

14. Examine a text and teacher's edition for your grade level interest to determine:

(a) How much discovery activity is included in the program

(b) What the authors' attitude toward discovery is

(c) How you might incorporate teaching for discovery into your program if you used that text

Hint for exercise 6: Recall the definition of greatest common divisor.

CHAPTER EIGHT

TEACHING FOR ORGANIZATION: DIRECTED LEARNING

DIRECTED LEARNING AS THE STANDARD CLASSROOM ROUTINE

In the two preceding chapters you met important but nonstandard instructional techniques: laboratory and discovery teaching. In this chapter we turn to the type of instruction that takes place day after day in over 95 percent of American classrooms. While we believe that the percentage is far too high, we feel that at least half of any instructional program should be class-organized, directed, developmental learning.

Directed learning involves the following components:

1. Carefully planned and organized activities that focus on specific learning objectives

2. Associated evaluation procedures that give students and teachers a measure of progress

3. Classroom procedures that develop understanding of skills and concepts as a cooperative activity, but under the teacher's direct guidance

Teaching in this way is important because of the nature of mathematics. Mathematics is hierarchical: that is, it builds concept on concept, skill on skill. Prerequisites are necessary to progress. It is a romantic fallacy to assume that students left to their own resources will rediscover and reorganize mathematics for themselves. Even if they could, imagine how inefficient and time consuming their progress would be. From the earliest grades, students meet ideas that demand prerequisite ideas and procedures. Learning to add requires the ability to count. Without the ability to order numbers correctly, students would never progress in learning addition.

In the interest of efficiency and orderly development, directed learning is adopted. Since this involves compromising freedom and openness for direction, teachers should be alert for opportunities to break this routine with other activities like those in chapters 6 and 7. At the same time, however, the teacher's control of the class (see point 3 above) can be so skillful and sensitive that neither the students nor outside observers can recognize the management. Directed learning should not imply heavy-handed imposition of discipline; rather it means a more subtle choice of activities and pedagogical techniques designed to move the class toward prior established objectives.

PLANNING, THE KEY TO ALL TEACHING

Too much teaching is ad hoc, off the cuff, or too lightly planned. Because of this, in far too many classrooms math is a daily set routine of teacher talk/student listen, followed by workbook drudgery.[1] Students respond with a growing dislike for mathematics when it is imposed upon them in this nineteenth-century format.

---

[1]In some classrooms, the basic role of mathematics is to keep students busy on workbook exercises (seat work) while the teacher meets with small reading groups.

The answer to this is, of course, carefully planned and designed purposeful activity. Overplanning and overpreparation *never* hurt. Teachers can always depart from well-laid plans to explore unexpected student questions or comments. But underplanning *always* hurts. It leaves beginners helpless with time on their and their students' hands; it leads experienced teachers to extemporize, which can be even worse. Planning is the key to all teaching, not just developmental teaching.

The key question is, How do you plan effectively? Planning is an idiosyncratic activity; some teachers use only a few notes on a scrap of paper or even unwritten organization, while others write out detailed procedures. In either case, there are certain well-defined aspects that we now consider: determining objectives, establishing procedures and activities, and evaluating progress.

DETERMINING OBJECTIVES

Certainly you must first decide what you wish to accomplish in a lesson or a unit of instruction. Behaviorists have substituted for the phrase "what you wish to accomplish" a more useful phrase, "how you want your students to behave," thus focusing on students rather than the teacher.[2]

It sounds easy; you want your students to be able to add, solve word problems, or master the long division algorithm. But unfortunately such objectives are hardly useful in short-range instruction, since they lack detail. Teachers should identify exactly what aspect of addition they wish to address:

> The student will be able to relate addition to exercises on the number line.
>
> The student will recall basic (one-digit) addition facts.
>
> The student will add two two-digit addends without carrying (regrouping).

---

[2]So-called behavioral objectives go further, demanding specificity beyond what we describe here. The interested reader may refer to Robert F. Mager, *Preparing Objectives for Programmed Instruction* (Belmont, Calif.: Fearon, 1962).

These are only a few of the many specific teaching objectives related to addition alone!

Note too that these three examples refer only to content at a level below that addressed in the previous two chapters. Consider in this regard the various levels of conceptual understanding concerning computational skill:

The student can add, relying on counters.

The student bases addition on memorized facts.

The student employs shortcuts in addition.

The student relates addition to the number line.

The student can estimate results and check accuracy.

The student can utilize structural properties of addition.

The student can explain the steps in the addition algorithm.

The student can prove why the algorithm works.

The student can develop an original addition algorithm.

The University of Chicago psychologist Benjamin S. Bloom has classified educational objectives into a hierarchy. His *Taxonomy of Educational Objectives*[3] lists the following general categories, for each of which we give an example:

Knowledge, ranging from specific facts and terminology to generalizations, theories, and structures. *The student will be able to identify triangles, squares, and rectangles.*

---

[3]Benjamin S. Bloom, et al., *Taxonomy of Educational Objectives: The Classification of Educational Goals, Handbook I: Cognitive Domain* (New York: Longmans, Green, 1956). See also, David R. Krathwohl, et al., *Taxonomy of Educational Objectives: The Classification of Educational Goals, Handbook II: Affective Domain* (New York: David McKay, 1964).

Comprehension, including translation, interpretation, and extrapolation. *The student will be able to translate statements like "John has 3 more marbles than Mary" into equations like* $J = M + 3$.

Application of mathematical ideas to real world problems. *The student will be able to measure the lengths of objects in the classroom in metric units.*

Analysis of elements, relationships, and organization. *The student will be able to justify the steps in multiplication of two-digit numbers.*

Synthesis or organization of ideas into a report, a plan, or a system. *The student will be able to teach a classmate how to regroup in addition.*

Evaluation on the basis of internal or external evidence. *The student will be able to disprove conjectures by producing counterexamples.*

These categories suggest some of the deeper thought patterns that should be addressed in instruction. Unfortunately, too much teaching and testing is focused exclusively on the knowledge recall level of learning. (We will return to this point when we discuss evaluation.)

No teacher, in developing classroom plans, should feel compelled to spell out goals in carefully worded sentences unless a supervisor requests it. A series of brief notes can carry the same meaning:

Number-line addition

Recording facts in table

Word problems

The time saved by making such notes can go into the other aspects of planning.

ESTABLISHING PROCEDURES AND ACTIVITIES

Now that we know our destination, we must plan our route. We must determine whether we want to follow the direct route to our objectives, or a scenic, meandering route that encourages us to pause along the way to experiment and discover new vistas.

Many experienced teachers follow established procedures in attacking major processes, for example addition in the first grade or addition of fractions in the fifth. Early lessons on the process are largely devoted to careful review of prerequisite skills and concepts. Within this sequence of lessons, a strong foundation is laid for the more formal development that follows. Next comes a period of transition from concrete to abstract. During this time algorithmic procedures are introduced, first as record-keeping devices for the concrete activities, and later as shortcut and timesaving procedures. During these lessons it is vital that students experiencing difficulties be allowed to regress to concrete activities to restore confidence. (Failure to allow for this kind of regression is one of the most common pedagogical errors. It leaves students with rote procedures for which they have no checking ability. For example, a student who forgets the memorized product of 4×3 often cannot recreate it.)[4] During the last lessons, applications are introduced (see chapter 9) and a variety of activities such as games and contests provide practice to help solidify and speed up understanding of the unit. Evaluation and any necessary reteaching should also take place at this time.

EVALUATING PROGRESS

Many teachers devise evaluation techniques at the same time they set up their objectives, in other words at the beginning of the development of a teaching unit. While this may at first seem out of sequence, reflection should suggest the strength of this idea. Our objectives are refined by our evaluation procedures. No matter how we teach a unit, if we evaluate student progress only by having students carry out algorithms, they will quickly learn to focus their attention largely on those aspects of instruction. This is exactly what

[4]Evidence related to this may be collected by asking several adults if they can show you why $9 \times 7 = 63$.

happens in many classrooms, and the tendency becomes increasingly apparent in higher grades and secondary schools when students become more "test sophisticated" and begin to ask the question, "Will this be on the test?"

In planning instruction then, the teacher should associate specific evaluation procedures, even test items, with objectives. Returning to the hierarchy of objectives on pages 226–227, note the following illustrative exercises:

Knowledge: The meter is a unit of

(a) Area
(b) Weight
(c) Length
(d) Volume

Comprehension: Write an equation relating the data

x	3	4	5	6	7
y	4	5	6	7	8

Application: Find the area of your desk top in square centimeters.

Analysis: If $(x + 5)/2$ is equal to a whole number, then x can be

(a) Any integer
(b) Any even integer
(c) Any odd integer
(d) Any multiple of 5

Synthesis: Suppose that instead of having ten digits, we had only six: 0, 1, 2, 3, 4, and 5, and we counted 1, 2, 3, 4, 5, 10, 11, 12, etc. Continue counting to 100 in this system and complete one-digit addition and multiplication tables.

Evaluation: You have learned two methods of division in class. Tell which method you prefer and why.

Here are some things to take into account in evaluation:

1. You will find it most useful to begin accumulating test items, filed on 3″ × 5″ cards by topic or even objective.[5]

2. Be sure evaluation questions are clearly stated. Too often an incorrect response is a correct answer to what the student thought was being asked.

3. Avoid trick questions. If you use them, do so in a nonevaluation setting.

4. Employ observation techniques as well as written tests to evaluate student progress.

There are two aspects of evaluation that should be carefully taken into account. These have been defined as *formative* evaluation, whose purpose is to influence teaching procedures, and *summative* evaluation, which is designed to rank students or otherwise measure their progress. A useful formative evaluation procedure is to give a pretest on a unit, designed to provide two kinds of information: (1) what additional review of prerequisites is needed, and (2) how much students already know about the topic to be taught. To use the grades on such a test, which would contain items on content not yet taught, for student evaluation would be patently unfair. But its value in helping design instruction should be evident.

PLANNING FOR THE BEGINNING TEACHER

Often beginners who observe a master teacher orchestrate a lesson in an excited class are overwhelmed.[6] There is so much to know and to prepare. Beginners should realize that becoming a master teacher is an incremental process that usually takes several years.

---

[5]Plan to save copies of tests you administer for revision and possible reuse another year. By recording remarks about item difficulty at the time you give the test, you will help yourself in this process.

[6]One of today's finest classroom expositors, Arthur Engel of Stuttgart, West Germany, said of his first observation as a student teacher: "My master teacher was so good that I decided I could never become a satisfactory teacher. I almost quit that day."

There is, however, a useful base from which the beginner can work. With the contemporary stress on alternate styles of teaching, a great deal of criticism has been directed at the elementary school mathematics textbook. Too rigid, not appropriate to poor readers, unrealistic problems, no opportunity for discovery, say the critics. But a textbook provides any teacher, not just a beginner, with a carefully organized program, just what the teacher needs to plan activities.

Anyone familiar with the writing and editing process involved in producing an elementary textbook series knows the careful attention that is paid to development and sequence, balance and maintenance. Any major textbook today also provides in text and teacher's commentary:

Chapter and lesson objectives

An evaluation program often including pretests, chapter summary exams, and skill maintenance quizzes

Carefully structured lesson materials usually covering two to four pages of text

Detailed plans for teaching those pages

Suggested nontext activities

Additional review exercises and tests for evaluation of reteaching

Remediation exercises

A realistic amount of work for a school year

A program integrated from grade level to grade level

Here then is a *foundation* on which beginners can build. You can usually trust the overall organization of such a text because significant organizational errors are usually picked up in prepublication trials. But no teacher should feel rigidly tied to the lesson structure of even the best texts. To do that would be to suppress your own personality and to misdirect many of your own personal teaching strengths. From your very first day of teaching you should seek to modify the lessons of the basic text to make them more appropriate for your class and for yourself.

Good teaching involves more than a search for excellence. Following a text too closely leads rather quickly to sterile presentations. A significant result of this, which becomes more apparent in secondary schools, is that students learn *not* to read their math texts. Their texts become mere exercise books. This happens because the teacher's classroom development often duplicates too closely the text presentation. (Some teachers so lack creativity that they use the same examples displayed in the text!) Unfortunately the only students who are willing to duplicate the teachers' efforts by reading the text are those who least need to do so.

The teacher should seek out alternate approaches to those of the basic text in developing the ideas of a lesson. Then a student reading the text will have two supportive activities rather than one repeated. Although creative teachers can devise alternative approaches themselves, creative teachers are usually experienced teachers. The beginner is left in real trouble. There are, however, resources available to help respond to this problem. Creative teaching ideas are found in such sources as: other texts, especially experimental programs like the English Nuffield Project or School Mathematics Project materials, journals like the *Arithmetic Teacher* and the *Grade Teacher,* and in content books for elementary teachers. We will return to this topic in chapter 12.

QUESTIONING

If planning is the key to teaching, questioning is the hinge on which the door swings open. We have stressed that development of material by the teacher should be sensitively imposed in directed learning. This is largely a matter of appropriate questioning.

Questions have traditionally been asked of students to determine what they have learned. But there are better uses of questions, including: to stimulate thinking, to check understanding, to guide problem solving, to arouse curiosity, to provide practice, and to suggest discovery activities. Only when these aspects of questioning are considered do they contribute in a substantive way to directed learning. You should think of levels of questioning in much the same way you thought of levels of objectives and evaluation levels.

Some characteristics of good questions are:

1. The question is clear and understandable.

2. The language and difficulty is appropriate to the student.

3. The person to whom the question is directed is usually not identified until the end of the question. "Can you tell me, John?" Not "John, can you tell me." In this way, the question is addressed first to the class.

4. Both convergent (single-answer) and divergent (open-ended discussion) questions are utilized in balance.

Here are some examples of questions that aid directed learning:

1. Can you tell the class how you worked out that answer?

2. Do you agree with that answer? (asked occasionally after correct as well as incorrect answers)

3. Who can make up another example?

4. Each of these figures is a rhombus. None of these other figures is a rhombus. Let's see if you can work out the mathematician's definition of a rhombus.

5. I'm too lazy to write all that down. Can anyone suggest how we could abbreviate that process? (An example would be omitting the zeros in the multiplication algorithm.)

6. How would you explain that to a younger brother or sister?

7. Where do you suppose you could use that?

8. I don't believe it. Convince me.

9. Can anyone find an exception?

10. We have disagreement here. Mary says yes, Patty no. Let's vote. [*After the vote*] Now let's have an argument for each position. [*After the argument*] Now let's vote again to see if any of you have changed your minds.

11. That is excellent but complicated. Can anyone give a more elegant solution?

12. Has Bill forgotten anything?

13. That procedure continues. Can anyone take over from here?

Notice how these questions (1) say to the students, "Keep thinking!" (2) are encouraging, (3) treat students as partners in the learning process, (4) tend to apply equally to right and wrong answers, (5) encourage interaction among students, (6) soften the teacher-leading aspects of directed learning, and (7) are designed to increase the ratio of student to teacher talk.

One other useful type of question is the psychoanalyst's implied question: raised eyebrows or "Oh?" followed by silence. To the students, as to the patient, this means "Go on." It is an effective technique with an alert class.

What you are trying to accomplish in a directed learning lesson is cooperative student and teacher development of mathematics. You must use great care not to let it become a teacher-telling/student-listening situation. It is best to have the leading or directing aspects of this method tied to the teacher's choice of examples; examples provide better transition points than questions.

Experienced teachers can usually come up with the right question at the right time; beginners often have more difficulty. You will find it most useful to incorporate several key questions in your lesson plans. These should include not only major content questions, but also questions that will raise the level of discussion and involve more students.

DIRECTED LEARNING AS AN APPLICATION OF BEHAVIORISM

Recall now our discussion in chapter 2 of behaviorist and gestalt psychology. Laboratory learning and discovery learning have obvious gestalt aspects, while directed learning leans more heavily toward the incremental aspects of behaviorism. This means that teachers should attempt to break down the directed learning process into manageable steps.

Consider in this regard teaching the long division algorithm. Your students can compute the quotient for exercises like 3,105 $\div$ 7 and now must turn to divisors with two or more digits. They are faced now with one of the most complicated algorithms in their elementary school program.

To attack it directly without breaking the problem into reasonable learning steps would mean losing all but a few of the best students. Your question then is how to organize a program in logical sequence to take the students up a gentler slope.

You must ask yourself where the difficulties lie in moving from the left example to the right:

```
     443 R4           171 R13
  7)3105           27)4630
    28                27
     30               193
     28               189
      25                40
      21                27
       4                13
```

Analysis suggests that the difficulty relates to multiplication. Students know the multiplication facts for single digits, so they can readily produce the quotient figures on the left. They do not know the products for the factor 27. Why not at first provide those products? Then the students will see that the two processes are exactly the same. Write on the chalkboard:

```
  27     27     27     27     27     27     27     27     27
 × 1    × 2    × 3    × 4    × 5    × 6    × 7    × 8    × 9

   27)4630    27)10085    27)24652    27)993004
```

First work out the products together and then turn to the division exercises. Now the division exercises are very similar to the familiar exercises with one-digit divisors. Students can see that the process is the same before they turn to the next step of estimating partial quotients.

It is this kind of careful rethinking of the learning steps that led B. F. Skinner to suggest that classroom instruction is very much like step-by-step programmed instruction. Thus the teacher breaks each learning task down into small steps, each of which is mastered en route to criterion task mastery. Perhaps, but this comparison falls far short. Classroom instruction can go far beyond programmed instruction as a result of the teacher's ability to modify a route at any time. In addition, programmed instruction fails to account for student initiative and intuition.

EXERCISES

1. Use an elementary school textbook series and associated teachers' manuals to trace the following developments:[7]
   - (a) Addition in grade one
   - (b) Multiplication in grade three
   - (c) Division in grade five
   - (d) Addition and subtraction of fractions in grade six
   - (e) Percent in grade seven or eight

2. Compare one of the developments in exercise 1 to the same development in a different text for the same grade. Note both similarities and differences.

3. Choose one of the topics of exercise 1 and plan the following lessons:
   - (a) An introductory lesson
   - (b) A lesson that would be taught about midway through the unit
   - (c) A concluding lesson

   Include in your plans, your objectives, a sequence of content, and some key questions and examples.

4. Prepare a summative examination on the topic of exercise 3.

5. Compare your exam of exercise 4 with the objective hierarchy on pages 226–227. If you have not already done so, devise questions that respond to each level of this taxonomy.

6. Briefly describe what you feel are the major differences between discovery teaching and directed learning.

7. How can discovery teaching be used to support directed learning?

8. Which step in Bloom's *Taxonomy of Educational Objectives* do you find to be the most important? Discuss your answer.

9. Examine carefully a text for your chosen grade level in order to determine:
   - (a) The major new algorithms taught
   - (b) The sequence of steps in developing one of the algorithms
   - (c) Key steps and stumbling blocks in (b)
   - (d) Modifications you would make in your teaching program to respond to (c)

---

[7]Note: The developments may be extended over several parts of the books.

CHAPTER NINE

TEACHING APPLICATIONS AND PROBLEM SOLVING

MATHEMATICS AND THE REAL WORLD

Today many mathematicians, especially those who consider themselves pure (as opposed to applied) mathematicians, consider their subject completely abstract and divorced from the real world. Based on the following figure, they would consider their work to be associated only with the upper rectangle, not with the lower one.

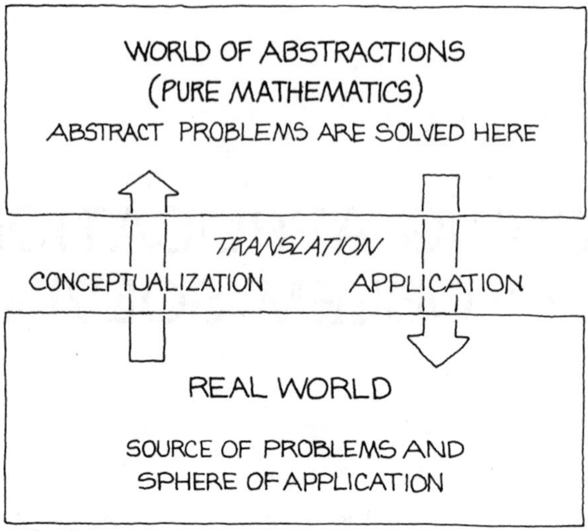

At the most elementary level we could have the following example:

Real World Problem: We see 3 cows and 2 horses in a field and wonder how many animals there are in all.

Conceptualization: $3 + 2 =$ ____.

Abstract Solution (pure mathematics): $3 + 2 = 5$.

Application: There are 5 animals in the field.

While the example leaves much to be desired, it does suggest the limitation of pure mathematics to dealing with the *abstract* concepts of numbers (arithmetic and algebra) and space (geometry).

Most people—and indeed most mathematicians—do not view mathematics in this narrow sense. They see mathematics as including the entire cycle of problem solving.[1]

[1]It should be noted that a great deal of mathematics development and proof does indeed take place almost exclusively at the abstract level. Our discussion here is concerned specifically with the problem-solving aspects of mathematics.

1. Defining significant problems in the real world

2. Data collection (when necessary)

3. Conceptualization

4. Solution of the abstract problem

5. Application to the original problem

6. Extension to other problems

One of the fairest criticisms of the new math of the 1960s is that it reflected too strongly the pure math point of view, thus isolating mathematics from both its source and its application in the world around us. We need not review further this intramural argument among mathematicians; we should instead draw from it an understanding of some of the processes involved in problem solving.

Exercises in school mathematics often lack significant aspects of real life problems. Specifically they often ignore:

Developing the problem from a real situation

Abstracting from the problem the part that is amenable to attack

Collecting data

Sorting applicable data from information that does not relate to the defined problem

---

Judging the reasonableness of the solution

Making decisions on the basis of the solution

Exploring related problems and extending the solution

Generalizing the solution

Generating related problems

It is clear that standard textbook problems touch only on the points at the middle of this list. The laboratory method of teaching responds to much of the first part of this list. Other activities should be developed to respond to the last part.

TRANSLATION: A CENTRAL ASPECT OF PROBLEM SOLVING

On the diagram at the beginning of this chapter a feature that may have been overlooked is the nature of the transition between the real and the conceptual worlds. That transition is accomplished by translation. In other words, the original problem appears in essentially nonmathematical form. In a textbook word problem, for example, the student is given an informative paragraph followed by a question. He must translate that English statement into a mathematical statement. And after he manipulates the mathematical statement, he must translate his result back into English. Although the latter part of the solution raises some problems and should be considered, we focus here on the former part.[2]

The process of translation is a familiar one to teachers and students of foreign languages:

English	*French*	*Spanish*	*German*	*logic*	*mathematics*
and	*et*	*y* or *e*	*und*	$\wedge$	$+$

There are, however, two important differences between verbal and mathematical translations, one of which works in favor of mathematics and one against:

1. There are far fewer translations to be made in mathematics because there are fewer symbols.

2. Translation into mathematics is far from word-for-word.

---

[2]See exercises 1 and 2 on page 265.

The first point simplifies our memory problem, but the second can lead to difficulties. For example, consider the difference between:

Mary *and* John bought two marbles.	2
Mary bought two marbles *and* John three.	2 + 3

Whereas translated into French, Spanish, or German, the *and* would be the same in both phrases, in mathematics it plays a tangential role in the first but a central role in the second. Of course the matter is not even that simple:

Mary bought two marbles while John bought three.	2 + 3
Mary bought two marbles, John three.	2 + 3
Mary and John bought two marbles each.	2 + 2 (or 2 × 2)

There is some value in comparing translation from English into mathematical statements with translation from English into a foreign language. But serious differences should be recognized. To go much beyond this table would not be of much assistance to students.

English	*mathematics*
and	+
is	=
of	×

(Note that "is" refers to any form of the verb *to be:* was, should be, and so on.)

There is one other important lesson that mathematics teachers have only recently learned from teachers of foreign languages. That is the idea that translation is a two-way process, each direction reinforcing the other.

English ⟷ *French*

English ⟷ *mathematics*

Just as translating from French into English helps us to translate English into French, so too translating mathematical statements into English statements can help students to translate English statements into mathematical statements. Students should be encouraged to make up stories that relate to the following kinds of mathematical statements:

$$2 + 3 = 5 \qquad 3 \times 5 = 15 \qquad 3\overline{)10}^{\;3\ R1} \qquad (5 \times 7) + 3 = 38$$

as well as

$$2 + 3 = \_\_\_\_ \qquad 3 \times 5 = \_\_\_\_ \qquad 3\overline{)10} \qquad (5 \times 7) + \_\_\_\_ = 38$$

Teachers who have used this technique are usually surprised and delighted with the results. Their students make up remarkable stories showing real creativity, suggesting how important the provision for alternative ways of thinking may be for students. But their diverse stories should make clear another important difference between translation to a foreign language and translation to a mathematical statement. Any mathematical statement represents the basic structure for an infinite number of possible verbal statements. Translating from verbal language to mathematics then is what mathematicians call a *many-one relation.*[3]

Some authors have suggested a nice way to use these ideas in the classroom. They suggest that students write news stories that go with headlines, such as the above equations. Similarly, students are asked to write the headlines for news stories, thus leading them to the heart of the matter. Here are a few examples from children for the headline $2 + 3 = 5$.

> *The two brothers went to visit their three cousins on the farm. The five children played with the animals there.*

---

[3]We do not intend to make an issue here of whether this statement is universally true, that is, that a given sentence could be translated to either $2 + 3 = x$ or $2 = x - 3$. We feel that argument is unnecessary, so in this context we will consider the two equations equivalent.

Billy had two marbles. He won three more playing hi-dobs. Then he had five.

The two astronauts landed on Mars. They found three Martians there. That made five people.

The range of answers from youngsters is constantly being extended in surprising directions by travel and television.

THE SEPARATION OF TRANSLATION AND COMPUTATION

Until about twenty years ago students attacked word problems directly. For example, given the word problem:

Seven boys each had 34 marbles and an eighth had 57. How many marbles did they have in all?

students would be expected to set up the problem:

$$\begin{array}{r} 34 \\ \times\ 7 \\ \hline 238 \end{array} \qquad \begin{array}{r} 238 \\ +\ 57 \\ \hline 295 \end{array} \text{ answer}$$

There is a basic difficulty with this. The student must either completely internalize the problem statement or move back and forth several times between computation and statement. As a response to this, the so-called equation method was introduced to the elementary school. The idea is to separate translation from computation. To solve the same problem now, a student would first write:

$$(7 \times 34) + 57 = x$$

Carrying out the computations to simplify the equation, the work might appear like this:

$$(7 \times 34) + 57 = x \qquad \begin{array}{r} 34 \\ \times\ 7 \\ \hline 238 \end{array} \qquad \begin{array}{r} 238 \\ +\ 57 \\ \hline 295 \end{array}$$

$$238 + 57 = x$$

$$295 = x$$

Answer: 295 marbles

The value of this separation process should be evident. Reading continues to be a serious problem for all students (more of this in the next section), so steps like these that help students to organize their thinking in systematic ways should not only improve their mathematics but may also help their reading. At the same time, this equation method lays important groundwork for solving more complex problems by the same technique in secondary school and college.

PROBLEM SOLVING AND THE CALCULATOR

A specific aspect of problem solving that should be explored by classroom teachers of all grades is the use of calculators to carry out computations. We believe that all students should continue to learn computational algorithms. The mathematical understanding embedded in the process will continue to justify teaching them. But we must teach problem solving too, since it is far more important. Outside of school today it is the rare student who does not have access to a calculator (or cash register). Students will need to know what to do with the calculator to solve their problems.

Use of the calculator in school allows introduction of more complex problems much earlier. Consider, for example, the following possibility. A first-grade class has learned what addition is about early in the school year. Now, without waiting for the long process of learning the sums, the children attack rather complex problems. They add shopping lists. They find the total weight of their entire class. In the process they:

Solve realistic problems

Have more opportunity to read large numbers and in the process learn about place value

Meet decimals in the natural setting of prices

Become interested in how the process works, and thus motivated to learn the algorithms

The same kind of argument may be made for topics at higher grade levels.

But there is a much more important reason for using the calculator. Many students lose their way in problems, forgetting the path to be followed as they carry out calculations. This is often the source of those wildly incongruous answers that students come up with, such as 3 seconds to walk a mile or a man 278 years old. By eliminating the conceptual detour into calculations, the calculator allows the students to focus on the problem itself. This can make two-, three-, or four-step problems accessible to the middle grades. Here, for example, is the kind of exercise that fourth- or fifth-grade students can answer once they have met the concept of average.

EXAMPLE

During the first semester Jerry received test grades of 76, 95, 82, and 87. During the second semester his test results were 88, 98, 77, 91, and 93. How much better was his test average the second semester?

Without a calculator many students would find Jerry's first semester average and fail to continue; with the calculator they are better able to command the entire problem. The ability at all grade levels to process problems of higher complexity is a valid goal to which the calculator responds in a useful way.

READING VERSUS MATHEMATICS

Studies of elementary school students have shown that there is a high correlation between reading achievement and problem-solving ability in mathematics. Students certainly cannot solve the problems if they can't read them.[4] What are some possible responses to the problems this correlation imposes? One response, which was discussed in preceding sections, is to work on reading skills, especially those relating to problem solving. But another less obvious response is to try to separate the mathematics from reading.

We seek to cut down the reading necessary to solve some problems. There are several ways to do it. One method is to present the problems orally. (For individuals this can be done using tape cassettes. See chapter 11.) Another method is to present problems with concrete objects (laboratory teaching) or in pictorial form. Consider two presentations of the same problem:

PROBLEM Four boxes, each weighing the same amount, are placed together on a scale. The scale registers 76 grams. How much does each box weigh?

PROBLEM

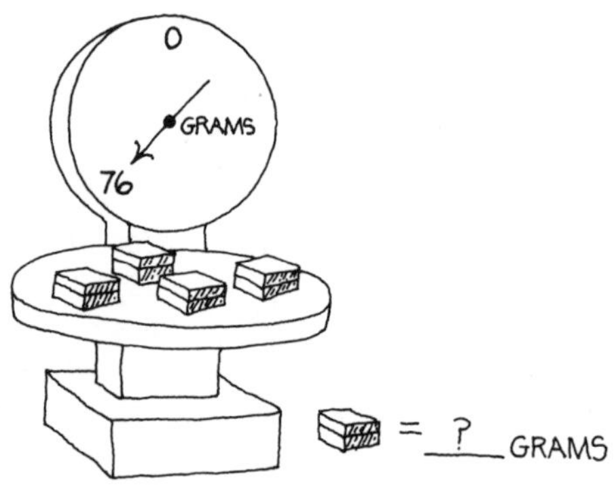

---

[4]There is a second factor operating as well, which statisticians call the law of regression. That law would predict a positive correlation, but it is not of interest in this discussion. We will comment further on this law in chapter 10.

The pictorial representation reduces the number of words from twenty-three to two. Here is a case where a picture is worth, if not a thousand, at least twenty-one, words. Note that in the pictorial representation students are forced to make an assumption, possibly unwarranted, that all the boxes weigh the same. This is a typical kind of problem that this procedure introduces.

Teachers should not misunderstand or misapply the point here. It is important that students learn to solve problems expressed in words on a page, and teachers should continue to address this pedagogical problem.[5] But at the same time they should also seek ways to give students with weak reading skills a chance to perform the mathematical aspects of problem solving.

PROBLEM SOLVING AND LOCAL RESOURCES

How are problems presented to us outside of school? Certainly they are not often stated in words on a page. More often they are presented in symbolic or concrete form. Whenever possible, these should be brought into the classroom so that students can see the application of their work. Consider here two third-grade activities:

1. The teacher has distributed order blanks obtained from a local short-order restaurant at which many students have eaten. Students are invited to choose their own meals. Then, the teacher asks them to calculate the cost of the meal. (The teacher may discuss the tax as an enrichment activity.)

2. Another teacher has obtained a number of state road maps from a local filling station. The maps have already played a useful role in social studies. Now, the students are invited to design trips of their choice to various parts of the state and to determine total mileage.

Although these two examples impose on local merchants, they produce a kind of contact that is important to students.

---

[5]An argument could be made that this is more important to reading than to mathematics, but that kind of argument is not productive; both are very important.

A more extensive problem-solving activity that also has social studies connotations is a market survey. Fifth- or sixth-grade students can devise a "market basket" list of groceries and then check the cost of that market basket in several local stores. This kind of activity should be carefully handled so that students make true comparisons of brand, size, and quality of items. The teacher may wish to generate the list in a class discussion, have a team of students check stores for specific items, and, based on their results, make a mimeographed list of specifics for other teams to price. Finally, if the project is undertaken early in the school year, the results can be retained for comparison with a later survey. Price increases can be compared with reported national trends.

STUDENT-GENERATED PROBLEMS

We have mentioned the value of having students devise word problems to fit given equations. This technique may be used in any problem-solving setting. Students are directed to make up a more interesting problem that will involve similar computations. Given this instruction students usually devise not only interesting but often quite challenging exercises. By collecting the student-generated problems and constructing an assignment from the most interesting ones, the teacher can not only provide more practice but also reward creative students. Some teachers list names with the exercises:

3. Theresa's problem. Three dolls have four skirts each. . . .

Another way to generate problems is to distribute old newspapers to the class, asking students to cut out articles or advertisements that suggest problems of the type being discussed. This technique is especially useful in the sixth and other grades when percent is the topic, but it also applies to activities at all levels.

DIMENSIONAL ANALYSIS

Several decades ago an acrimonious debate was aired in mathematics and science teaching journals about the use of labels in mathematical equations. Scientists promoted the use of labels, while the purists among the mathematicians threw up their hands in shock. But the matter is essentially settled today, as a full mathematical basis has been provided by Hassler Whitney, a mathematician with the Institute for Advanced Study at Princeton.[6] All the advantages of dimensional analysis for checking labels and procedures are available to teachers of both science and mathematics.

Here are some examples of dimensional analysis in use:

$$2 \text{ cows} + 3 \text{ cows} = (2 + 3) \text{ cows} = 5 \text{ cows}$$

$$2.5 \text{ m} = 2.5 \text{ m} \times 1 = 2.5 \not{\text{m}} \times \frac{100 \text{ cm}}{1 \not{\text{m}}} = 250 \text{ cm}$$

$$30 \text{ mph.} \times 4 \text{ hr.} = 30 \frac{\text{mi.}}{\not{\text{hr}}.} \times 4 \not{\text{hr}}. = 120 \text{ mi.}$$

The volume of an 8 foot long 2″ × 4″ board:

$$8 \text{ ft.} \times 2 \text{ in.} \times 4 \text{ in.} = 48 \text{ ft. in.}^2$$

but since ft. in.^{2} is not a standard unit, 48 ft. in.^{2} may be converted to in.^{3} (cubic inches) or ft.^{3} (cubic feet) as follows:

$$48 \text{ ft. in.}^2 = 48 \not{\text{ft}}. \text{ in.}^2 \times \frac{12 \text{ in.}}{1 \not{\text{ft}}.} = 576 \text{ in.}^3$$

$$48 \text{ ft. in.}^2 = \overset{4}{\cancel{48}} \text{ ft. } \cancel{\text{in.}^2} \times \frac{1 \text{ ft.}}{\cancel{12} \cancel{\text{in.}}} \times \frac{1 \text{ ft.}}{12 \cancel{\text{in.}}} = \frac{4}{12} \text{ ft.}^3 = \frac{1}{3} \text{ ft.}^3$$

The basic idea of dimensional analysis is that labels cancel and otherwise operate by the same rules as numbers. In any measurement problem, units can always be determined by this means, in this way giving the students

[6]See Hassler Whitney, "The Mathematics of Physical Quantities," *American Mathematical Monthly* 75(1968): 115–38, 227–56.

a check on their work as well as the correct label in their answers. Note that when units are to be converted, a unit multiplier is always used. Thus both

$$\frac{12 \text{ in.}}{1 \text{ ft.}} \quad \text{and} \quad \frac{1 \text{ ft.}}{12 \text{ in.}}$$

equal one, since numerator and denominator are equal measures. Multiplying by such a fraction does not change the measure; it merely changes the type of unit.

Another benefit of dimensional analysis is its reduction of memory load. For example, students need only remember the first of each of the following groups:

12 in. = 1 ft.	3 ft. = 1 yd.	10 mm = 1 cm
144 in.^{2} = 1 ft.^{2}	9 ft.^{2} = 1 yd.^{2}	100 mm^2 = 1 cm^2
1728 in.^{3} = 1 ft.^{3}	27 ft.^{3} = 1 yd.^{3}	1000 mm^3 = 1 cm^3

The second entry is found merely by squaring the first, the third by cubing the first.

CREATIVE PROBLEM SOLVING

Until now in this chapter we have discussed standard textbook word problems and modifications of those problems. It is important that all students be challenged to go beyond these problems to tackle interesting and unique exercises. Problem solving should overlap with discovery, since both have a gestalt character. But there is another aspect of creative problems that you should consider. Bright students become especially bored with routine textbook problems. You will find some students whose interest rises remarkably when an element of contest is part of problem solving. A student who is now a teacher told one author that the challenge problems in his elementary school classes were responsible for his initial interest in mathematics.

Learning to solve problems is a key activity for the elementary school student. Too often we hear the lament: I can do the computations, but I can't solve the problems. We must be concerned about the students' ability to function *outside* the mathematics classroom, where no one can tell them which operations to perform. Continuing attention must be paid to problem solving. As George Polya, the famous mathematician and writer about problem solving, has said, "The best way to teach students to become problem solvers is to have them solve many problems."[7]

LITERATURE AND MATHEMATICS

A rather different approach to mathematical applications is being utilized by Frederique Papy in the Comprehensive School Mathematics Program. (See Appendix C for the CSMP address.) This method was used earlier by Paul Rosenbloom in the MINNEMAST Program. We will reprint Rosenbloom's delightful story from that program here. This story has anthropological antecedents and illustrates how mathematics relies on primitive ideas *even more basic than counting.* Frederique Papy's stories are equally intriguing to children. They are based more on fantasy and involve anthropomorphizing numbers themselves; characters like "1" and "0" have central roles. Students are often encouraged by the stories to create things themselves.

Following is the Rosenbloom story. Teachers and parents know that this kind of charming story may be read over and over again to young children. You might sometimes want to tell the story presenting Ugboo as a little girl.

---

[7]Polya's little book, *How to Solve It* (New York: Doubleday, 1957), is well worth reading for ideas about solving creative problems.

UGBOO'S BIG PROBLEM

Paul C. Rosenbloom

HERE IS UGBOO.

Here is Ugboo. He lived a long, long time ago. This is the way he counted: "One—two—many." He did not know any other way to count more than two. At that time no one knew how to count more than two.

Ugboo had a job. He watched sheep. He watched the sheep of the whole tribe. Every morning he would let them out of the fold (sheep pen). He would take them to a grassy place. Ugboo had to watch the sheep while they ate grass. He had to keep his eyes open because the lions and the wolves liked to eat sheep. They would steal sheep and eat them if Ugboo wasn't looking. At night Ugboo would take the sheep home and put them into the fold again.

One evening when Ugboo came home with the sheep, the chief of the tribe met him. The chief's name was Zarathustra. In those days the chief of the tribe always had a long name to show that he was important. Zarathustra looked at the sheep. He said, "Are these all the sheep of the tribe? Don't you have more?"

Ugboo answered, "These are all the sheep of the tribe. They are the same sheep we had this morning."

Zarathustra said, "There don't seem to be as many sheep. Did you fall asleep today while you were supposed to be watching them? I think you did."

Ugboo began to cry. "I did *not* fall asleep. I kept my eyes open all the time."

Zarathustra was angry and shouted, "I think you fell asleep and a wolf or a lion stole some sheep. It looks as though there are fewer sheep than there were before. If you lose any more sheep, I will punish you, Ugboo! The tribe needs the sheep for wool, skin, and meat." Then the chief went away.

Ugboo was very sad. He said to himself, "How can I be sure that there are as many sheep now as there were before? How can I show big chief Zarathustra that I did not lose any sheep? There were many sheep before and there are many sheep now. How can I, or anyone else, tell the difference between many sheep and many sheep?"

Ugboo was afraid of Zarathustra. The chief was the biggest and strongest man in the tribe. All the others were afraid of him, too. Ugboo did not want Zarathustra to punish him.

Ugboo thought and thought. He thought all evening about his problem. At supper his mother said, "Ugboo, why are you so quiet? On other nights you chatter all the time."

"I am thinking," Ugboo answered. Then he told his mother about his problem.

She said, "You are wasting your time. Everybody says, 'one—two—many,' and that's all there is. More than two is many. But now let's stop and eat. Here's a stone knife and a big piece of deer meat. Cut off a small piece for each of your brothers and sisters."

Ugboo did as his mother told him. He began to cut the meat and said, at the same time, "One piece for brother Nip, one for sister Snip, one for sister Snap, and one for little Norum." Then he carried the meat to the other children and gave one piece to each one. He gave himself a piece, too.

While they were eating, Ugboo said to himself, "One piece of meat for each child, one child for each piece of meat. No children left over. No pieces left over. There are just as many pieces of meat as children and just as many children as pieces of meat."

Suddenly he felt as though a light had lit up in his head. He felt as though he had been in the dark until now.

He jumped up and yelled, "I've got it! I've got it!"

His mother asked, "What have you got? A stomach ache?"

Ugboo said happily, "I know how to find out whether there are fewer sheep at night than in the morning. I know! I know!"

What answer do you think Ugboo found to his problem?

Let the children make suggestions.

As soon as Ugboo woke the next morning, he went to the edge of the lake near his cave. He took with him a sheepskin bag which his mother had made for him. He began looking for

I THINK YOU FELL ASLEEP AND A WOLF OR A LION STOLE SOME SHEEP.

little stones and pebbles on the shore. He picked up every one he found, and put it in his bag. When the bag was full, he threw it over his shoulder and carried it to the sheep fold. He emptied the bag on the ground, and then let the sheep out of the fold, one at a time.

As each sheep left the fold, Ugboo put one pebble in the bag. Then he led the sheep to the big chief, Zarathustra.

"What do you want?" growled the chief.

"I want to give you this bag of stones," said Ugboo. "There is one stone in this bag for each sheep in the flock and one sheep for each stone. There are just as many stones as sheep. You can see for yourself."

The chief went back with Ugboo and began pairing the stones with the sheep. Sure enough, there was one stone for each sheep and one sheep for each stone.

Zarathustra muttered to himself. "Let's go over this again very slowly. I want to be sure—really, really sure I understand this. Let me see. If there is one stone for each sheep, then there are at least as many stones as sheep."

AS EACH SHEEP LEFT THE FOLD, UGBOO PUT ONE PEBBLE IN THE BAG.

He sat down and wiped the sweat from his forehead. He said to Ugboo, "This thinking business is hard work. I'm tired already—I had better rest awhile."

After a few minutes he said, "Where was I? Oh, yes. There are at least as many stones as sheep. But there might be more stones than sheep. We might have one stone for each sheep, and still have some stones left over. Let us look. Are there any stones left over?"

Zarathustra started to look to see whether there were any stones left over. Ugboo reminded him, "Don't you remember, chief? There is one sheep for each stone. So there can't be any stones left over."

Zarathustra was puzzled. He wrinkled his eyebrows and thought. He thought very, very hard. Suddenly he began to smile.

"That's right!" he said. "That's absolutely, positively right! It is hard to think of all these things at one time. But once you do put it all together, it is really easy to see. Since there is one stone for each sheep, there are at least as many stones as sheep. Since there is one sheep for each stone, there are at least as many sheep as stones. As many stones as sheep . . . as many sheep as stones . . ." He looked from the stones to the sheep, to the stones, to the sheep, thinking.

Suddenly he pounded one fist into the palm of his other hand and shouted, "Of course! There are just as many stones as sheep!"

THIS THINKING BUSINESS IS HARD WORK.

Then he turned to the boy and asked, "What of it? Why are you taking up my whole morning with all this stuff? Why haven't you taken the sheep out to the grassy place yet? They must be hungry already."

Ugboo answered, "Don't you see? When I bring the sheep home tonight, you can pair the stones with the sheep again. You can put down one stone for each of the sheep. If there are no stones left over, then you will know that I have brought back all the sheep. If there are some stones left over, you will know that I have lost some sheep, and you can punish me."

Zarathustra said, "How is that again? If there are some stones left over, then . . . Let me think it over . . . Oh, don't bother me any more! Go tend your sheep right now, or I won't wait until tonight to punish you. Get going. Scoot! I have to go hunting. Do you think I have all day to talk to little boys?"

Then Zarathustra went hunting with some of his friends. During the hunt, he told the other men about what happened. "You know that boy, Ugboo? He came to me this morning with a long story about stones and sheep."

The chief began explaining to the men about one stone for each sheep and one sheep for each stone, but—wouldn't you know—he got it all mixed up! "I'm sure I understood it this morning," he said. "Now I am so dizzy, I am not sure of anything. Let's hunt now and talk about it at supper tonight."

That night the chief talked it over with all the other leaders in the tribe. They were sitting around the fire in a circle, each one eating a chunk of meat he held in his hand, and they were arguing.

Finally, the chief said, "Let's call Ugboo," and he pulled Ugboo into the circle of men. "Explain what you told me this morning, Ugboo," he said.

Ugboo began to tell, slowly and shyly, how he had cut up the meat for his brothers and sisters. "There was one piece of meat for each child and one child for each piece of meat," Ugboo began, "and none left over."

"We don't want to hear about that," the chief said. "Tell the men about the sheep and the stones!"

"Well, the meat gave me the idea," Ugboo said. "I thought if it would work for the children and the pieces of meat, I might be able to pair each sheep with something, too. Then I thought of the stones. I collected a lot of stones and put them in this bag my mother made for me. When I went to the sheep fold this morning, I dumped all the stones on the ground. Then, for every sheep that came out of the fold, I put one stone in the bag. There were just as many stones in the bag as there were sheep—one stone for one sheep.

"And tonight, when I brought the sheep back to the fold, I took a stone out of my bag each time a sheep went in the gate. When all the sheep were back in the fold, my bag was empty. There was exactly one stone for every sheep—just as there had been in the morning. There were no sheep left over and there were no stones left over. That's how I know I brought back just as many sheep tonight as I took out this morning."

When Ugboo finished, all the men were quiet for a while, thinking. Then they began to ask questions.

"Would this work with other things, too?" one of the men asked. "If there is one spear for each man, and one man for each spear, then are there just as many spears as men?"

Another man asked about people and noses. Another one asked about knives and bones.

At last Zarathustra said, "This is a wonderful discovery and I have thought of another way to use it. If we have two sets and want to know which one has more in it, all we have to do is pair one thing in the first set with one thing in the other. We keep on matching one for one. When we are done, if there are any left in one set, then we know that *that* set has more. If there is nothing left over in either set, then there are just as many in one set as in the other."

All the men agreed that this was a very good idea. One of the men said, "Ugboo is a very clever boy. We ought to do something for him." The others said, "Yes, he deserves a reward."

Then the big chief, Zarathustra, said to the boy, "We are going to give you a great honor. We are going to give you a name just as long as the big men have. Then everyone will know that you are a very important person. From now on, we will call you 'Uggabugaboo.'"

Uggabugaboo's mother and brothers and sisters all ran up to him and hugged and kissed him. His father patted him on the back and shook hands with him. No other boy in the whole tribe had ever had such an honor.

When he grew up, Uggabugaboo became a very big chief himself. Then he was called Uggabuggabuggabuggaboo. He was *really* important then.

Historical basis for the theme of *Ugboo's Big Problem* is to be found in a book by Richard Starr, *Nuzi: Report of the Excavations at Yorgan Tepa, near Kirkik, Iraq* (Harvard University Press, 1939). The report notes the finding of "a large number of inscribed clay texts, one of which was the extraordinary tablet of 'Zikarri the shepherd.'" Roughly egg-shaped and hollow, with a hole at its pointed end, it bears the inscription "stones of the sheep" followed by a list of animals given to "Zikarri the shepherd," presumably for grazing. Inside the tablet were forty-nine pebbles.

FLOWCHARTS

At the beginning of this chapter we suggested that our school view of problem solving and applications was too narrow. A useful tool to broaden that view is the flowchart. Flowcharts are often associated with computers, since their use was motivated by computer programming. But their value is more extensive. Flowcharts provide a visual tool to regularize any procedure, in effect to turn a procedure into an algorithm. Even young children view them as tools to explain tasks to still younger brothers and sisters.

As an illustration of this, consider the following nonmathematical flowchart produced by a fifth-grade student for using the telephone to call a friend.

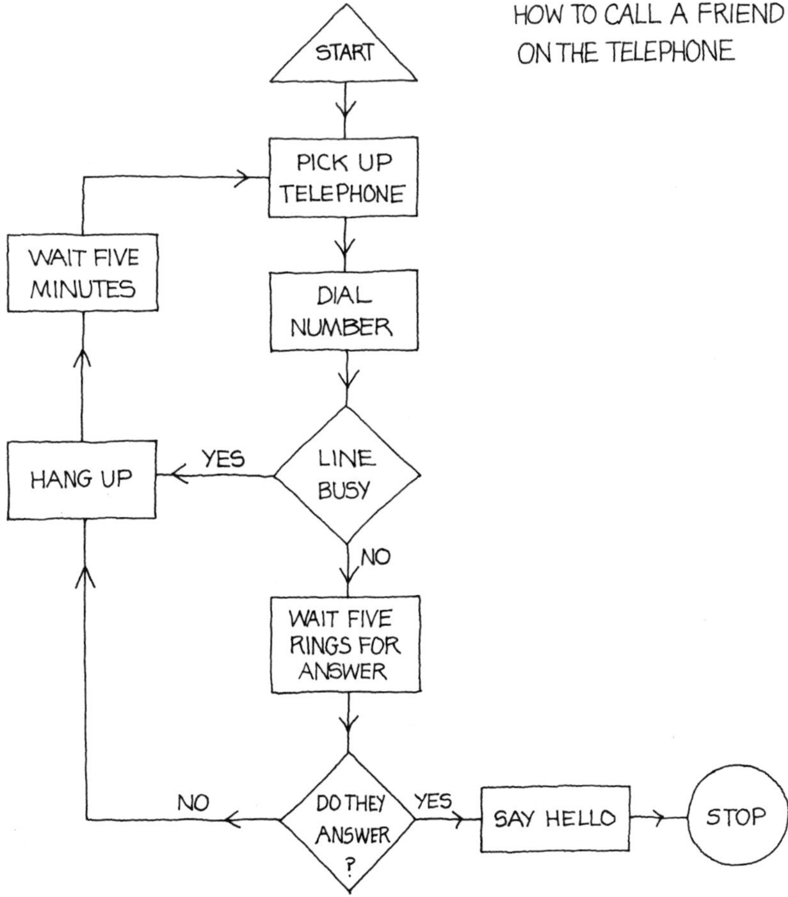

How is this tool applied? As mathematics becomes increasingly complex, it is important to be able to translate the procedures for their solution into easily followed steps. This is as important to a nonmathematical assistant as it is to a computer. It is for this reason that many applied mathematicians say that a problem is never really solved until the solution process is regularized in a flowchart or computer program. In this section we briefly introduce this tool and suggest some of its uses in problem solving and elsewhere in the mathematics curriculum.

Here are some flowchart symbols and the parts of the process they represent. You can see them in use in the telephone example.

The triangle is the entry point, the starting point of the problem.

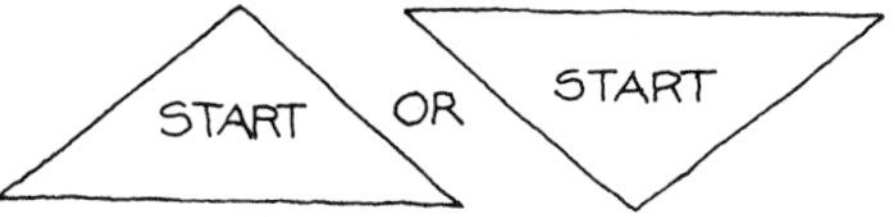

The rectangle is a process box where all the processes will be performed (mathematical or otherwise).

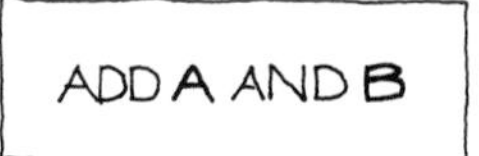

Another box based on the rectangle is a rectangle with a curved bottom. This box is used when one is told to "output," which means to write an answer or a result.

The diamond is where decisions are made. A yes-or-no answer is always required. The answer determines which arrow to follow.

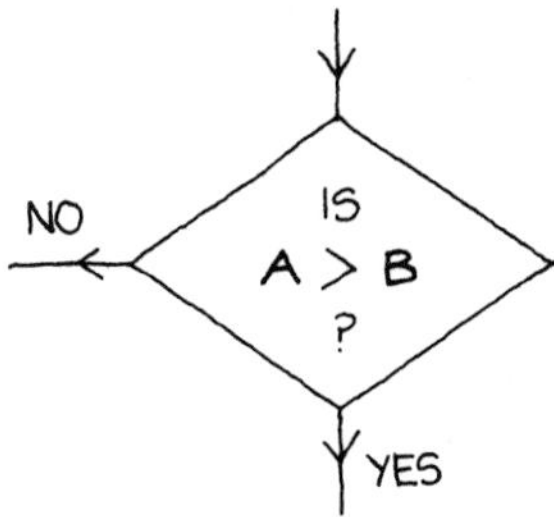

The circle is the exit or stopping point.

These different figures are connected with arrows. The only symbol type on this list that may cause problems is the diamond or branching symbol. Illustrations of both mathematical and nonmathematical flowcharts will further demonstrate the importance of this aspect.

TO WATCH TELEVISION

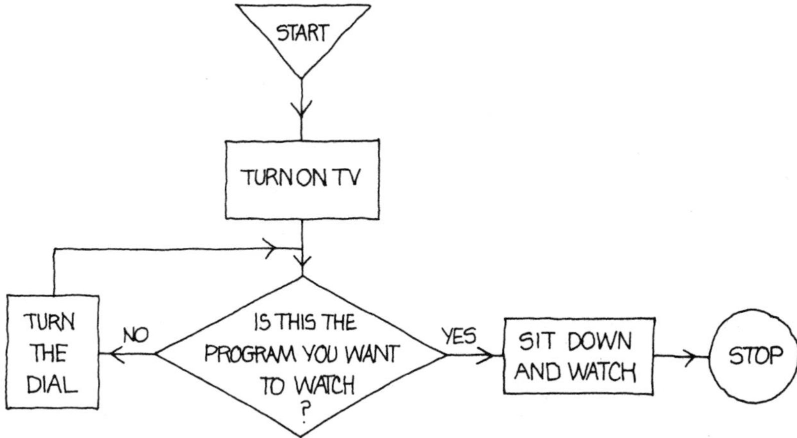

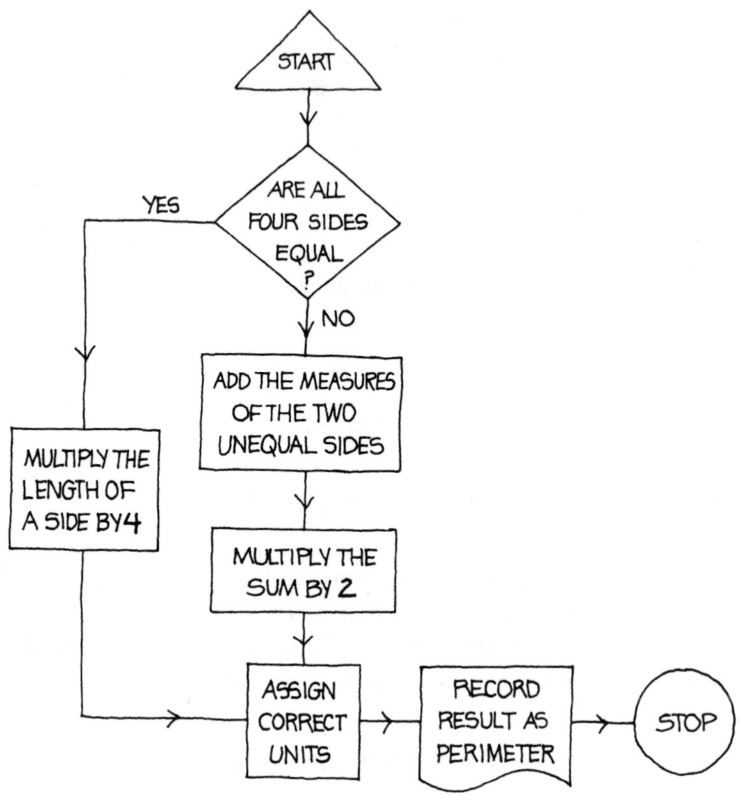

Some additional nonmathematical examples are:

1. Sharpening a pencil
2. Tuning a radio to a favorite station
3. Calling a friend long distance
4. Getting to class in the morning
5. Washing dishes after dinner

6. Returning a book to the library

7. Changing a flat tire

8. Giving a dog a bath

9. Washing hair

10. Putting shoes and socks on in the morning

11. Buying a new jacket

12. Choosing a television program

13. Having a tooth pulled

14. Returning home from vacation

15. Making your bed

16. Eating an orange

17. Starting a car in the winter

18. Making a tape recording

19. Making a peanut butter and jelly sandwich

20. Catching a fish

A useful way to attack a programming problem is to brainstorm a list of steps related to an activity, initially ignoring the order. Later these steps can be compressed and reduced to the essentials of the process.

Important note: Once a mathematical flowchart is constructed, it is necessary to have students test their programs by running several numbers (data) through the program. This activity helps to turn up flaws in the flowchart, and allows the student programmers to "debug" their programs.

Here is another program:

TO FIND THE GREATEST COMMON DIVISOR (GCD)

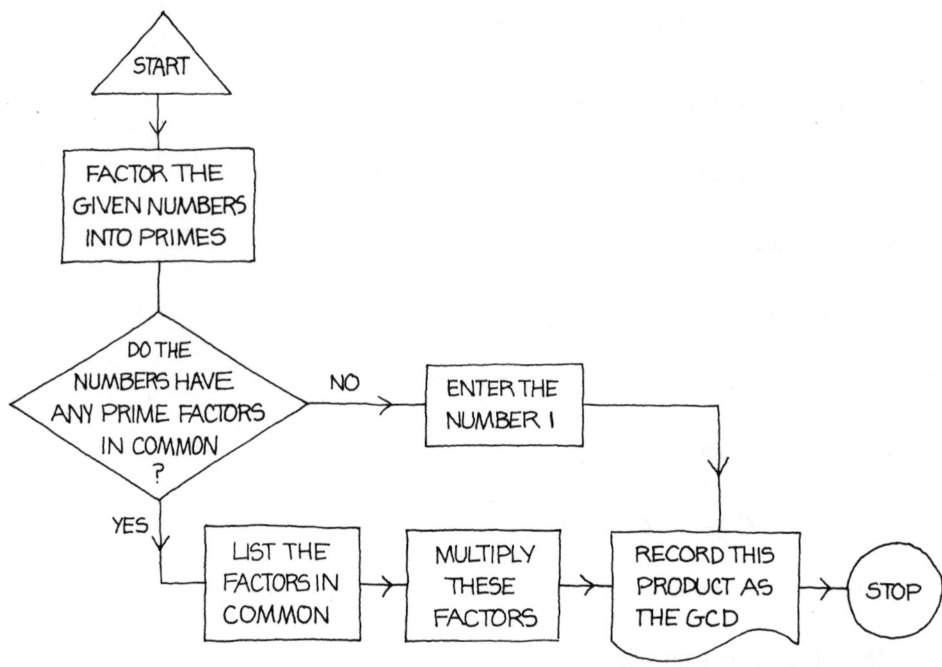

These examples will suggest that besides providing a tool for regularizing the processes involved in problem solving (as in finding the area of a rectangle) the flowchart is also useful for recording the steps in a mathematical procedure. Some examples that invite programming are:

1. Adding two numbers of two digits each
2. Reducing a fraction to lowest terms
3. Subtracting two two-digit numbers
4. Multiplying two two-digit numbers
5. Changing a decimal to a common fraction (and vice-versa)
6. Multiplying two fractions
7. Dividing a four-digit number by a two-digit number

In fact, any common arithmetic procedure lends itself to this approach.

EXERCISES

1. A common difficulty in classroom problem solving is failure to translate a correct mathematical solution back into a response to the original question. How would you respond to this difficulty?

2. Too often students fail to notice obviously inappropriate answers. For example, a student may answer $564 instead of $5.64 for a grocery bill, and not be struck by the fact that the answer is unreasonable. (Hopefully that answer will still be unreasonable when this book is published.) Discuss what you believe is the difficulty and suggest some techniques to attack this pedagogical problem.

3. Make up a word problem for each of the following equations. Exercise your creativity here; try to be as exotic and freewheeling as possible:

(a) $13 + 12 = 25$

(b) $7\overline{)32}$ with quotient 4 R4

(c) $7\overline{)32}$ with quotient $4\frac{4}{7}$

(d) $13 + 7x = 34$

(e) $x^2 + 5x = 36$ (x^2 means x times x)

4. Do you think you could use some of your answers to exercise 3 as word problems in an elementary school classroom? Why or why not?

5. Find two problems expressed in words in an elementary school text. Present those same two problems by means of pictures, reducing some but not necessarily all of the vocabulary load. How many words did you save? Did you lose anything in the process?

6. Look up in an upper-grade mathematics text five problems involving measurement units. Try to include several different types, such as ratios, percent, area, and store purchases. Use dimensional analysis in solving these problems.

7. Try to solve the following: In olden times movies were cheap: adults paid 10¢, teen-agers, 4¢, and children twelve and under entered at 10 for a penny. If a hundred people attended a show for a dollar, how many of each—adults, teen-agers, and children—were there?

8. Describe your experience working on the problem of exercise 7. Include in your discussion what you found out about the problem and about yourself.

9. Is the problem of exercise 7 an appropriate challenge for sixth-grade youngsters? Why or why not?

10. Test the mathematical flowcharts used as examples in this chapter by running data (numbers) through them. Where you encounter problems try to debug the program by adding steps.

11. Write a flowchart for one of the examples on page 264 appropriate to your grade interest. Test your program and debug it.

12. Obtain a "four-banger," a hand-held calculator that carries out the four basic operations (+, −, ×, ÷). Learn to calculate with it. Use it to calculate answers to a variety of exercises in a text for the grade level of your interest. Which exercises are simpler with a calculator? For which exercises is the calculator not suited? Why? (If you find none in the latter group, try your calculator on some of the exercises in chapters 1, 3, and 7 in this text.)

13. Review a text at your grade interest to locate five places where you could use a calculator to supplement the text and five places where you think the calculator would be of no use or even a disadvantage.

PART 4

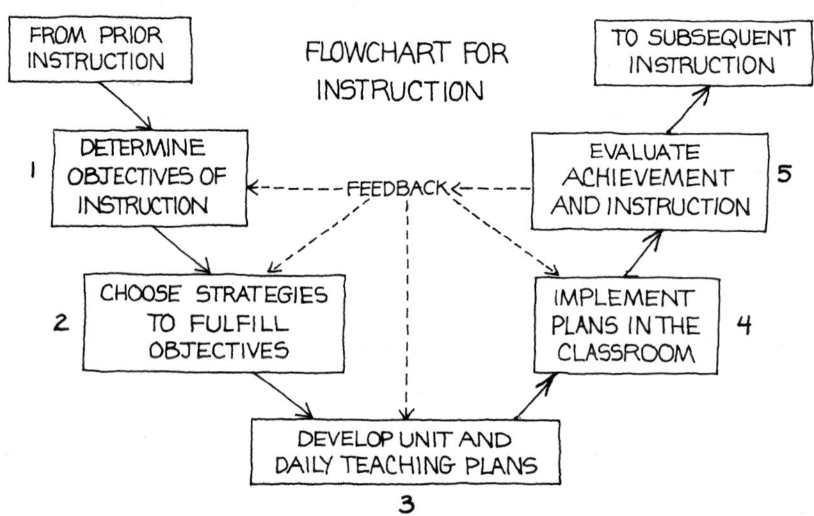
FROM PRIOR INSTRUCTION
FLOWCHART FOR INSTRUCTION
TO SUBSEQUENT INSTRUCTION
1
DETERMINE OBJECTIVES OF INSTRUCTION
FEEDBACK
EVALUATE ACHIEVEMENT AND INSTRUCTION
5
2
CHOOSE STRATEGIES TO FULFILL OBJECTIVES
IMPLEMENT PLANS IN THE CLASSROOM
4
DEVELOP UNIT AND DAILY TEACHING PLANS
3

CLASSROOM AND STUDENTS

In this final section we move from planning and organizing to the classroom itself. In chapter 10 we will seek ways of reaching each youngster in our charge, the weakest student as well as the strongest. We will then, in chapter 11, briefly review classroom materials and equipment available to mathematics teachers in most schools. In chapter 12 we will seek to place all that has gone before into the perspective of the individual teacher in a classroom situation. In this last chapter you will be encouraged to evaluate your own strengths and weaknesses in order to best fit what you have learned with your own personality. It is important for each person entering teaching to maintain and even strengthen his or her individuality. Teachers are not peas in a schoolhouse pod.

CHAPTER TEN

INDIVIDUAL DIFFERENCES IN THE CLASSROOM

THE CLASSROOM SETTING

Most teachers will deal with twenty to thirty-five students in their classrooms. In some ways those two or three dozen youngsters will be as alike as kernels on an ear of corn. They will all respond in predictable ways to the latest television idol and to other current fads and fashions, seemingly programmed directly into their nervous systems. They will tend to dress alike and to respond to you in established patterns. They will use the same pop vocabulary. Unless they change drastically from the time of this writing, their speech will abound with *you know* and *like,* and they will substitute the verb *go* for *say* as in "So I go, 'How are you doing, Sam?' and he goes, 'I'm okay.'"

But at the same time, each child will be unique. Each will have a distinct personality, positive and negative attributes, and personal problems brought into your classroom from home or from the playground. Second in priority only to planning and implementing your instructional program will be your responsibility to respond to your students as individuals; some would even place this first. In this text we limit our concern to curricular problems relating to mathematics, but we remind teachers that their concern should extend beyond subject matter. Your influence on youngsters with whom you have daily contact is so great that you should think deeply about how to respond to them.

Differences will not merely develop in your classroom; many will be brought there. Even kindergarten youngsters enter school that first autumn with widely differing backgrounds. In every grade there will be children (most often girls) who seem mature beyond their years, and there will be others (both boys and girls) who seem to be placed above the grade in which they belong. You must sort out these differences and respond to them in positive ways.

THE BASIC QUESTION: DO YOU WANT YOUR STUDENTS ALL ALIKE?

Do we want to try in our instruction to make students alike? This is a most important question, the answer to which too few teachers understand and apply. There is a great temptation to encourage all students to move forward together at an equal pace, learning together, achieving together. And of course curricula and textbooks are organized in just that way. In fact, group organization of the mathematics program is so widely imposed that it is reasonable to predict what topics a majority of students in this country will be working on in any given week of the school year.[1] For example:

First grade, fifteenth week: addition and subtraction sums to 6

---

[1]It should be noted here that we do not imply criticism. The social mobility of modern society, which leads to many student transfers is only one of many reasons supporting structured progress along similar curricular lines.

Second grade, twenty-second week: two-digit addition and subtraction

Fourth grade, thirtieth week: fractions

Sixth grade, thirty-seventh week: ratios and percent

It would seem from this that we would answer—or have answered for us—the question of this section in the affirmative. In fact, much nineteenth- and early twentieth-century teaching did indeed aim for this goal. For example, choral response, children chanting answers as a group, was one of the standard teaching techniques of those years.

But think about the problem carefully. We have a classroom full of unique individuals with differing abilities and differing backgrounds. (It is not inegalitarian to note that basic ability—IQ, if you will—varies markedly among individuals. To pose an extreme case, quite obviously a brain-injured child has less ability to achieve academically than a healthy youngster. The wide range of student abilities, whether inborn or a result of early environmental experiences, is apparent to any classroom teacher.) To expect these widely diverse children to achieve alike is nonsense. Compare in this regard a recent model car with a Model T Ford. Surely we would expect the modern, more powerful car to move to an early lead in a race. Even more importantly, we would expect the gap between the two cars to widen as the race continued.

This last is an essential point. You should expect the differences between "slower" and "faster" youngsters in your classroom to increase rather than decrease. Herein lies the error so often found in remedial programs: the expectation that such programs will help students to catch up with classmates of better ability. Such programs would do better to expect weaker students to move forward at a pace somewhat less than that of stronger students; to expect more is folly.

Beware of classroom settings in which individual differences are minimized. In such classrooms the teachers "teach to the middle," the average-ability students of the group. Meanwhile what happens to the half-dozen or more bright youngsters and the equal number of weak students? The first group is bored to tears. (Some teachers further contribute to this boredom by assigning such students extra routine problems, effectively encouraging them to keep their talents in low profile.) Meanwhile, the weaker students are floundering.

Our answer then to the question, "Should you seek to homogenize your students into a classroom of smooth consistency?" is a resounding no. Rather you should encourage all children to achieve to their full potential, to develop and grow not at their neighbor's pace but at their own. This does not rule out competition among students, but it stresses instead competition with oneself, the kind of competition that the lone runner faces when striding for the four-minute mile.

ACCOMMODATING DIFFERENCES TO THE COMMON CURRICULUM

Accepting the need to challenge all students to work to their full potential, how does a teacher respond to what is called by its critics the lock-step curriculum? A number of answers are worth considering.[2] We will examine two:

1. Allow students to progress at their own pace through the curriculum. We will refer to this as *total individualization.*

2. Keep the class together on units of work, but provide differential activities within each unit. We will refer to this as *enrichment* (for lack of a more specific designation).

The first of these two choices, total individualization, is one of the major educational fads of the 1970s. All across the country students are working alone on mathematics lessons in programs like IPI (Individually Prescribed Instruction) or PLAN (Planned Instruction According to Need). Although students do learn in such programs, we feel that the losses inherent in total individualization offset many of the gains. The key lies in the word *alone.* Interaction, testing one's ideas against those of the teacher or one's peers; development by other than worksheet; activities that range beyond the standard computation-oriented aspects of the curriculum—these are either lost or curtailed. In particular, the withdrawn student who needs, but does not seek, help is too often lost in this kind of program.

---

[2]In particular we consider here a self-contained classroom. Some larger schools group by ability, thus reducing the classroom range, but never, of course, eliminating it.

The achievement of students in such programs can best be described as mixed. As of this writing, no strong case can be made for the major individualized programs even when the basis for comparison with traditional instruction is computation, on which the individualized programs focus.

Turn then to the second approach, the one we quite frankly advocate. The class does not abandon the set curriculum; the work of the school year is still separated into ten or twelve major units. But within each unit there is wide diversity of program. Some specific aspects of the enrichment approach are:

1. The students all start all units together. Introductory work, with the full class, includes pretesting (to determine individual problems with prerequisite skills and concepts as well as prior familiarity with the content of the unit) and early exploratory and concrete-oriented lessons.

2. As the work moves ahead to more conceptual and abstract-oriented activities, the class begins to diverge. Weaker students are given more practice with basic concepts and may approach these basics in more than one way. They spend much longer on concrete activities. Meanwhile, stronger students are given the opportunity to explore related areas not in the basic program, to attack challenging problems, and to work on larger projects. They do not, however, move on to subsequent units.

3. Despite the differing programs, the full class continues to meet for some sessions throughout the instructional program. In particular all students take unit tests together.

4. At later stages of the unit program, student tutoring is arranged. Capable students at this time provide remedial assistance for students having difficulty.

5. Throughout the instruction program certain activities bring the whole class together. These activities may be outside the regular day-to-day work. Games, lab exercises, and enrichment problems taken from current events in school and the world are useful here. Such activities help all students to see themselves as part of the ongoing class group.

It should be immediately apparent that a great deal of work is involved in organizing such a program, something that is true of all quality teaching. Planning requires differentiation of activities and preparation of methods of identifying student problems (formative testing). But these tasks fall within a reasonable framework. Students are all working on the same tasks during a substantial part of the time. They are not, as in the case of total individualization, essentially isolated from each other. In fact, only extremely bright students, capable of going far beyond their classmates, will be encouraged to work entirely on their own.[3] You should be able to plan much group work within this framework; it is a manageable kind of program.

A TESTING TECHNIQUE

One problem associated with the enrichment program described in the last section is that of testing. For groups with a wide range of abilities you want to administer tests that reasonably reward those who do satisfactory work but still offer some challenge to the best students. Many teachers find this a difficult task. If the test challenges the best, the weakest fail miserably; if, on the other hand, weaker students do satisfactorily, the brighter students are bored or finish early and create discipline problems.

Too much attention has always been given to numbers on test scores. Some people even fall into the trap of believing that a test grade of 80 percent means that the student knows four-fifths of the material. Such beliefs are illusory. Consider for example a test of ten multiplication items each of the form:

$$\begin{array}{r} 37 \\ \times\ 56 \\ \hline \end{array}$$

Careful inspection of the steps in such a calculation shows that there are about ten, so the entire test includes about a hundred small steps, an error in any one of which will make an exercise incorrect. This means that a student who errs in one of a hundred steps will receive a grade of 90 instead

---

[3]In such extreme cases, you may wish to accelerate beyond what is described here, but always ensuring that such youngsters are exposed to a broad enriched program.

of 99. It is also possible for two errors to cancel out. For example a student may write:

$$\begin{array}{r} 13 \\ \times\ 5 \\ \hline 65 \end{array}$$

He may have made two errors: (1) forgetting to carry the 10 in his partial product 15, and (2) confusing addition with multiplication for a moment and writing the sum 6 instead of the product 5 for 5 × 1. Assuming for the moment that errors do not cancel out in this way, we have the following possible scale. (Note that there is a range of possible grades because several errors might have been made in the same exercise.)

errors among 100 small computations	*test grade range*	*true percent correct*
1	90	99
2	80–90	98
3	70–90	97
4	60–90	96
5	50–90	95
6	40–90	94
7	30–90	93
8	20–90	92
9	10–90	91
10	0–90	90
11	0–80	89

Testing creates certain difficulties, which are aggravated by an overall misunderstanding of the meaning of grades. A grade of less than, say, 60 is considered failing. And whenever you include challenging test problems, most of your weaker students drop below 60. Here is a way to circumvent that problem:

1. Construct items that will test basic understanding of the unit. Assume that there are ten of these.

2. Construct additional challenging exercises for brighter students. Assume that there are five of these of increasing difficulty.

3. Administer a scaled scoring procedure. For the example given it might be:

number of correct answers	*grade*	
15	100	
14	98	
13	96	
12	94	
11	92	↑
10	90	2 points each
9	81	
8	72	
7	63	↑
6	54	9 points each

In other words, the first ten correct answers count 9 points each, and additional correct answers count 2 points each. (Note: this does *not* refer to exercises 1-10 and 11-15, respectively, but to the total number of correct answers in any order.)

This kind of test will let you fairly determine the ability of average students, while at the same time challenging brighter students. Of course the scoring system can be varied according to the number of exercises, the number of challenge problems, and the teacher's choice of point range. Two additional advantages of this scoring system are: more students will attempt difficult problems, and you will find that students pay more attention when you review the tests.

THE VALUE OF TUTORING

We have indicated that tutoring by fellow students is an appropriate technique in the enrichment classroom. Some criticism has been directed at this technique because, critics say, it is a misuse of the brighter students' time, all benefits accruing to the weaker students. As it turns out, nearly the opposite is true. Any observer of student peer tutoring is struck by the fact that the real beneficiaries are the tutors. The tutors have an opportunity to reexamine, review, and even reorganize content with which they are partly familiar. In this process, they clarify the topic for themselves. Teachers should recognize this from their own experience; they learn a subject well by teaching it.

Student tutoring must be carefully monitored in order to ensure that important aspects of the process are conveyed to the students being tutored. Tutors should be counseled to assist by having the students work exercises, picking out errors for explanation, and directing attention to other examples that focus on these same problem areas. In other words, you must train your tutors in the fundamental arts of teaching.

ACCELERATION VERSUS ENRICHMENT

We have suggested that the class should move forward as a group. Now the question arises: How fast should the group progress? This question is especially important in homogeneously grouped (ability-sectioned) classes. Should the stronger students cover more than a year's work. Or, as the question is so often put by classroom teachers, "Can we move on to the text of the next grade?" This question is asked almost exclusively by beginning teachers, whose lack of experience limits the breadth of the instructional program. Teaching only the most narrowly defined content of the text, these teachers can only see extending their programs by moving ahead to new material. Meanwhile, their coverage of basic work is too superficial.

As experience is accumulated, teachers realize that mathematics appropriate to a given grade is far broader than what they will ever have time to cover except with truly gifted students. They must *always* choose a program somewhat less than the full content of the figure:

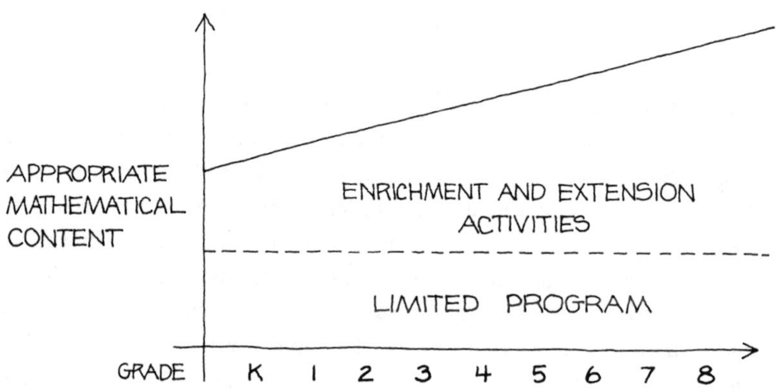

Given this view of mathematics, acceleration (moving ahead of the curriculum sequence) is usually inappropriate. What should be emphasized is the development of strong enrichment activities that support and extend the basic program.

Time is a key factor here. Too much valuable school experience is lost because "there just wasn't enough time." Laboratory activities and discovery lessons take time. So any "surplus" time is of great value, and should not be lost by moving ahead too rapidly to the next topic.

And finally in this regard we counsel any beginning teachers who feel they should move more rapidly to construct and administer a fair but challenging test on the content they have taught during the previous two weeks. In every case that teachers followed this advice, the test results forced them to rethink their teaching velocity.

THE UNSUCCESSFUL STUDENT

Until now this chapter has dealt with the total spectrum of students, in fact leaning toward problems related to better students. But better students have the ability to make their own way if necessary. A more immediate if not a more serious problem is the unsuccessful student, the youngster who experiences great difficulty in the classroom.[4] We turn now to this important problem.

A multiplicity of names has been used to describe unsuccessful students: low-ability students, slow learners, underachievers, reluctant learners, disadvantaged, culturally deprived, disaffected, rejected, non-college bound. One colleague has even suggested *deliberate abstractor*. But while each of these designations indicates a slightly different aspect, they all come together in the fact that these students are unable to succeed at the pace of their peers.

Instead of considering all the different types of unsuccessful students, we note two in particular:

1. Students who lack the ability of their classmates.
2. Students who have the ability to perform but for one reason or another will not or cannot do so. (By *cannot* we mean a lack not of ability but of something else like prerequisite skills or desire.)

The more accurately teachers can place students in the correct category the better they can assist them, but it takes extremely sensitive teachers to distinguish the two groups. An interesting study by Rosenthal and Jacobsen, reported in their book *Pygmalion in the Classroom*, indicates how teachers' perceptions of students affect the students' progress.[5] The authors found that when they misrepresented weak students to their teachers as type 2 rather than type 1 above, the students began to achieve better. The teachers in some way communicated their belief in the students' ability to succeed, raising their self-image and subsequently their achievement.

---

[4]It is as much an error to focus all attention on the weaker students as it is to neglect them. *All* students deserve the best possible program suited to their abilities.

[5]Robert Rosenthal and Lenore Jacobsen, *Pygmalion in the Classroom* (New York: Holt, Rinehart, and Winston, 1967).

There is another important lesson in this experiment. Students are sensitive to what their teachers think of them. If, even in the most difficult setting, you can maintain a positive view of each student, by that act alone you will contribute to their learning. In particular you should avoid concerning yourself with whether type 2 students will not or cannot perform (that is, whether to place the blame on them or others), but should instead seek to help them in the best way you can.

One other point about weak students should be considered. They tend to be weak in everything and do poor work in all subjects. They usually have a short attention span and lack social and athletic skills. A common misbelief about weak students is that they would be better suited to manual skill activities; with few exceptions they are not. In this way they are the unfortunate victims of the statistical law of regression: below average in one dimension, they tend to fall below in others. Those at the opposite end of the spectrum derive all the benefits of that law.

THE INNER-CITY STUDENT

One kind of unsuccessful student comes from the central city ghetto. Such students have particular learning problems that require special attention.

Since most mathematics teachers have grown up in cultures different from those of inner-city students, they need to develop an understanding and acceptance of the students' culture. Teachers must also recognize the attitudes, aspirations, and pressures on such students. Often these students are assigned to low-achievement classes because the usual mathematics course, text, and instruction turn them away. Many of them have mathematical ability, which they use to solve day-to-day problems, but such problems are different from the suburb- and country-oriented problems of most texts.

Many inner-city students have grown up in crowded cities where housing is substandard, and where families are likely to have limited resources. Spare time is usually spent in crowded, noisy conditions both at home and on the street. Such students have rarely known privacy, and hence may often interrupt school activities. Crowding and lack of privacy have also given them information about the inner motives of others, so such students may be overly sensitive to actions of teachers. To survive in a crowded, rejecting society, on the other hand, they have resourcefulness and creativity that teachers can capitalize on.

Their crowded environment may also make such students irritable and touchy; classroom tensions may lead to temper outbursts. They have learned to distrust adults, to expect failure in school, and to settle many difficulties by physical means. They often resort to daydreaming to shut out the uninteresting activities of the classroom.

Students from the inner-city may have few possessions of their own; hence they may show little concern for school property or the property of others. Such students may come from large families in which they do not feel wanted, and hence may feel that no one really cares about them, or that they never will have an opportunity to improve their lot. Consequently, they may lack motivation in the classroom and frequently be absent. Communication at home and on the street is not in the language of the school; thus reading and listening levels are low and vocabulary may appear shocking.

The first step in dealing with inner-city students is to build confidence in the teacher. Teachers must show that they accept all students as they are. Teachers must show they appreciate the students if they expect the students to like themselves. They must show faith in the students and in their ability to learn. Students must be convinced that they are important, and that mathematics offers opportunities for change. If the students sense that the teachers value them, it will be more difficult for them to reject the teachers and the activities they propose.[6]

We have singled out here inner-city students because there are so many of them and because so few teachers have had adequate preparation to meet their special problems. But there are also rural children with special problems and minority groups with special problems and—yes—even suburban children with special problems. The lesson to be extracted from this section is that teachers must sensitize themselves to the specific problems of their charges.

Some readers will have such backgrounds themselves. We believe that they have extra importance in the schools. They can help others to join them in identifying and attacking these special problems.

---

[6]An especially useful book for city teachers is Herbert L. Foster, *Ribbin', Jivin,' and Playin' the Dozens: The Unrecognized Dilemma of Innercity Schools* (Cambridge, Mass.: Ballinger, 1974).

RESPONDING TO THE UNSUCCESSFUL STUDENT

The unsuccessful student needs exactly what all students need: good, sensitive teaching. If there is a difference in the approach to instruction for weaker students, it should lie in greater concentration on the concrete and semiabstract aspects of instruction. This is what Larry Couvillon of Florida State University calls "delayed conceptualization." Too often teachers move to abstract levels too quickly, assuming that students are following them. This can be especially tragic for weaker students. All students need to be comfortable with one level of learning before moving to the next. Rushing them can be synonymous with failing them.

Even more important to the long-term welfare of low-ability students is that the program should focus on *concepts rather than on specific techniques.* This is a controversial view that is not widely held. In fact, most teachers give up on teaching concepts to unsuccessful students, and turn to teaching them rote facts and procedures. The mathematics literature abounds with articles that support this approach.

But it is wrong on logical grounds to ignore the study of concepts. Conceptual learning is efficient learning; it reduces the number of things to be learned. In fact a case could be made that conceptualization, and even civilization, is a direct result of man's inherent laziness, his determination to seek shortcuts and labor-saving devices. Here is a comparison of the approaches of conceptualizing and nonconceptualizing students:

Conceptualizer	Rote learner
Learns conceptual basis	Fails to conceptualize
Builds techniques on concepts; learns with understanding	Memorizes with no understanding
Remembers through practice	Recalls correct and incorrect facts
Can check errors against concepts	Cannot reconstruct errors

Consider an example: learning the addition facts. Conceptualizers understand "what addition is about." They think of addition in terms of counting, combining groups of tokens, and the number line. They develop facts from these ideas, knowing that if they aren't sure of the sum 7 + 6 they can reconstruct it. In this particular case, they might well relate 7 + 6 to the more familiar 6 + 6.

Meanwhile, the teacher has given up on some of the weaker students, and turned them to the task of memorizing the addition table. From the students' view, this means learning many three- and four-digit combinations like 7613, 459, and 9918. Their task is not so different from memorizing the license plate numbers in a parking lot. By failing to attack concepts, teachers have increased extraordinarily the memory load on just those students who can least support the load. No one would disagree that it is difficult to teach concepts to weaker students. But the problem here involves choosing between two fundamentally different learning approaches. This becomes increasingly important as students progress through school. There is no firm ground on which to build multiplication if addition is not understood. The rote memory process becomes further complicated: is it 8756 or 8715, the multiplication fact or the addition fact that is called for? And without conceptual understanding of the process, how can students decide when and where to apply these processes in the real world.

One reason that teachers have been tempted to focus on rote learning of facts and algorithms is the ubiquitous standardized test on computation. "If they can't learn why, I'll drill computation into them," is their response. But in the end this method is inefficient. Greater stress on concept learning would have better served these students for the immediate as well as the long-term learning process.

Some years ago several primary-grade teachers in the inner-city schools of Norwalk, Connecticut, decided to try a change of focus with even their weakest students. They aimed for concepts rather than memorized facts, and spent most of their time working with the concrete and semiabstract in the classroom. Their success was striking and encouraging. Computation ability on standardized tests rose sharply, many students exceeding the standards expected of them. But not everyone was satisfied. One school administrator complained about "the marks all over the papers." Students' answer sheets often appeared like this:

23. 8 + 7 = <u>15</u> 00000000 0000000

37. 3 × 4 = <u>12</u>
XXXX
XXXX
XXXX

GIVING REMEDIAL ASSISTANCE

There has been a long and honored tradition of remediation in the teaching of reading. Only recently has progress been made in developing a parallel program in mathematics. In any case, basic responsibility for math remediation in most schools is left to classroom teachers.

Remediation can be quite naturally separated into *diagnosis,* and *providing assistance.* Diagnosis, it turns out, is more than half the battle. Once the teacher knows quite specifically what the student's difficulties are, developing and implementing an assistance program is reasonably straightforward. It is not enough, however, to know that Johnny can't add. A diagnosis is a determination of much more specific malfunctions. In the same way, "It doesn't work right" offers little help to someone making repairs. To assist students having difficulty with addition, you should know the following:

Do they lack prerequisite skills like counting?

Do they understand addition as it relates to concrete objects?

Can they relate addition to semiabstract devices like the number line?

Are their difficulties restricted to errors among the addition facts?

Do they have specific difficulty with some step in the algorithm?

Do they understand and correctly apply regrouping?

The answers to a written test are never enough to provide a basis for adequate diagnosis. The teacher should observe students as they calculate and work problems. The teacher should be prepared to ask questions and to pose additional problems to focus further on specific difficulties. Sometimes direct assistance can be offered at this time, but more often a fuller assistance program must be worked out. In either case, follow-up activities are necessary to ensure that there is no regression to old habits and to assure understanding.

Many contemporary textbooks have keyed additional computation exercises to specific topics. Workbooks also provide drill on specifics, sometimes introduced in novel and interesting ways. These may prove useful to the teacher in providing practice once a difficulty is diagnosed and treated. But a word of warning is in order here: the teacher should check students' work continuously. It is bad for any student to practice incorrect concepts or skills; for the weak student it can be catastrophic.

LEARNING HIERARCHIES

Psychologists Robert Gagné and David Ausubel have stressed the useful idea of learning hierarchies, structures of concepts and skills that build to a specific concept or skill. (See chapter 2.) The figure shows part of a possible learning hierarchy for adding two fractions:

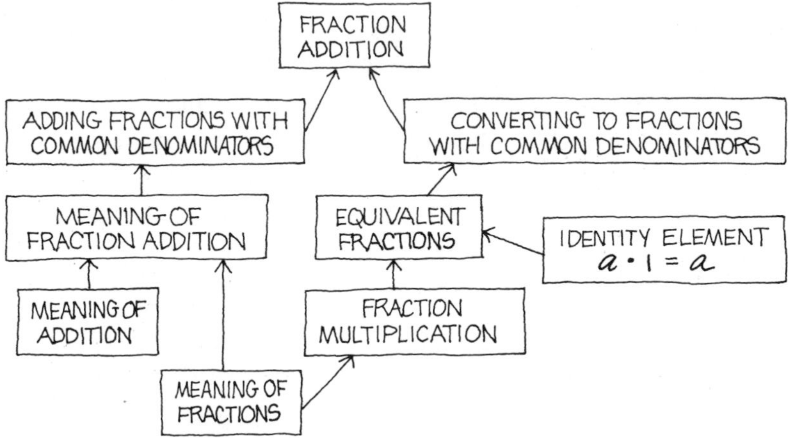

One use of such structures is for remediation. To help a student having difficulty with addition of fractions, you "back down" the hierarchy by asking appropriate questions for each box until you reach boxes that represent concepts the student understands. Those boxes provide you solid ground for remediation.

Researchers and some classroom teachers have found this a useful device. If the hierarchy is relatively complete and accurate, it provides a road map for concept development, and it is possible to retrace the paths to identify levels of understanding. Some proponents of the idea make the additional claim that it is then easy to lead the student back up the paths by instruction. In fact, some go still further, claiming that once prerequisite skills are mastered, the final step is virtually automatic. (See exercise 10.) Unfortunately it is not nearly as simple as that.

A WARNING

In this chapter we have adopted an oversimplified categorization of students into a weak, average, strong trichotomy. This is misleading for two reasons. First, the categories are arbitrary and their borders very difficult to define. Second, and far more important, the categories as they apply to students are unstable and elusive.

As a case in point, we suggest that the phrase "average student" is a misnomer. No human being is average; each exemplifies infinite variations on the general theme of humanity. On Tuesday a person is different from what he was on Monday, what he will be on Wednesday. Each person responds in a unique way to different topics, different teachers, and different peers. Change a student's seat in the classroom, and he becomes a different child. Weather affects students. So do problems at home. Gifted, stupid, irritating, affectionate–a student can be all of these, and everything in between. To fit youngsters into tight categories is to stifle them. We have then categorized students only to provide a basis for discussion. We recognize this as an over-simplification that is of use in planning an instructional program.

EXERCISES

1. Review your own elementary school mathematics experience in regard to your class standing, how your teachers seemed to perceive you as an individual, and how you performed independent work.

2. Based on your answer to exercise 1, indicate how your own experience will help you to understand and work with children, as well as what problems it may cause for you.

3. Talk with the best math student you know among your peers. Determine from him his opinion about:
   (a) Why he is a good math student
   (b) Which teachers helped him most and *how* (consider also teachers in fields other than math)
   (c) Which teachers he disliked and why
   (d) How to improve mathematics teaching in elementary schools

4. Talk with a peer who thinks of himself as a weak math student. Determine from him his opinion about:
   (a) Why he is a weak math student
   (b) Which teachers helped him most and why (consider also teachers in fields other than math)
   (c) Which teachers he disliked and why
   (d) How to improve mathematics instruction in elementary schools

5. Do you identify yourself as a conceptualizer or a rote learner? Identify the teacher you most associate with each learning style.

6. Construct a diagnostic test on some aspect of the standard curriculum at the grade level of most interest to you. Administer your test to a single student in an interview context. Identify the student's weaknesses and indicate how you would respond to them. (You may wish to share your findings with the child's teacher.)

7. Give exercises associated with each of the boxes of the learning hierarchy on page 287 that would provide information about a student's understanding of each concept.

8. Based on the exercises you developed for exercise 7, suggest some additional boxes that could be added to the learning hierarchy. Give exercises for each of those boxes.

9. Construct a learning hierarchy for a concept at the grade level of most interest to you. You will probably find it useful to refer to a textbook for the chosen grade to help organize your thinking.

10. With which psychological group (behavioral or gestalt) would you associate learning hierarchies? What kinds of learning would be difficult to fit into this kind of framework?

CHAPTER ELEVEN

CLASSROOM MATERIALS AND EQUIPMENT

Schools vary widely in the materials and equipment they provide for the classroom teacher.[1] In some schools teachers are encouraged to order whatever will support and extend their instructional program; in others they must make do with minimal facilities or may even be expected to provide their own. Most schools fall between these two extremes. One rule that applies almost universally, however, is that teachers who don't ask for supplies get very little and certainly less than those who do. The lesson in

[1]In many school systems any increase in teachers' salaries cuts into other budgets so that materials and equipment become increasingly difficult to obtain.

this is that teachers should carefully appraise their needs and prepare requests for equipment and materials to fulfill them.

In this chapter we make no attempt to survey this extensive topic completely. Instead we focus on the role of materials and equipment in the mathematics instructional program. We feel that it is most important for a classroom teacher to develop an attitude toward support systems that is not only informed and positive, but also carefully critical and realistic.

AUDIOVISUAL AIDS

The name audiovisual implies sensory input through hearing and seeing. A well-known mathematics educator, Robert E. K. Rourke, has referred to the textbook as the greatest visual aid known to man. By the same token, the teacher's voice may well be the finest audio aid. Many fine teachers function well by relying almost exclusively on these two basic tools. But the basic question each teacher must ask is whether supplementary aids would improve instruction. No one else can decide whether a fine teacher can become even better or a weak teacher more competent by using supplementary devices; they must answer this question for themselves. For one teacher the break in pace or the change of classroom tone may be just the thing; for another that may not be exactly what is needed.

And the answer must be specific. Too often beginners feel that they should use films or that they should have students build models, attitudes that are too global to be useful to them. As it happens, the number of good mathematics films is very small, so the first attitude could be counterproductive if applied without appropriate discretion.[2] Decisions about supplemental devices are much more specific anyway; they relate to immediate, rather than long-term goals.

At the same time it is impossible to make a case for not using good audiovisual aids. Consider in this regard a specific experience of the senior author. In classroom tests of a map-reading unit for the MINNEMAST Program, we found that some primary-grade students had difficulty visualizing what things looked like viewed from above. For example, the children drew a "map" of their classroom with their bodies and faces appearing in

---

[2]It is worth noting that this number is growing. Scattered among the many poor films are a few of excellent quality.

side-view profile. In order to respond to this kind of problem and to its extension to map-reading in general, we decided that a film would best suit our purposes. The film would show a youngster standing on a street corner. The camera would be mounted on a helicopter, which would take off and rise straight up, but the camera would remain focused on the waving boy. As the helicopter rose, of course, the boy would be seen from above, and in addition the pattern of streets and buildings would soon appear. At an appropriate point the picture would dissolve into a map of exactly the same region as the picture.

What does the film do? It responds to a specific instructional problem, in fact to several problems about teaching map-reading.[3] More importantly it does so in a way that the classroom teacher would be hard-pressed to duplicate (without access to a helicopter). The lesson of this film leads to the following two questions that you should ask of any supplementary device:

> Does it make a contribution to my instructional program?
>
> Is this the best solution available to me?

A third question that most teachers must also ask relates to priorities:

> With available resources, is this specific expenditure justified?

Other more important aids may have to come first, but this need only delay acquiring an aid you need.

A wide variety of materials and equipment is available to classroom teachers. In the sections that follow are some of the major types.

CHALKBOARDS

To older teachers the ubiquitous chalkboard would seem so much a part of the classroom as to be beyond mention here. Today's classrooms have made it less so; occasionally teachers must even seek out portable chalkboards for use. Chalkboards provide a place for students to practice, and a place for you to display work in progress, points to be emphasized, key questions, and assignments.

---

[3]A recent National Assessment of Educational Progress showed that only about one in three 17-year-olds and adults had mastered basic map-reading skills.

OVERHEAD PROJECTORS

The overhead projector has now replaced many functions of the chalkboard. The overhead projector (see figure) is so named because the teacher, facing the class, can use a transparency or write with a felt pen or wax pencil on the machine, projecting an image overhead onto a screen, wall, or chalkboard. Today these machines are available to most mathematics classrooms.[4] One particular advantage they enjoy over chalkboards is their flexibility: transparencies may be prepared before class; material may be displayed, "erased," and later recalled if necessary.

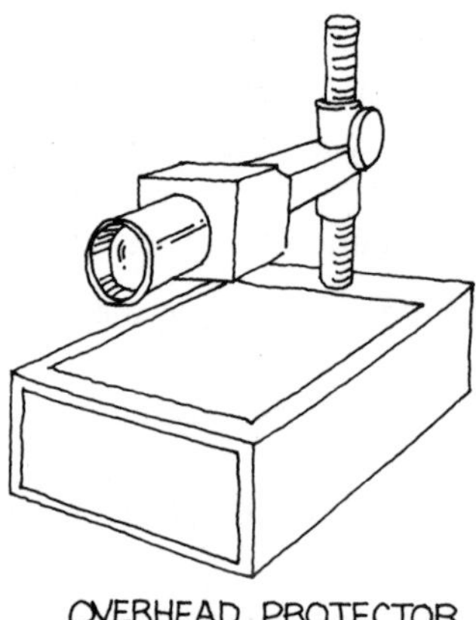

OVERHEAD PROJECTOR

BULLETIN BOARDS

Bulletin boards provide display space for a wide variety of items. They may be used for student honor work, theme presentations, enrichment topics, recreational exhibits, and pictures showing mathematical applications. Many teachers work cooperatively with student teams to make bulletin board exhibits a learning enterprise as well as a teaching tool.

---

[4]For an excellent pamphlet on use of this piece of equipment, see S. Krulik and I. Kaufman, *How to Use the Overhead Projector in Mathematics Education,* rev. ed. (Reston, Va.: National Council of Teachers of Mathematics, 1975).

MOTION PICTURE FILMS

Twenty years ago educators thought that films would revolutionize teaching. Today, many fads later, films play a minimal role in instruction. One reason for this is the fact that many films duplicate activities that teachers are well able to perform on their own. Many math films, for example, show a classroom teacher lecturing on a topic—something most classroom teachers can do as well or better. More recently films have turned to tasks difficult to carry out in the classroom. The best known of these, a Disney film called *Donald in Mathemagic Land,* uses animation and other specialized film techniques to provide an exciting and highly motivating mathematical experience.

FILMSTRIPS AND SLIDES

Literally hundreds of filmstrips are available for projection in the classroom. These provide sequenced presentations of specific content. Many teachers find them especially useful for review and remediation, particularly for students who have been absent. Some may be used by students for self-teaching.

TELEVISION

Several public television programs on mathematics are currently broadcast during school hours. "Infinity Factory" and "Sesame Street" have been particularly good in providing some of the reinforcement children need in an imaginative and attractive format. Although closed-circuit television has provided little for mathematics teaching, some teachers have made good use of this tool, especially when videotape facilities are available.

TAPE RECORDERS

The audio tape recorder and the individual tape cassette provide an important teaching tool. When utilized with earphones, students, even in crowded and noisy classrooms, are able to concentrate on taped lessons. Most tapes are carefully prepared to parallel worksheets, which students complete as they are directed to by the voice on tape. Current procedure has the students turn off their tape recorders as they work out assigned exercises. Upon completion, they restart the recorder to learn whether they are right or wrong. If they have missed an idea, they can rewind the recorder to an earlier point to replay the sequence.

OPAQUE PROJECTORS

The opaque projector allows the teacher to project opaque objects, as opposed to transparencies, on a screen. It is especially useful for displaying student papers for group reaction, as well as textbook pages for purposes of discussion.

MODELS

Models form a major category of visual and tactile aids for teaching. While models are usually considered in connection with geometric topics, they may also be used for other representations. For example, the concept of ratio may be displayed with models.

MULTIPLE-USE AIDS

Perhaps the best kind of audiovisual aid is one that has many uses. We shall consider one of these. At the time of this writing, several thousand wooden cubes with volumes of one cubic inch could be purchased for less than fifty dollars. Here are *some* of the uses for these cubes in elementary school classrooms:

Counting.

Estimating. (Estimate the number of blocks in the first pile. Check your guess by counting. Now try the other pile.)

Checking or justifying the answers for simple addition, subtraction, multiplication, or division exercises.

Displaying place value. Blocks may be glued to represent tens and hundreds.

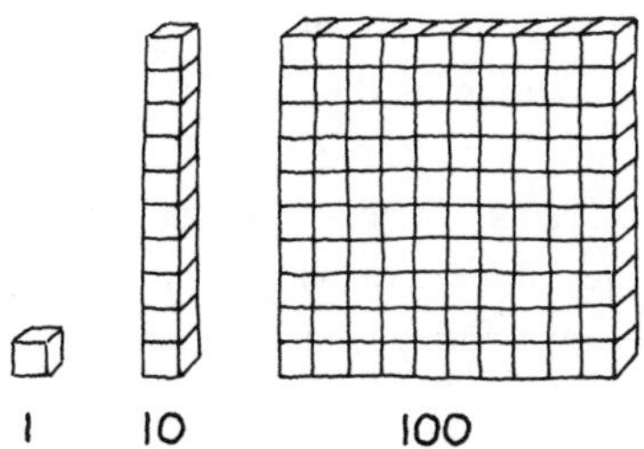

Higher decade addition and subtraction. The place-value blocks may be used for this purpose.

Area and volume problems.

Development of area and volume relationships for rectangles and rectangular prisms.

Pattern duplication. (Arrange your blocks exactly like these.)

Data collection and discovery activities. (One block has a surface area of 6 square inches. Two separate cubes would have 12. Can you put them together so that they have less outside surface area? What is the least you can get? Can you get 11 square inches? $11\frac{1}{2}$? Make a table showing the least surface area for 1 to 30 blocks. Try to guess beforehand, but always check carefully. Do you see patterns?)

Form and solve puzzles. (The seven shapes of the figures below are glued and students are challenged to form a cube using all of them.)

There are special advantages to aids like these cubes, which can be reused for many purposes. Students gain confidence through familiarity with the aid. This same familiarity makes it easier for students to regress to concrete activities with these materials when necessary. Teachers also gain certain advantages from the use of aids. Our observations suggest that teachers become more creative in their use of specific aids the more they use them. This is not just a matter of number of uses: the proportion of insight-generating uses seems to rise as the teachers' familiarity with the aid increases. Some examples of aids for which this is true are: Cuisenaire rods, Montessori materials, Stern and Dienes blocks, place-value charts, Wirtz's bean sticks, and geoboards or Burns boards.

Finally there is the matter of storage. An expression familiar to experienced teachers sums it up well: Teachers' closets are full of last year's aids, now only accumulating dust. The one-shot aid should be acquired only if its value merits at least annual use.

USING MATERIALS AND EQUIPMENT IN THE INSTRUCTIONAL PROGRAM

Once again, planning is the key to instruction. Appropriate use of audio-visual aids should be worked out carefully in advance. If this is not done, precious class time is wasted locating materials, models may be used inefficiently, or someone may have already borrowed the equipment. These logistical problems are best responded to by looking ahead.

In terms of ordering materials and equipment this means looking ahead to the full year. An annual review of necessary aids will save much later grief for classroom teachers. The new teacher should do this during the summer before entering the classroom; after the first year it is usually done at the end of the school year in preparation for the next. Here are the steps that may be followed:

1. Review available materials and equipment. Include in this inventory not only what previous teachers have accumulated but also what the school already has on order. The school secretary or principal can help you with the latter.

2. Page through the textbook you will be using to determine what aids relate directly to the instructional program of the text. Note them.

3. Refer to catalogs of major supply houses (available in your school offices) noting items you want. Also useful here is the 34th yearbook of the National Council of Teachers of Mathematics, *Instructional Aids in Mathematics.* This book provides extensive lists of available materials and equipment as well as sources; it also relates many of these aids to classroom instruction.[5] Add appropriate items to your list.

4. Carefully reorder your list according to priorities. When you have finished this you should have a list of items, including cost and source, in priority order. For major items representing substantial costs you may wish to provide a rationale.

5. Review this list personally with the school administrator responsible for purchase of these items. In most schools this is the building principal; in others it is either the mathematics supervisor or a team leader. If possible, at this time determine which items on your list you can count on in order to plan your program.

Now hopefully you have your supplies and equipment. How can you make best use of them? Here we note several points that you should consider in utilizing supplementary aids:

> Concrete materials make their greatest impact in the hands of the children. In this regard, it is well to recall the adage:
>
> *I hear and I forget,*
> *I see and I remember,*
> *I do and I understand.*

Here is an example from a sixth-grade classroom. Students are working individually at their seats on addition of mixed numbers. Exercises are of the form:

---

[5]We caution you to be prepared for an excessive behavioral orientation, which detracts from the otherwise high quality of this publication.

$$\begin{array}{r} 1\tfrac{2}{3} \\ +\ 2\tfrac{1}{2} \\ \hline \end{array}$$

Most of the children are performing well, but as the teacher circulates around the classroom he directs students with difficulties to check their work at one of the three flannel boards in the classroom. Their hands-on work at flannel boards with pie-shaped cutouts clarifies the process in a way that a teacher's demonstration could not.

> When devices are used that involve only part of the class you must plan other activities for the rest.
>
> You should work out housekeeping and other management procedures to use devices most efficiently. While each student should be expected to help keep order, you may wish to assign specific responsibilities for individual items.
>
> You should provide and encourage student access to appropriate aids outside the regular instructional program. Related puzzles and games are helpful for encouraging this.

EXERCISES

1. Read several reviews of audiovisual materials in the *Arithmetic Teacher.* Based on your reading and your own preferences, select two aids that you would use and one that you would not. Justify your decisions.

2. Add three specific uses to the list for the inch cubes.

3. Review a textbook for a grade level of interest to you in order to list materials and equipment that relate directly and indirectly to that program. Do *not* merely copy the list from the teacher's edition.

4. Develop a series of three lessons on a topic of your choice in which audiovisual materials or equipment play a central role. You will find the text used in exercise 3 helpful.

5. Recall and describe a lesson in which audiovisual aids were used effectively by one of your teachers.

6. Identify your own attitude toward audiovisual materials. How will this affect your teaching?

CHAPTER TWELVE

PUTTING IT ALL TOGETHER: ORGANIZING AND MANAGING MATHEMATICS INSTRUCTION IN THE CLASSROOM

In the preceding chapters we have reviewed psychological and philosophical bases for mathematics instruction, sketched in broad strokes elementary school mathematics content, highlighted some teaching procedures, and discussed materials and equipment. The responsibility associated with the content, procedures, and materials may appear especially overwhelming to the beginner. At the same time the beginner may not see how it all fits together. The reader may feel that he is missing the forest for the trees. For that reason we append this final chapter to place the other eleven in perspective.

PERSONAL ASSESSMENT

At the outset we urge you to assess your personal resources. Throughout this text we have recommended that you confront teaching techniques with your own personality and personal style. To do this you should reflect on both your assets and your weaknesses. Teaching ability is a gift. Some have this gift in great measure, some far less, but most find themselves well between the extremes. But in any case this gift provides a wide range within which you can function. The diagram suggests a sample range of achievement potential typical of a beginning teacher. A teacher could devote minimum effort and thought to teaching and drift to the bottom of the range. At that point, the minimum effort, perhaps even imposed by external constraints, could carry the teacher. Most schools have a few teachers who have followed this inexcusable course. They soon find themselves trapped in the same kind of negative reinforcement cycle as that of their nonachieving students. Their poor teaching encourages poor student attitudes and results, which discourages such teachers further, leading them to even poorer teaching, usually with attendant complaints about students, colleagues, school, and community. They do not, and usually cannot, understand that teachers down the hall may be succeeding with identical resources.

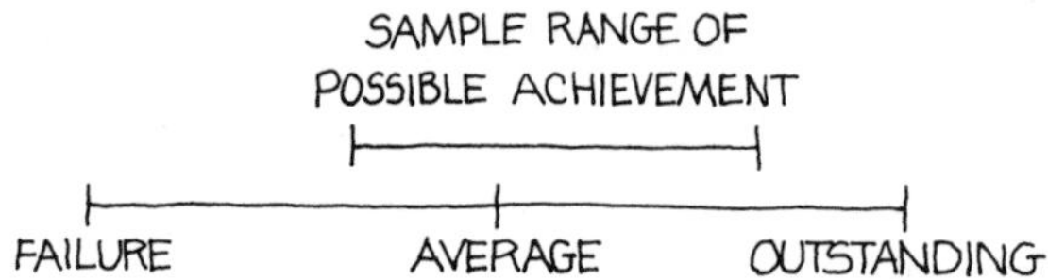

THE RANGE OF TEACHING ACHIEVEMENT

Consider those other teachers. They work hard to achieve at the top of their range. Though they may not have the type of personality or the ability to be the best in the school, they make maximum use of their talents, extending them wherever possible to their limits. This kind of teacher is usually reinforced positively. Students recognize the hard work and repay in kind. Certainly these teachers have some problems, and on some days may be discouraged and enervated by the hard work involved in teaching. But they learn from their failure as well as their success, and soon become smoothly functioning professionals.

RESOURCES FOR IMPROVEMENT

Few teachers who have made their way through college academic programs lack the ability to become excellent teachers. Many can be outstanding. From our observations, the qualities that take these teachers to the top of their range are:

1. *Effort:* These teachers recognize that teaching requires hard, disciplined work. They do not shrink from it but attack it head-on.

2. *Organization:* Time is a serious problem for all teachers, especially beginners. Without careful organization with recognized priorities and use of procedures that promote efficiency, time rapidly drains away. Even hard work will not make up for the loss.

3. *Positive attitude:* It comes as a shock to beginners, and to us, to find that there are teachers who don't like teaching or, worse, who dislike children. Certainly all teachers experience moments when anger, self-doubt, or resentment bubbles to the surface. To make headway, however, the teacher must be able to concentrate on the satisfactions of the job: the gains in achievement, the innocent gestures of affection that often come at unexpected times, and the times when plans work, experiments succeed, and decisions are right.

4. *Introspection:* Self-evaluation and analysis is necessary to improvement. If things do not work, it is important to seek ways to improve procedures. Blundering ahead without rethinking rarely does any good. A fragment of an overheard statement to a class is to the point: "Yesterday I wasn't satisfied with how our math lesson went. Today I'm going to ask you instead to. . . ." This teacher has responded to a difficulty in a way that at least shares with students the fault for lack of success.

5. *Help-seeking:* It is a serious error for beginners to assume that principals, supervisors, or colleagues will seek them out to provide help. This does happen, but far less often than it should. If teachers have problems on which they need help, they should seek it out. This represents a positive step to confront reality. The

alternative is to allow wounds to fester. Postponement rarely helps; more often it contributes to further difficulties.

6. *A sense of humor:* This involves more than an extension of positive attitudes. Teachers who can laugh at their own mistakes, and who can laugh *with* students about the class mix-ups, the foolishness, even the pomp and pretension of many aspects of school are better equipped to tolerate the continuing pressures of thirty or more human dynamos, a half-dozen subjects, and a world that rarely seems to understand. Without a sense of humor a teacher is doomed, not necessarily to failure, but to an unhappy life.

7. *A sense of worth:* This most important characteristic is often forgotten. Quality teachers know the value of learning, and through that, the value of teaching. They recognize the intrinsic value and potential danger of every child, as well as the importance of the teachers' powerful role *in loco parentis.* They respect not only the subjects they teach, but also the quality of the subject matter at their respective teaching levels. (Communicating this kind of respect has been a central aim of this text.) And finally, while recognizing the faults and shortcomings of the school, they still recognize the importance of this institution to society and civilization.

ANALYZING YOUR CLASSROOM TEACHING

Experience helps. Most teachers show marked improvement during their first few years. Others, however, merely repeat their poor quality first experience over and over. The key here is *reflection.* In order to place your background, personality, prior learning, and teaching experience into reasonable perspective, you should force yourself to reflect on these aspects of your personal teaching philosophy. Failure to do this or to incorporate your thoughts into your planning will reduce your effectiveness in the classroom. Yet few teachers take time to ponder their professional activities. The following are some aspects of teaching on which you should reflect.

ORGANIZATION OF THE TEACHING PROGRAM

The following figure illustrates a flowchart for organizing instruction. You should review this chart in order to assure yourself that you understand the discrete steps in the instructional process. You should then review each step in order to determine which components will require the most work.

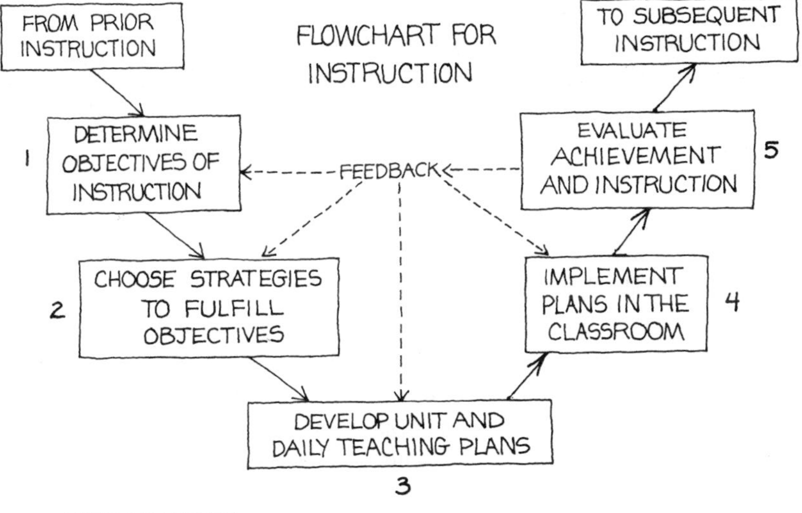

MATHEMATICS

If you are like most elementary school teachers your mathematical background does not extend far beyond (or in some cases even into) secondary school mathematical competence. This need not disturb you. But you should be seriously concerned about what mathematical understanding involves. Too much elementary school mathematics teaching begins and ends with computational algorithms. You must see to it that your mathematics teaching is less limiting, that in fact you give your students some feeling for the breadth and scope of this important subject. There is a great deal to reflect on here. How can I locate or devise interesting problems? How can I encourage creative, independent thinking and alternate ways of approaching mathematics? What is the best way for me to introduce a topic, motivate study of an algorithm, or extend study for gifted children? How can I communicate the consistency, the logic, and the pervasive nature of mathematics?

PROGRAM BALANCE

A balanced mathematics program provides students with a strong base in computational skills, while at the same time offering them discovery opportunities and exploratory exercises. Unbalanced programs lean too heavily toward one or the other of these extremes. While a program aimed solely at computation can be dry, sterile, and boring, a program directed solely toward discovery can also create problems. Students who lack computational skills soon find themselves too ill-equipped to master more than routine exercises. One of the major sources of discovery actually lies within computation, where rich patterns emerge. Many of the important number theories of Gauss, Euler, Fermat, and others evolved from calculating activities.

EVALUATION AND MAINTENANCE

"They were very poorly prepared when they came to me" is a common comment of classroom teachers at all levels. The complaint is usually unfair and fails to recognize the continuing responsibility of all teachers to maintain and if necessary remediate. In particular, students returning from summer vacations will have become rusty. Part of the ongoing program must include review and practice with the teacher's assistance. Ways of providing this reinforcement become central concerns of classroom teachers. Of course, this problem occurs not only at the beginning of the year, but must be confronted throughout. As each topic is completed, it becomes a part of the maintenance load.

In fact, review and maintenance work, which the English call *revision exercises,* provides an opportunity to retrace the steps in new ways. Review is especially challenging, since new and different approaches to common material are necessary to prevent boredom. The review should be a time of coordination so that separate topics are viewed in a unified way. Review of topics *A, B,* and *C* is enhanced by problems in which *A, B,* and *C* interact and complement each other. For example, in a sixth-grade review of area, ratio, and proportion, questions can be introduced that explore the effects of increasing width while length remains constant (and vice-versa) on the area of a rectangle. Consider in this regard the following questions that would ultimately lead to quite different answers:

What is the effect on the area of a rectangle of doubling the length and halving the width? Of doubling width and halving length?[1]

What is the effect on the area of a rectangle of increasing the length by 2 cm and decreasing the width by 2 cm? Of increasing the width by 2 cm and decreasing the length by 2 cm?

MATHEMATICS AND THE TOTAL PROGRAM

Most elementary school teachers still teach all—or at least several—subjects. This offers them an excellent opportunity to correlate various subjects. It is important to stress the contacts that mathematics makes with science, social studies, literature, and even physical education. Opportunities to do this abound, and provide students with a sense of the cohesiveness of their education, helping them to see how mathematics and other subjects apply to the real world.

Almost any unit of any subject has potential for mathematization. It takes only a few minutes reflection to generate these ideas. Some examples are:

Timing children as they run the fifty-yard dash interrelates physical education, science, and mathematics. For example, measuring time in seconds may be used to determine first how long at that speed the individual student would take to run one mile and then how many miles per hour that represents. For a sixth-grade girl who runs the fifty-yard dash in 12 seconds the calculation would be:

$$\frac{50 \text{ yds.}}{12 \text{ sec.}} = \frac{1{,}760 \text{ yds.}}{x} \qquad x = 422.4 \text{ sec. (or dividing by 60) about 7 min.}$$

Her speed is 1 mile in 7 minutes.

[1]It is common but not necessary to consider $l \geq w$. Without that restriction the two parts of each problem become one.

$$\frac{1 \text{ mi.}}{7 \text{ min.}} = \frac{x}{60 \text{ min.}} \qquad x = 8.5 \text{ mi.}$$

Her speed is about 8.5 miles per hour.

A social studies unit on Columbus's voyages to the New World can provide a source for many numerical problems. If a classroom globe is available, distances can be determined and ship speeds calculated. The size of the boats in the fleet may be compared with the size of the classroom to show how remarkably small these tiny vessels were. (The Santa Maria was 117 feet long and the Nina and Pinta each about 50 feet in length! On Columbus's first voyage he took from September 6 to October 12 to sail from the Canary Islands to San Salvador.)

Literature too may offer sources of mathematics exercises. In the Bible (Revelations 13:18) is the admonition: "Let him that hath understanding count the number of the beast: for it is the number of a man; and his number is six hundred three score and six." This statement was used by numerologists during the Middle Ages to assign to enemies evil characteristics related to this number of the beast: 666.[2] (Various popes and Martin Luther were so attacked.) Students can determine their own "number" to see if a multiple of it is 666. They merely sum the numbers corresponding to the letters in their names using the code:

A – 1	F – 6	K – 11	P – 16	U – 21	Z – 26
B – 2	G – 7	L – 12	Q – 17	V – 22	
C – 3	H – 8	M – 13	R – 18	W – 23	
D – 4	I – 9	N – 14	S – 19	X – 24	
E – 5	J – 10	O – 15	T – 20	Y – 25	

[2]The authors have seen this technique applied to the name Henry Kissinger. This suggests that we cannot entirely divest ourselves of old ways.

> For example, John Denver would be 10 + 15 + 8 + 14 + 4 + 5 + 14 + 22 + 5 + 18 = 115. Multiplying by 6 gives 690, far from 666. Students could then look for the "dangerous" numbers, the factors of 666. Thus even starting from an astrological base (some would say metaphysical), mathematics of interest to students can be developed. (Our experience with this exercise suggests that far from being threatened by the danger of one's number, students whose names lead to 666 become instant class folk heroes, proud of their fortune.)

Sophisticated examples like these are matched in everyday lessons by equally interesting possibilities. The challenge is to take a lesson at random and see.

DAILY ROUTINE

Here again the teacher must reflect on balance. There are advantages to both consistency and variation. An unvarying program provides security to many students; they know what to expect and what is expected of them. But routine has within it the seeds of boredom. Change responds to boredom, but it creates transitional problems of insecurity that cause many teachers to give up on new programs before they have been given a fair chance. Such teachers are so overwhelmed by the transition problems, which will decrease or disappear once students are again secure, that they don't continue new programs long enough.

Another aspect of daily routine poses a dangerous trap: Whatever works seems right, whatever fails is wrong. Teachers are often led into sterile routines and even severely restricted curricula by this false assumption. Students often rebel against demanding aspects of the mathematics program. The trick is not to give up challenging parts, but to seek more palatable ways of teaching them. In the end, for all of us—teachers and students alike—some drudgery is necessary; to think otherwise is unrealistic.

DISCIPLINE

Many beginners foresee discipline as their most serious problem. Their favorite question is, "What do I do if a student . . . ," and the rest reads like an episode from *Blackboard Jungle.* Actually, discipline should be the beginner's last concern. Beginning teachers will have disciplinary problems solely because they have failed to plan adequately, to provide appropriate materials, or to move the program forward to account for slower or faster students. Busy children working on activities within their ability range are seldom discipline problems.

A teacher who has trouble with discipline should think carefully first about transition periods in the classroom. These are the times when children, like adults, let off steam. By shortening some transition times and eliminating others, the classroom teacher can significantly reduce problems.

This is not meant to suggest that there are not children who, no matter what you do, seem like a thorn in your side. Behaviorists suggest that we ignore their negative acts, since attention is what they seek, and reward only their positive efforts, no matter how rare. This is excellent advice, but virtually impossible to follow. All of us are tempted at some time to respond to attack with counterattack. To do otherwise requires stern self-discipline, even if we recognize that counterattack fails and that turning the other cheek is effective.

Whenever possible, a more reasonable approach is to respond thoughtfully rather than emotionally to student acts. And when you fail, as you sometimes will, you should analyze the situation in order to improve your response next time.

Some experienced teachers improve their skills in responding to troublemakers because they come to realize that these children are not nearly as bad as they at first appeared. Most teachers are shocked when they meet their worst students outside the classroom and find them to be friendly and approachable, often apologetic. This underscores the need to remove the element of conflict from the classroom.

Sometimes a useful device will occur to you on the spot. One of our favorite stories concerns a colleague who took over in midyear a Brooklyn junior high school class that had already driven several teachers from the school. When he first entered the classroom no students were in their seats. Over the din, he shouted, "Sit down, please." When only two students sat down, he took out his record book and asked them their names. He then informed them that they were each private first-class. The others immediately took their seats, asking as they did so what the teacher meant. "This is the army," he told them. By the end of the year, not only did he have a number of generals, but he also had his class in control.

Certainly this was positive reinforcement. (It was also extrinsic, that is, coming from outside the subject matter. Intrinsic motivation, generated by the subject matter itself, is preferable when it works.) But the point here is that the approach was effective because it was unexpected. Innovation is as effective in discipline as it is in other areas of education.

ORGANIZING MATHEMATICS LESSONS

It may seem a retreat now after introducing you to so many interesting and challenging aspects of mathematics to restress the view expressed in chapter 8 that you should rely on a textbook for your instructional program organization. But we shall do exactly that. Beginning teachers would be most unwise to start teaching mathematics by organizing the program entirely on their own. Such a course would add a tremendous burden to their already full teaching responsibilities.

A textbook provides a secure base for inexperienced teachers. Given that starting point, you can later extend and enrich the textbook program. As you become comfortable with your own program, you can modify the textbook development and depart from it in more significant ways.

In particular we recommend to all teachers of upper grades, beginners as well as experienced teachers, that they do not start their teaching programs from page one of any text. They should take advantage of the motivation students bring to school in September and start on newer material, returning later to review the content of earlier grades. They should recognize that students need to settle back into the school routine before testing to determine how much review will be necessary.

Now let us assume that the teacher has a teachers' edition (TE) of a text and has decided on a lesson. That much was easy, but now he must begin to plan in greater detail. Here are some things he can do:

1. Read the TE plan and the student text carefully, making note of any additional preparation required.

2. Organize the total class period around a series of activities. The 30–60 minutes alloted to mathematics moves rapidly and the teacher needs to take advantage of every minute of that time. Such an organization might include:

   (a) A motivating problem to introduce the new concept or algorithm (5 minutes)

   (b) Developing the logic of the new content using concrete materials (10 minutes)

(c) Regularizing the procedures through observed seat-work, providing assistance where necessary (10 minutes)

(d) Students explaining the procedure: what to do and why (5 minutes)

(e) Review of questions from the previous day (10 minutes)

(f) Assignment of new work (5 minutes)

3. Once the overall organization is noted (often following the TE plan rather closely), it is especially important for the beginner to flesh this out with specific exercises and examples, in particular with well-worded questions. (A serious error of many teachers is to use the same examples as the ones in the student text. Even where procedures are followed in detail, it is wise to choose different exercises to illustrate them.) Key questions are especially useful, since they neatly supplement questions that will occur naturally to the teacher as the lesson develops. By this means, the teacher sees to it that important details and special cases are not overlooked.

4. Concrete materials and audiovisual devices are located and made available. If, for example, paper is to be cut, both paper and scissors must be accessible. It is amazing how often such common sense details are omitted, ruining a part of a lesson.

5. Procedures for quick review of previous work are identified.

6. The out-of-class assignment is detailed.

7. Transition stages between steps of the overall plan are reviewed to seek ways to smooth these discipline-problem periods.

Many experienced teachers carry out these preparatory details informally without making records. (Some go too far in this direction and their lessons take on an off-the-cuff character, which detracts measurably from the quality of instruction.) Beginners will want to overplan. The recurring nightmare of beginners is finding themselves finished with their lessons before time has elapsed, and standing tongue-tied before their classes. Such episodes do occur, most often when beginners race through lessons too fast and superficially. To meet such a contingency, it is well for the beginner to prepare something extra to fill such gaps: a trick, a game, an enrichment problem. Dozens of these are provided in this text.

A SAMPLE LESSON

Here is a second-grade lesson plan in which "carrying" is introduced, and a narrative account of some parts of that lesson as it was taught:

PLAN

1. Tongue depressor example: 25 + 37. How can we find the total number? Direct counting, etc. Time how long it takes with a stopwatch.

2. Overhead projector transparency showing 25 + 37. Meaning of 25, 37. Group tens: 50. How can we deal with 5 and 7 left? Fifty-twelve: 512! Dealing with the 12 as 10 + 2.

3. Recording these steps

$$\begin{array}{r} 25 \\ +\ 37 \\ \hline \end{array} \qquad \begin{array}{l} 20 + 5 \\ \underline{30 + 7} \\ 50 + 12 = 50 + 10 + 2 = 62 \end{array}$$

4. Seat-work problems

$$\begin{array}{r} 46 \\ +\ 58 \\ \hline \end{array} \qquad \begin{array}{r} 73 \\ +\ 19 \\ \hline \end{array} \qquad \begin{array}{r} 28 \\ +\ 64 \\ \hline \end{array} \qquad \begin{array}{r} 55 \\ +\ 35 \\ \hline \end{array}$$

5. Race the clock. Compare time on exercise with direct counting time (from start of class).

6. Homework from yesterday.

7. Assignment: read pages 112–13. (Is there a misprint on one of these pages?) Exercises 1–12 on page 113.

NARRATIVE ACCOUNT

Before class the teacher has placed two piles of tongue depressors (25 and 37 in each) on a table at the front of the room beside the chalkboard. He has also prepared several overhead projector transparencies for use in class. Toward the end of the reading lesson, before the math class, he had two students count the number of tongue depressors in each pile and record the figures on the chalkboard. Now it is time for math.

Teacher: Some of you probably heard me ask Mary and Billy to count the number of tongue depressors in each of the two piles on the table. They've written their totals on the chalkboard. Sam and Loretta, will you please check their counts? While they're doing that, I'll tell you what we want to do. We want to find out how many sticks there are in all. Tell me how we could find out. Hands. Yes, Jane.

Jane: Count them all.

Teacher: Good. Just a minute. Your totals check? Fine. Thanks, Mary and Billy and Sam and Loretta. I'll rewrite them over here on the chalkboard so we can all see. [*Writes*]

25
37

Now, Jane, I'm sorry I interrupted. You said?

Jane: Count them all.

Teacher: Excellent, Jane. Now can anyone suggest a shortcut to save time?

Roscoe: [*The class brain*] Add the numbers.

Teacher: Good, Roscoe, but you're getting a little ahead of us. How could we find the answer by simplifying Jane's procedure?

Carl: You could start with 25 and count the second pile.

Teacher: How does that work?

Carl: That just saves you from counting the 25 pile again.

Teacher: Good. Could we start with 37 instead?

Several: Yes!

Teacher: Which is better? Yes, Flora?

Flora: Start with 37 because you have fewer to count.

Teacher: Good Flora. Now will you do that for us while I time you with this stopwatch. Ready. Go. [*Pause*] Very good, Flora. You took just about 28 seconds. Last year's record was 31 seconds. Now let's see if we can find a way to beat even Flora's record. [*Displays transparency on screen*]

```
||||||||||         
||||||||||  |||||        25

||||||||||  ||||
||||||||||               37
||||||||||  |||
```

On the screen I have represented the 25 and 37 sticks in groups. How did I do that?

Tammy: You have 25 as two tens and five more, and you have 37 as three tens and seven more.

Teacher: Everyone at your seat copy this picture except Mike. Mike, will you use these rubber bands to group the tongue depressors into groups of ten? Now loop the full groups of ten. How many are there, class?

Class: Five. (A few students say six at this point.)

Teacher: How many sticks are left over in the top group?

Class: Five.

Teacher: The bottom group?

Class: Seven.

Teacher: That means how many left over in all?

Class: Twelve.

Teacher: Is there another ten there?

Class: Yes.

Teacher: And how many more still?

Class: Two.

Teacher: Very good. So now we have. . . .

Class: Six tens and two ones.

Teacher: Or. . . .

Class: Sixty-two.

Teacher: Now let's try to do the same thing without the sticks. (*Displays new transparency.*)

$$\begin{array}{r} 25 = 20 + \\ +\underline{37} = \underline{\qquad} \end{array}$$

Teacher: Copy that on your papers carefully and see what you can do with it. Francine will you write on the overhead, please? [*Passes around room giving encouragement, assistance, and praise. Most papers show the expected response.*]

$$\begin{array}{rl} 25 & = 20 + 5 \\ +\underline{37} & = \underline{30 + 7} \\ & \quad 50 + 12 = 62 \end{array}$$

You're all doing quite well. [*Passes out mimeographed seatwork*] Now try these exercises in the same way. [*After about five minutes*] Now Flora, let's see if this way helps you to improve your speed. [*Flora is timed by the new method.*] Finished? Let's see: 21 seconds, the new 2-B record for 25 + 37. [*To the class*] Your assignment is on the chalkboard. Do it carefully and tomorrow we'll set out to improve even further on Flora's record.

Recall now our discussion of behavioral objectives in chapter 8. From the sample plan it is clear that the basic goal of the lesson was to have students take the first step in conceptualizing an addition algorithm. By focusing on the students, this teacher thought of the timing trick for motivation, and having the student finish the overhead transparency for others to use as a comparison. Had he completed his slide it might have been neater, more artistically satisfying, but far less so pedagogically.

There is one last point that should be made here. All teachers find that they actually learn a great deal about the content of their courses during the first year of teaching. This is because they are deeply involved in organizing the content. This argues strongly for increased student involvement so that they too can share in this learning. A case in point: when one student helps another, the student who gains most is invariably the tutor.

BECOMING A MASTER TEACHER

During the first weeks of classroom teaching, beginners must spend their full energy organizing and managing the activities of the next minute, to say nothing of the next day or week. Teaching soon settles into routine, however; it remains hard, enervating work, but at least manageable. Immediately, teachers should set their sights on becoming master teachers. From the outset, they should begin to develop and implement an improvement program.

We have already discussed at length two aspects of that program, reflection and introspection. Other aspects include further study, professional involvement, and working with other teachers and supervisors. In particular we stress the latter. It has been our observation that supervisors, no matter how overextended or overworked they are, are delighted when teachers seek out their assistance. They will go out of their way to assist anyone who takes this kind of initiative.

Teachers need not seek such assistance only when teaching problems arise. They should begin to think of ways to improve even lessons that have gone well. They should look for ways to modify classroom organization. They should seek ways to become involved in various teacher organizations. They should find better avenues for interaction with parents and others in the community. They should search for new mathematical examples. They should, in other words, become steeped in, and further committed to, their teaching profession. Supervisors can be of great help in all of these.

SATISFACTION COMES FROM STUDENT ACHIEVEMENT

Teaching is hard, often exhausting, work. It is constantly demanding, even threatening to teachers because of its importance to the future of children. But it is also exhilarating to quality teachers. No one and no problem, no matter how difficult, can detract from the great pleasure that master teachers take from knowing they have helped students learn.

EXERCISES

1. Analyze yourself as you confront teaching. What attributes will provide you with most support in teaching? What attributes will stand in your way?

2. Indicate some good characteristics of the best classroom teacher you have known. How do you think he or she developed those characteristics?

3. From a textbook for the grade you plan to teach, select three widely separated activities.
   (a) Using the teachers' manual as a source, develop careful plans for those three classes.
   (b) For each lesson prepare display materials, overhead projector transparencies, worksheets, and other supplementary teaching aids.
   (c) Prepare three test exercises that would be useful in evaluating student progress on each topic.
   (d) Devise five key questions for each class.

4. Indicate three ways that you could improve the lesson plan on page 315 to make it more useful for yourself.

5. Visit a mathematics class and examine the teacher's plans for that class.
   (a) Describe briefly the plan and the lesson.
   (b) Indicate ways you would modify the plan.
   (c) Suggest ways that the teacher could have involved more students in implementing the plan.

6. Develop a self-improvement program related to your teaching of mathematics to extend over the next five years. Include in your plans both formal and informal activities as well as your short- and long-range goals.

APPENDIX A

MATHEMATICS BOOKS FOR THE ELEMENTARY SCHOOL LIBRARY

The following books represent a starter set of books for children. Individual titles are annotated P for primary grades, K–3 for kindergarten through grade 3, and I for intermediate grades 4–8.

Adler, Irving. *The Giant Golden Book of Mathematics.* Golden Press, 1960. P, I

Adler, Irving, and Adler, Ruth. *Magic House of Numbers.* John Day, 1957. I

Adler, Irving, and Adler, Ruth. *Numbers New and Old.* John Day, 1960. I

Asimov, Isaac. *Realm of Numbers.* Houghton Mifflin, 1959. I

Bakst, Aaron. *Mathematical Puzzles and Pastimes.* 2d ed. Van Nostrand, 1964. I

Bakst, Aaron. *Mathematics: Its Magic and Mystery.* Van Nostrand, 1941, 1952. I

Barnard, Douglas St. Paul. *It's All Done By Numbers.* Hawthorn, 1968. I

Bergamini, David et al., eds. *Mathematics.* Time, 1963. I

Branley, Franklin. *Measure With Metric.* Crowell, 1975. P

Charosh, Mannis. *The Ellipse.* Crowell, 1971. P

Charosh, Mannis. *Straight Lines, Parallel Lines, Perpendicular Lines.* Crowell, 1971. P

Diggins, Julia E. *String, Straightedge and Shadow: The Story of Geometry.* Viking, 1965. I

Freeman, Mae. *Finding Out About Shapes.* McGraw-Hill, 1969. P

Froman, Robert. *Bigger and Smaller.* Crowell, 1971. P

Gallant, Roy A. *Man The Measurer: Our Units of Measure and How They Grew.* Doubleday, 1972. I

Gardner, Martin. *Mathematical Puzzles and Diversions.* Simon and Schuster, 1959. I

Gardner, Martin. *Mathematics Magic and Mystery.* Simon and Schuster, 1956. I

Glenn, William H., and Johnson, Donovan A. *Exploring Mathematics on Your Own.* Dover, 1960. I

Glenn, William H., and Johnson, Donovan A. *Invitation to Mathematics.* Doubleday, 1962. I

Heath, Royal V. *Mathemagic: Magic Puzzles and Games with Numbers.* Dover, 1933. I

Hogben, Lancelot. *The Wonderful World of Mathematics.* Random House, 1955. I

Jonas, Arthur. *New Ways in Math.* Prentice-Hall, 1962. I

Land, Frank. *The Language of Mathematics.* Doubleday, 1963. I

Linn, Charles F. *Estimation.* Crowell, 1970. P, I

Lowenstein, Dyno. *Graphs.* Franklin Watts, 1969. I

Luce, Marnie. *Math Concept Series:* (1) *Zero Is Something,* (2) *One Is Unique,* (3) *Primes Are Builders,* (4) *Sets: What Are They?,* (5) *Points, Lines and Planes,* (6) *Polygons: Points in a Plane,* (7) *Polyhedrons: Intersecting Planes,* (8) *Measurement: How Much? How Many? How Far?,* (9) *Counting Systems: The Familiar and the Unusual,* (10) *Ten: Why Is It Important.* Lerner Publications, 1969. P, I

Luce, Marnie, and Lerner, A. B. *Math Concept Series:* (11) *Infinity, What Is It?* Lerner Publications, 1969. P, I

Menninger, Karl. *Number Words and Number Symbols: A Cultural History of Numbers.* M.I.T. Press, 1969. I

O'Brien, Thomas C. *Odds and Evens.* Crowell, 1971. P

Ravielli, Anthony. *An Adventure in Geometry.* Viking, 1957. I

Razzell, Arthur G., and Watts, K. G. O. *Circles and Curves.* Doubleday, 1969. I

Razzell, Arthur G., and Watts, K. G. O. *Symmetry.* Doubleday, 1967. I

Reid, Constance. *From Zero to Infinity: What Makes Numbers Interesting,* 3d ed. Crowell, 1965. I

Shimke, William. *Math Concept Series:* (12) *Patterns: What Are They?* Lerner Publications, 1969. P, I

Sitomer, Mindel, and Sitomer, Harry. *Circles.* Crowell, 1971. P

Sitomer, Mindel, and Sitomer, Harry. *What is Symmetry?* Crowell, 1970. P

Srivastava, Jane Jonas. *Weighing and Balancing.* Crowell, 1970. P

Wahl, John, and Wahl, Stacey. *I Can Count the Petals of a Flower.* National Council of Teachers of Mathematics, 1976. P

Weyl, Peter. *Men, Ants and Elephants: Size in the Animal World.* Viking, 1959. I

APPENDIX B

SELECTED BOOKS FOR TEACHERS

The books preceded by an asterisk represent the most important listed. Addresses for publishers marked by an asterisk are listed in Appendix C; others may be easily obtained.

Berger, Emil J., ed. *Instructional Aids in Mathematics: NCTM 34th Yearbook.* National Council of Teachers of Mathematics, 1973.*

Biggs, Edith. *Mathematics for Older Children.* Citation Press, 1972.

Biggs, Edith. *Mathematics for Younger Children.* Citation Press, 1971.

Bitter, Gary G.; Mikesell, Jerald L; and Maurdeff, Kathryn. *Activities Handbook for Teaching the Metric System.* Allyn and Bacon, 1976.

**CSMP Mathematics for Primary Grades.* Comprehensive School Mathematics Program, 1975.*

**CSMP Mathematics for Kindergarten: Teachers Guide.* Comprehensive School Mathematics Program, 1976.*

Fletcher, Harold, and Howell, Arnold A. *Mathematics with Understanding.* Books 1 and 2. Pergamon Press, 1970.

Frederique and Papy. *Graphs and the Child.* Algonquin Publishing, 1970.

Frederique. *Mathematics and the Child 1.* Cuisenaire Company of America, 1971.

Gattegno, Caleb. *The Common Sense of Teaching Mathematics.* Educational Solutions, 1974.*

Greenes, Carole E.; Willcutt, Robert E; and Spikell, Mark A. *Problem Solving in the Mathematics Laboratory: How to do it.* Prindle, Weber and Schmidt, 1972.

Grossnickle, Foster E. et al., eds. *Instruction in Arithmetic: NCTM 25th Yearbook.* National Council of Teachers of Mathematics, 1960.*

Henderson, George L. et al. *Let's Play Games in Mathematics.* Vol. 1–6. National Textbook, 1971.

Hlavaty, Julius H. et al., eds. *Enrichment Mathematics for the Grades: NCTM 27th Yearbook.* National Council of Teachers of Mathematics, 1963.*

*Hlavaty, Julius H. et al., eds. *Mathematics for Elementary School Teachers: The Rational Numbers.* National Council of Teachers of Mathematics, 1972.* (Associated films available.)

Holt, John. *How Children Fail.* Dell Publishing Co., Inc., 1964.

Kline, Morris. *Why Johnny Can't Add: The Failure of the New Math.* St. Martin's Press, 1973.

Lovell, Kenneth. *The Growth of Understanding in Mathematics: Kindergarten through Grade Three.* Holt, Rinehart and Winston, 1971.

Mathematics—The First Three Years. A Nuffield/CEDO Handbook for Teachers. Wiley, 1970.

Mathematics: The Later Primary Years. A Nuffield/CEDO Handbook for Teachers. Wiley, 1972.

Moore, Carolyn C. *Why Don't We Do Something Different? Mathematical Activities for the Elementary Grades.* Prindle, Weber and Schmidt, 1973.

Mueller, Francis J., ed. *Updating Mathematics: Elementary School Edition.* Croft Educational Services, 1964.*

Nelson, Doyal, ed. *Measurement in School Mathematics: NCTM 1976 Yearbook.* National Council of Teachers of Mathematics, 1976.*

*Payne, Joseph N., ed. *Mathematics Learning in Early Childhood: NCTM 37th Yearbook.* National Council of Teachers of Mathematics, 1975.*

Problems: Red Set, Green Set, Purple Set. (Nuffield/CEDO) Wiley, 1970, 1969, 1971. (Laboratory activity cards.)

Reys, Robert E., and Post, Thomas R. *The Mathematics Laboratory: Theory to Practice.* Prindle, Weber and Schmidt, 1973.

*Ruderman, Harry D. et al., eds. *Mathematics for Elementary School Teachers.* National Council of Teachers of Mathematics, 1966.* (Associated films available.)

Skemp, Richard R. *The Psychology of Learning Mathematics.* Penguin, 1971.

Smith, Seaton E., Jr., and Backman, Carl A., eds. *Games and Puzzles for Elementary and Middle School Mathematics.* National Council of Teachers of Mathematics, 1975.*

Stern, Catherine, and Stern, Margaret B. *Children Discover Arithmetic.* Harper and Row, 1949, 1971.

Wenninger, Magnus J. *Polyhedron Models for the Classroom,* 2d ed. National Council of Teachers of Mathematics, 1966, 1975.*

*Williams, Elizabeth, and Shuard, Hilary. *Primary Mathematics Today.* Longman (Addison-Wesley), 1970.

*Wirtz, Robert W. *Banking on Problem Solving in Elementary School Mathematics.* Curriculum Development Associates, 1976.*

*Wirtz, Robert W. *Drill and Practice at the Problem Solving Level: An Alternative.* Curriculum Development Associates, 1974.*

*Wirtz, Robert W. *Mathematics for Everyone.* Curriculum Development Associates, 1974.*

Wirtz, Robert W.; Botel, Morton; and Nunley, B. G., *Discovery in Elementary School Mathematics.* Encyclopedia Britannica Press, 1963.

Wolf, Frank L. *Number Systems and Their Uses.* Xerox, 1971.

Zaslavsky, Claudia. *Africa Counts: Number and Pattern in African Culture.* Prindle, Weber and Schmidt, 1973.

APPENDIX C

SELECTED SOURCES OF MATERIALS FOR MATHEMATICS TEACHING

Many schools have on file catalogs from major distributors and publishers. A postcard to others will bring descriptive literature.

The Arithmetic Project
55 Chapel Street
Newton, Massachusetts 02160

CDA Math
Curriculum Development Associates
Suite 414
1211 Connecticut Avenue, N.W.
Washington, D.C. 20036

or

CDA West
P.O. Box 5335
Carmel, California 93921

Childcraft Equipment Company
155 East 57th Street
New York, New York 10010

Comprehensive School Mathematics Program
3120 59th Street
St. Louis, Missouri 63139

Creative Playthings
Princeton, New Jersey 08540

Creative Publications
P.O. Box 328
Palo Alto, California 94302

Croft Educational Services
100 Garfield Avenue
New London, Connecticut

Cuisenaire Company of America
12 Church Street
New Rochelle, New York 10805

Educational Solutions, Inc.
80 Fifth Avenue
New York, New York 10011

Math Media
P.O. Box 345
Danbury, Connecticut 06810

Midwest Publications Company
P.O. Box 307
Birmingham, Michigan 48012

Milton-Bradley Company
74 Park Street
Springfield, Massachusetts 01105

National Council of Teachers of Mathematics
1906 Association Drive
Reston, Virginia 22091

SEE: Selective Educational Equipment
3 Bridge Street
Newton, Massachusetts 02195

TUF: Avalon Hill Company
4517 Harford Road
Baltimore, Maryland 21214

Yoder Instruments
East Palestine, Ohio 44413

INDEX